A PERFIDIOUS DISTORTION OF HISTORY

Jürgen Tampke

A Perfidious Distortion of History

**THE VERSAILLES PEACE
TREATY AND THE SUCCESS
OF THE NAZIS**

SCRIBE
Melbourne • London

Scribe Publications
18–20 Edward St, Brunswick, Victoria 3056, Australia
2 John St, Clerkenwell, London, WC1N 2ES, United Kingdom

First published by Scribe 2017
Reprinted 2017

Copyright © 2017 by Jürgen Tampke

Printed and bound in the UK by CPI Group (UK) Ltd, Croydon CR0 4YY

Scribe Publications is committed to the sustainable use of natural
resources and the use of paper products made responsibly from those
resources.

CiP records for this title are available from the National Library of
Australia and the British Library

9781925321944 (Australian edition)
9781925228953 (UK edition)
9781925307948 (e-book)

scribepublications.com.au
scribepublications.co.uk

To Bruce Kent
teacher and friend

Contents

The arguments used in Germany against the Treaty of Versailles were so absurd that one could not help but wondering. Two officers' widows—this was not in Berlin but in Wiesbaden and was perhaps typically provincial—fiercely announced to me that it was all my fault (because I was English) that they now had to have their linen washed once a fortnight. It emerged that their stocks, which had formerly been generously sufficient for a month, had been depleted by post-war conditions. This they attributed solely to the *Versaillerdiktat*.

ELIZABETH WISKEMANN,
THE EUROPE I SAW

Preface

The Versailles Peace Treaty, the pact that ended the First World War between the German empire and the Allies, has not enjoyed a high reputation among politicians, historians, and opinion makers since its signing in June 1919. Conventional wisdom has it that, guided by motives of punishment and revenge, and based on the untenable claim that Germany had caused the war, the treaty's chief instigators—United States president Woodrow Wilson, British premier David Lloyd George, and French prime minister Georges Clemenceau—imposed a Carthaginian peace upon the defeated enemy. Loss of vital industrial and agricultural regions and the imposition of massive reparation payments, it is claimed, crippled the economy of the Weimar Republic, as post-World War I Germany came to be known. This in turn constantly destabilised the Republic's political life.

Thus the gentle seeds of democracy that are said to have been sown in the aftermath of the Great War were not allowed to flourish. Instead, the fourteen years of the Republic were marked by perpetual confrontations, setbacks, and unsurmountable difficulties — all linked to the harshness of the Versailles Peace — which in the end drove the German people into the arms of Adolf Hitler, whose evil potential no one could foresee, of course.

It is the intention of this book — with the Versailles Peace nearing its centenary — to show that these accounts constitute a falsification of history. Contrary to the widespread belief, the treaty with Germany did not break Wilsonian principles, and none of the president's Fourteen Points was violated. Rather, it was Germany's presentation, or more correctly its deliberate misinterpretation, of the Fourteen Points that stood at the heart of the matter. Claims that the German empire lost 13 per cent of its territory and 10 per cent of its population are based on phony statistics. Article 231 of the treaty, the much maligned 'war guilt paragraph', did not assign war guilt to Germany. Above all, it was not the 'burden' caused by reparation demands that stood behind the calamitous collapse of the Weimar economy which accompanied the massive defection of middle-class voters to the Nazi Party from the late 1920s onward.

Just as the Versailles Treaty is approaching its hundredth anniversary, so too is the chief monograph upon which much of its vilification is based, a book which has become a kind of bible of the anti-Versailles industry — John Maynard Keynes' *The Economic Consequences of the Peace*. That a book is one hundred years old does not mean per se that it loses its value. But Keynes's assessment of the Versailles Treaty was flawed from the beginning. Keynes was among the outstanding economists of his time, without doubt, but there is equally no doubt that *The Economic Consequences of the Peace* was not his best work—it was his poorest. In fact, not two decades had passed before Keynes himself regretted having written it.

It is true that 'the war to end all wars'—as a legion of hack novelists, moviemakers, singers, and textbook-writers have lamented—did not end all wars. But that was not the fault of the peacemakers.

CHAPTER ONE

Imperial Germany

Count Otto Eduard Leopold von Bismarck, minister-president of Prussia and chancellor designate of a newly united German empire, was a deeply worried man as the year 1870 drew to its close. Although the Prussian-led German armies had decisively defeated the French on the battlefields—indeed, Emperor Napoleon III had been captured and his government had collapsed—the enemy stubbornly kept fighting. For three months, heads of the German states and their representatives had been waiting at Versailles to prepare for the celebration of German unification, set to take place in the palace's grandiose Hall of Mirrors as soon as hostilities ended. Alas, the French did not yield, but kept up a desperate resistance.

Bismarck could have had his peace in early September, when a hastily formed Republican government was willing to negotiate a settlement after the battle of Sedan. However, the Prussians' demand that the provinces of Alsace and

Lorraine be ceded rekindled the French fighting spirit. Regular armies and *francs-tireurs* (fighting units first formed in 1792, when irregular forces and volunteer levies were raised to assist in the early campaigns of the revolutionary wars) put up a dogged resistance, as did Paris. Following the example set by the Revolution's Convention in 1793, the Republican government called for a people's war—an arming of the people (*levée en masse*) to save the French nation from defeat. The war dragged on.

The Prussian minister-president was at loggerheads with the army command about the most effective tactic to subdue the Parisians. To bring about the end to the war, Bismarck wanted to shell the city with heavy artillery, killing civilians indiscriminately in the process. Army chief General Field Marshal Count Helmuth Karl Bernhard von Moltke (commonly referred to as the elder Moltke), worried that the bombardment of civilians would outrage international opinion, preferred to force the Parisians to their knees by starving them. As his assistant, General Albrecht von Blumenthal, put it bluntly, '… the inhabitants shall cop it like mad dogs. We don't give a damn about what happens to the Parisians. They bought it upon themselves.'[1]

Quarrels with the army were not the only problem for Bismarck. International opinion had begun to turn against Prussia. In particular, the Gladstone government in Britain had become critical of the annexation of Alsace-Lorraine. In Germany, too, the mounting costs caused by the continuation of the military campaign and the entertaining and upkeep of the aristocratic dignitaries at Versailles had begun to sap enthusiasm for the war. There was no end in sight to the haggling over the entry conditions of the

South German states to the new Germany. Aware that the Prussian minister-president was under great pressure to finalise the unification of Germany, the regents of Bavaria, Württemberg, Baden, and smaller states used every opportunity to strike a favourable bargain.

Worn out by so much stress, Bismarck was confined to bed for several days during December 1870. He had recovered by New Year, but news from the French countryside, where *francs-tireurs* continued to harass German troops, did not lift his spirits. He demanded that towns and villages which had co-operated with or sheltered *francs-tireurs* be burned to the ground and all male citizens hung. There was no need to take prisoners of war. Enemy soldiers should be mowed down, as taking prisoners would only hamper Germany's war effort. Delinquents who spat on German soldiers from bridges were to be shot; so were the women and children who scavenged for potatoes on the fringes of Paris. His wife, Johanna von Bismarck, showed even less mercy: all the French, down to the little babies, should be shot or stabbed to death.[2]

The German soldiers did not need much prompting. The burning of towns and villages and mass killings of civilians had become widespread by the end of 1870. The longevity of the conflict, coupled with the serious supply problems that had arisen by the late autumn, rekindled a level of savagery reminiscent of the seventeenth century. The spirit of the eighteenth-century Enlightenment had not failed to have an impact on military conduct. While, for example, there were no international treaties regulating warfare, by the nineteenth century it had become a convention that private property was not to be appropriated, that there was to be no plundering, and that the occupying power was to maintain law and order—for example, that there was to be no theft or rape on the part of the soldiers. The Prussian armies, since the wars of Frederick II in the eighteenth century, had stood out for their strict discipline on and off the field. In this tradition, the Prussian King Wilhelm I reminded his army at the beginning of the 1870–71 war that he expected orderly conduct on their entering enemy territory. They were not to turn upon the civilian population; rather, it was the duty of every honourable soldier to protect private property and not to damage the reputation of the Prussian army by lack of discipline.[3]

By this time, however, the king's admonitions were falling on deaf ears. The siege of Strasbourg in mid-August 1870 gave the first indication that the Franco-Prussian War was to evoke the savagery that had marked the Thirty Years' War and would foreshadow the barbarism of twentieth-century warfare. The commander in charge of the Prussian army units, General von Werder, ordered a bombardment of the city. Four nights of continuous pounding with high explosive and incendiary shells destroyed a large part of Strasbourg, including some of its finest buildings. The Museum of Fine Arts, the Library with its treasures, the Palais de Justice, the Arsenal, and the Huguenot Temple Neuf were all burned to the ground, and fire also destroyed the roof of the Cathedral. Thousands of civilians were left dead or injured, and the killing or maltreatment of defenceless non-combatants, including women and children, quickly spread.

Paul Baron von Collas, *Generalstabsoffizier* in the First Prussian Army, regularly wrote to his parents in Kassel. His letter of 31 December 1870 illustrates the deterioration that had occurred in the conduct of the war:

> Our war is taking on a rather strange character now, and will become much crueller, if the [French] people won't come to their senses. Yesterday between Amiens and Abbeville a detachment of ours ran into enemy troops who were supported by inhabitants of a neighbouring village. The Commander of the detachment had immediately all 60 male inhabitants shot. Fortunately we have now reached a stage where we execute without fuss or delay anyone causing any kind of harm, and we now burn down whole villages. To force the fortress Peronne to surrender we shot within 48 hours 8000 shells into the town which is now ablaze with a gigantic fire.
>
> Tomorrow evening I will be back in Rouen where I have a very comfortable quarter.[4]

By the opening of 1871, the behaviour of von Collas's unit had become the norm. Châteaudun, a town of 7,000 people, was burned to the ground.[5] Near Toul, the Prussian 57th Regiment, pursuing *francs-tireurs*, burned the village of Fontenoy-sur-Moselle, but, finding no 'citizen soldiers', bayoneted all the inhabitants and threw them into the flames.[6] On the river Loire, collective reprisals had become commonplace. Near Orleans, the town of Ablis was razed, and all males killed, in retaliation for an attack by irregulars. There is little evidence that the non-Prussian army corps behaved any better.[7]

By mid-January, it was obvious that capitulation by the Republican government was imminent. Now the formal unification of Germany could at last take place at Versailles. King Ludwig II of Bavaria, whose consent to his country's admission to the German empire had netted him a large cash handout and an annual payment of 300,000 marks, had signed the official letter—drawn up by Bismarck—that offered King Wilhelm I of Prussia the Kaiser's crown on behalf of the German princes.[8] As Ludwig, the king of Saxony, and the king of Württemberg did not attend the coronation ceremony, it fell upon Grand Duke Frederick of Baden as the highest-ranking potentate to proclaim 'His Imperial and Royal Majesty Kaiser Wilhelm'.[9] The latter accepted without great enthusiasm. He is reported to have grumbled to Bismarck that his old Prussia had come to an end.[10] Prince Otto of Bavaria, brother to King Ludwig, saw the ceremony as a pretentious, tasteless act on the part of an arrogant victor intent on demonstrating the absolute triumph of the Prussian military monarchy in the realms of both foreign and domestic policies. 'I cannot describe,' he wrote to Hohenschwangau, 'how immeasurably painful and distressing I felt about each act … everything was so cold, so painful, pompous and ostentatious—and yet so heartless and empty'.[11]

That the German unification was based on six years of success on the battlefield earned enormous admiration and prestige for the army leadership, not only in Prussia but among a large section of the German population. This encouraged a widespread, rapidly growing tendency to reduce politics to a simple matter of military might and strong-arm tactics. The notion of merciless warfare ('swift, decisive action') that accompanied the unification, so readily accepted in German military and civilian circles, was a sombre sign of things to come. Little more than a generation later, a publication of the German general staff on the conduct of war demonstrated the legacy of 1870–71. *Kriegsbrauch im Landkrieg* (published in English as the *German War Book*) was critical of the tendency to humanitarianism claimed to be common in the nineteenth century. Such considerations, it claimed, had 'degenerated into sentimentality and flabby emotions [*weichliche Gefühle*], leading to 'a desire to influence the usage of war in a way which was in fundamental contradiction to the nature of war and its object'. Hence the German officer must be wary of false views about the essential character of war. He will have 'to guard himself against excessive humanitarian notions' because 'certain severities are indispensable to war, as the only true humanity very often lies in a ruthless application of them'.[12]

This helps to illustrate what little impact the attempts in the early twentieth century to prevent a reoccurrence of the savagery of the Franco-Prussian war by way of international treaties would have upon the German military, its supporters, and theoreticians. Although Germany officially adhered to the Hague Conventions, the nation's military leaders and theorists had little respect for the limitations that the conventions' rules would place on warfare.[13]

Unification brought about by victory over France — allegedly Germany's arch-rival — led to an unparalleled level of national celebration and enthusiasm. According to a leading German historian, the *Bildungsbürgertum* (educated bourgeoisie) — academics, lawyers, high school teachers, high-ranking public servants, the upper level of the clergy, and other university-educated citizens — had been elevated into a 'highly emotional state of euphoria'.[14] German liberals who, ten years earlier, had seen Bismarck as their arch-foe, the reactionary personification of Prussian conservatism, now faced about: for the first decades of the new German empire, they became his firmest supporters in the Reichstag. The joy of sticking it to the French in no uncertain terms ('giving *saures* to the Frenchmen') was for a long time a favourite topic at the beer tables and in the choral, rifle, gymnastic, skittle, and countless other societies that made up Germany's rich club life. Imposing victory statutes were put up in every German town, followed by the construction of memorials recalling aspects of Germany's glorious past. The largest of these constructions, the Hermann Monument near Detmold, rose to 54 metres. Its purpose was to commemorate the annihilation of three Roman legions in the nearby Teutoburg Forest by the Cheruscan leader, Arminius (now renamed Hermann), in 9 A.D. Just as Hermann had united the Germanic tribes to defeat the Romans, various inscriptions now praised the Prussian king for having again united the German tribes (*Deutsche Volksstämme*) against the arch-foe, France.

Opera composer Richard Wagner provided the musical embodiment of this new Teutonic spirit. The titles and characters of his works—*Lohengrin, Ring der Nibelungen, Rheingold, Walküre, Siegfried, Götterdämmerung*—all harked back to Germany's mystical origins. His hero, *Lohengrin*, was the most popular figure of Germany's legendary past, the embodiment of all that was perfect (and hence German). His bride, Elsa, embodying in her purity the German folk-spirit, was devoted, loving, and—as long as she was not seduced by the cunning perfidy of dark and hostile forces—blindly trusted by her saviour and leader. Having achieved the financial support of King Ludwig II, Wagner in the mid-1870s was able to stage magnificent performances at the Bavarian town of Bayreuth. The Wagner festival there became a cult for music lovers and for German patriots.

Only two shadows fell upon this picture of Teutonic harmony.

In 1871, Pope Pius IX had issued a 'Declaration of Papal Infallibility' intended to strengthen Rome's hold over Catholic communities everywhere. This clashed with Bismarck's goal to bring the Catholic Church in Prussia under the control of the state. When Catholic clergymen refused to undergo training at state institutions and to submit church appointments for government approval, the chancellor turned upon them. Soon, nearly 1,000 parishes were without a pastor, most Catholic religious orders had been suppressed, over 200 priests jailed, three bishops and two archbishops removed from office, and the archbishop of Trier had died shortly after he was released from a nine-month imprisonment. Although resentment lingered, particularly among the Bavarians, the Catholic Church was beaten into submission and was transformed, through its political arm, the Centre Party, into a conservative institution and one supporting the German Reich.

The second shadow was cast by the German socialists. Founded in the 1860s, the German labour movement was peaceful and law-abiding. It hoped to improve the lives and working conditions of Germany's rapidly growing industrial population by peaceful means, through parliament. The socialists were seen, however, by the barons of

Germany's coal and steel industries—all close friends of the chancellor—as a threat to the unlimited power they wielded over their workforce as the *Herr im Hause*, the 'master of the house'. In 1878, two assassination attempts on Kaiser Wilhelm I led to a wave of hysteria. Although, in reality, the attempts had nothing to do with the German labour movement, but were staged individually by fanatics, the nation's foremost historian, Heinrich von Treitschke, called on employers to sack workers suspected of socialist sympathies. In the late 1870s, Bismarck introduced anti-socialist laws that were passed by both the conservatives and the liberals. Mass arrests and widespread imprisonment followed. The socialist party was outlawed, meetings banned, and newspapers suppressed, and capital punishment was reintroduced in Prussia and other German states.

Things were quiet domestically, at least for a while. Then, ten years later, a new wave of dissatisfaction and discontent swept the country, due not to new quarrels over church and religion, or even the socialist threat (the anti-socialist laws had been abandoned in 1890 after Wilhelm II had ascended to the throne and dismissed Bismarck). The new concern was that the young German empire was not enjoying the status it rightfully deserved among the world powers. In particular, the colonial carve-up of the globe was believed to have severely disadvantaged the Reich. To quote Max Weber's inaugural lecture at Freiburg University, 'the unification of Germany was a youthful prank' too costly to have been undertaken unless it marked the beginning of a German *Weltmachtpolitik* or 'world-power politics'.[15]

Imperial politics, parties, and pressure groups

The Reich that Bismarck had created ensured that power firmly rested with the crown. The kaiser could appoint and dismiss any member of cabinet at will. There was a parliament made up of an upper house (the Bundesrat) and a lower house (the Reichstag), but neither the chancellor nor ministers had to account to these houses or accept any resolution passed by either. The kaiser was also in charge of all the chief aspects of the political decision-making process. In particular, he held the right to declare war and peace, and he was in charge of the army. With the kaiser at its head, the army—virtually a state within the state—was the empire's most powerful institution. In cases of emergency, when it was believed there was a threat to the imperial establishment, the army had the power to declare martial law and suspend civil liberties. Its prestige after the unification wars was enormous. Most non-commissioned officers entered the German civil service after serving, and this meant that a pronounced spirit of Prussian militarism permeated the nation's everyday life. The kaiser had the support of the nobility, whose members were naturally keen to prevent any erosion of their privileges. Conservatism and conservative parties also had solid support in Protestant rural and semi-rural regions, and the Lutheran pastors ensured that nonconformist or dissident thought had little chance of infiltrating their communities.

Reichstag elections were based on direct, universal male suffrage. The Reichstag could debate all matters political, and the annual budget had to be passed by both the Bundesrat and the Reichstag. All decisions of the Reichstag, however, could be vetoed by the Bundesrat, which was the assembly of representatives from all states belonging to the Reich. Only the Bundesrat could initiate legislation, and Prussia clearly dominated this chamber. As elections in Prussia were conducted under a three-class franchise system based on title and wealth, significant social or political changes were not likely to occur. With the Reichstag holding no effective power, the German parliamentary system was less democratic than its British or French equivalent.

The German middle classes did not lack political influence, and were not altogether excluded from the decision-making process. They dominated Germany's rapidly growing industrialisation, were in charge of the nation's outstanding education system, accounted for the bulk of lawyers and public servants, and, as the twentieth century approached, controlled a large share of the media—which was rapidly becoming a key factor in influencing both domestic and foreign policies. In fact, the majority of Germany's middle classes (politically represented by the National Liberals) was opposed to any tampering with Bismarck's constitution. The National Liberals believed that political power was not a matter for the masses. To them, Reichstag membership was properly the domain of the educated and propertied. Hence they had no inclination to challenge Prussia's three-class franchise system or to support attempts to overcome the drastic inequalities that marked the distribution of electoral boundaries which discriminated heavily against the urban population.

A minority of so-called progressive or left liberals advocated that the Reichstag be given more power, and that the cabinet be responsible to the legislative assembly. Some left-liberals even argued that the working class should be socially and politically integrated.[16] However, most of middle-class Germany, regardless of its party affiliation, stood behind the empire that Bismarck had created. They had little respect for the Western political systems where, it was widely believed, parliaments held excessive power. They said that in France's Third Republic (where a popularly elected assembly could appoint and dismiss ministers at will), party bickering, personal ambitions, and a restless struggle for ministerial positions had led to widespread corruption, favouritism, nepotism, and administrative inefficiency. By contrast, they believed that in Germany a strong monarchy kept a check upon unlimited parliamentary power, and an incorrupt, independent civil service allowed for efficient and reliable government.

In the United States, because of the 'machine-like nature of American politics', the bureaucracy was seen as being widely corrupt, suffering from the 'domination of the stock exchange'.[17] The United Kingdom (commonly referred to in Germany as 'England'), which had earlier drawn admiration from some German political observers, was now seen as sinking into decline if not decadence. 'In the halls of Parliament', a leading German historian proclaimed, 'one heard only shameless British commercial morality, which, with the Bible in the right hand and the opium pipe in the left, spreads the benefits of civilisation around the world'.[18] Economically, too, Britain was said to be falling behind, and German exports had began to outstrip those of Britain.

Pressure for global involvement came from many directions. The *Zentralverein für Handelsgeographie und Förderung der deutschen Interessen im Ausland*, an umbrella organisation of industry and commerce, impressed on the government the economic advantages of colonies. The *Verein für Sozialpolitik*, a group combining anti-free-trade economists, intellectuals, and academics, and headed by Gustav von Schmoller, argued that the creation of an overseas empire would assist in solving the social problems that had emerged with rapid industrialisation. A broad section of the middle classes from *Kleinbürgertum* (the petty bourgeoisie) to the *Bildungsbürgertum* joined the chorus, as did most of the academic establishment.

By the mid-1880s, public pressure for overseas expansion had swollen immensely; moreover, the National Liberals, upon whose support Bismarck's government had been able to rely since unification, had suffered a massive loss at the 1881 Reichstag election. The acquisition of colonies, a major aim of the National Liberals, was bound to revive their electoral fortunes. In 1884, Bismarck gave his consent to the acquisition of colonies in Africa and the Pacific. Until then he had shown only limited interest in overseas ventures, which he considered unlikely to yield sound economic returns and which would entail the risk of costly and unnecessary involvement outside Europe. He allegedly claimed that his map of Africa lay in Europe.

The raising of the German flag in South-West Africa in March 1884, and at various locations in north-eastern New Guinea and surrounding islands in November 1884, marked the beginning of Imperial Germany's colonial enterprise. At its peak, the empire also included Togoland, the Cameroons, German East Africa, the Marshall, Caroline, Palau and Mariana Islands, part of Samoa, and Kiautschou Bay in China.

German expansion overseas was accompanied by the formation of a plethora of nationalistic and imperialistic pressure groups. Most vociferous was the Colonial Society, founded in 1882 by Carl Peters, a daring colonial adventurer who virtually single-handedly acquired the German colony of East Africa. Peters was also prominent in the foundation of the Pan-German League in 1894, which pushed for German expansion overseas, German dominance in Europe, and the Germanisation of ethnic minorities within the Reich. Active also was the 'Association for Germandom Abroad', which aimed to carry German culture to the remote corners of the globe, and at home the 'Society for the Eastern Marches' was set up to destroy Polish identity in Germany's eastern provinces. The largest of these imperialist organisations was the Navy League, whose membership was about 300,000 at the outbreak of World War I. The league was financially supported by the arms manufacturer Krupp, which was profiting from the construction of the German battle fleet.

Krupp's economic good fortune was one outcome of Germany's naval construction program; another was the increasing diplomatic, political, and military isolation of the Reich. Whereas Germany's colonial expansion did not cause overwhelming concern among the rival powers—they all were active in the global carve-up, and the best pickings had long been made—the construction of a large battle fleet soured relations with the British empire, still the world's leading power. The consequences of this were to prove fatal.

After unification, Bismarck's foreign policies became conservative, and—in contrast to his oppressive domestic actions—aimed to consolidate the status quo. He knew that rapprochement with France was out of the question because of Alsace-Lorraine. But he nurtured friendly relations with the Austro-Hungarian empire and, more importantly, with tsarist Russia. Hence France was left isolated, with little chance to pursue revanchist policies. He also continued Prussia's traditional policy of goodwill towards the United Kingdom.

After his dismissal from office by Kaiser Wilhelm in 1890, this changed. The Reinsurance Treaty with Russia, a cornerstone of Bismarck's foreign policy, was almost immediately abandoned by his successor, Leo von Caprivi. Worse, reciprocal treaties that lowered German tariffs on agricultural imports, particularly Russian grains, were strangled by the furious agitation of the Agrarian League (Bund der Landwirte). Made up chiefly of big East Elbian landowners, this organisation managed to recruit a multitude of members to campaign against any candidate opposed to agricultural tariff protection. The league has been seen as the first major step towards the formation of a radical political right bent on mobilising the masses for aggressive conservative ends—a precursor of twentieth-century fascism.[19] The tsarist government countered by entering a series of economic and military treaties with France.

By the mid-1890s, Germany's pursuit of Weltpolitik had gathered considerable momentum. In December 1897, the state secretary of the Foreign Office, Bernhard von Bülow, gave a memorable speech in the Reichstag's debate on foreign policy. Von Bülow left no doubt about the future course of the German empire:

Fears have been expressed that we are about to enter a risky venture. Don't you worry, Gentlemen. Neither the Chancellor nor his advisors are the kind of people that seek unnecessary conflict. We don't all feel the necessity to put our fingers into every pie. However, we do hold the opinion that it is not advisable to exclude Germany at the very beginning from the competitions of other countries.

(Bravo!)

The times when the Germans left the earth to the [the influence] of one of their neighbours, the seas to another, only reserving for themselves the heaven above where pure doctrine holds …

(Laughter, Bravo!)

… those times are over. We see it as one of our prominent tasks to support the interest of our navigation, our trade, and our industries … [and] we demand that German missionaries, German goods, the German flag, and German ships are treated with as much respect as those of other powers.

(Bravo!)

We are only too happy to allow for the interest of other nations, provided that our own nation's are treated with the same respect.

(Bravo!)

In a word: we demand a place under the sun.[20]

His were not just empty words. Von Bülow, on becoming chancellor two years later, presided over two initial navy bills that authorised an increase in German battleships from seven to 38. Plans for further enlargement of the battle fleet did not take long to follow. Not many outside Germany believed that this sudden build-up was needed to safeguard Germany's export trade or its overseas possessions. The broad belief in free trade that marked the Age of Imperialism meant that German trade did not need large-scale military protection. Some individuals and companies benefited from the colonial enterprise, but, by and large, the colonies were a financial liability. Costs of running them far outweighed the income they brought, and they did not provide raw materials or markets for industry—or an outlet for excess population.

The British empire had little doubt about who would eventually be on the receiving end of this naval build-up. In 1902, the British government ordered large-scale modernisation and expansion of the empire's battle-fleet. The launching of the all-big-gun *Dreadnought* in 1906 made all existing ships obsolete, and British naval construction over the subsequent years far outpaced Germany's. Equally important, Britain entered into the Entente Cordiale with France in 1904, and made a similar agreement with Russia in 1907.

Von Bülow's claim that Germany had no intention of putting her fingers into every pie also proved misplaced, as governments in the new century blundered from mistake to mistake. Their policies aimed at humiliating the French over Morocco failed, and their abrupt and negative stand towards the attempts of the Hague Conference to keep the arms race under control, establish a universal system of arbitration, put limits on the conduct of warfare, and refrain from violence against civilians all offended international opinion. Equally offensive was German support of Austria-Hungary's annexation of Bosnia-Herzegovina on the Balkan peninsula. The Habsburg monarchy was now its only ally.

This opposition to many of Imperial Germany's policies led to a popular belief, fostered by the bulk of the media, pressure groups, and politicians, that Germany was being encircled and that Britain, France, and Russia were preventing the German nation from taking up its deserved role in the world. France had stooped so low as to enter into an alliance with reactionary tsarism in pursuit of her revanchist policies. Russia, in her craving for a pan-Slavonic empire, was seeking a crucial showdown between the Slavonic and Germanic peoples. To complete this dark scenario, England, 'perfidious Albion', envious of Germany's economic growth (*Handelsneid*), had joined the international enterprise to prevent the proud German nation from taking its rightful place in the global community.

Only the Social-Democratic German labour movement seemed to stand apart from this growing bellicosity.

German social democracy

The foundation of the German Social Democratic Party dates back to the merger of the General German Workers Association (*Allgemeiner Deutscher Arbeiterverein*, ADAV) with the Social Democratic Workers Party

(*Sozialdemokratische Arbeiterpartei*, SDAP) in the Thuringian town of Gotha in 1875. The former organisation had been founded in 1863 by Ferdinand Lasalle, a lawyer and classical scholar, who had been active in the 1848 Revolution. To better the living conditions of the working population, it had advocated the introduction of universal manhood suffrage in free and equal elections; adequate salaries for elected deputies; a fairer wage system; the formation of independent workers' co-operatives; a reduction in daily working hours; a curtailment of female labour and the abolition of child labour; the introduction of a single progressive income tax instead of indirect taxes; and the supervision of work conditions in mines, factories, and workshops by worker-elected officials.

As its program was far too modest for Karl Marx, who had established himself as the most outspoken international socialist, Marx deputised two of his strongest supporters in Germany, Wilhelm Liebknecht and August Bebel, to set up the SDAP as a rival organisation in 1869. It was soon obvious, however, that the existence of two separate parties was counter-productive, and this led to their unification into the German Socialist Workers Party (*Sozialistische Arbeiterpartei Deutschland*, SAP), renamed in 1890 the *Sozialdemokratische Partei Deutschlands*, SPD, the title it still carries today. The Gotha conference reaffirmed the previous demands, but added the Marxist principles of class abolition, the overthrow of the capitalist system, and international workers' solidarity.

By the mid-1870s, Marx had become the leading theoretician of the Socialist International labour movements. Marx's key argument was that the capitalist system would collapse because of its cannibalistic nature. As he says in Chapter 32 of *Capital*:

> One Capitalist always kills many … Along with the constantly diminishing number of capitalist magnates, who usurp and monopolise all advantages, … grows the mass of misery, oppression, slavery, degradation, exploitation, but with this too grows the revolt of the working class, a class always increasing in numbers and disciplined, united, organised by the very mechanism of capitalist production … Centralisation of the means of production and socialisation of labour reach a point where they become incompatible with their capitalist husk. Thus they burst asunder. The knell of private property sounds. The expropriators are expropriated.

Once this happened, the gateway to the new Jerusalem would open to a socialist and, eventually, communist society, where there would be no more exploitation of one class by another. This did not mean that all were equal, an idea that Marx dismissed as utopian—it would be from each according to his ability, to each according to his need.

With hindsight, few would argue with his claim that capitalism is a fundamentally precarious economic system. If it has survived all challenges, it is certainly not because of its inherent strength. We should bear in mind, too, that the system we have today has little resemblance to the one Marx had analysed in *Capital*. It is his belief in the revolutionary nature of the workers' movement that did not eventuate. The workforce in the English-speaking world—Britain,

North America, Australia, and New Zealand—where industrialisation was most advanced by the second half of the nineteenth century, showed little inclination to work towards the overthrow of the capitalist system. This was in part because, bad as conditions were for the majority of workers, they did not become impoverished to the extent Marx had envisaged. Workers could vote for parliamentary candidates who promised to look after their needs. The formation of unions strengthened their cause, and their own political parties sprang up. By the turn of the century, in some Australian states and in New Zealand, for example, Labour parties had already gained office. All of this led to slow, gradual improvements.

Developments in the English-speaking world did not go unnoticed in Germany. The Gotha program had made a nominal commitment to Marxist principles, but the policies pursued by the SAP were reformist and not bent on confrontation. However, when the full weight of Imperial Germany's ruling establishment descended upon the Social-Democratic labour movement after the introduction of Bismarck's anti-socialist laws, the new Erfurt program, introduced in 1891, made a far stronger commitment to Marxist ideals. In line with Marx's demand for a 'dialectic unity of theory and practice', the party's chief theoretician at the time, Karl Kautsky, drew up a theoretical and a practical part. Emphasis was firmly on theory, which committed the SPD to work towards a proletarian revolution. The practical part reiterated pragmatic, everyday policies to improve the living and working conditions of the workforce.

Yet the ink on the Erfurt program had scarcely dried when the theoretical part was severely questioned. The most outspoken of the critics was Eduard Bernstein, a journalist and a leading member of the party who, living in London during the 1890s, entertained close contacts with the British labour movement.

Bernstein questioned Marx's predictions of the impeding collapse of capitalism. To him, the growth of cartels and trusts did not mean that capitalism was becoming exclusively a system of a few large-concern owners; nor did he agree that the members of the lower middle class were being proletarianised. Hence, he thought, the claim that the rich at the top were getting fewer and fewer and the exploited at the bottom more numerous was incorrect. He questioned the assumption that there was a system of rigid division between classes, and the notion of class struggle altogether. He did not see evidence that the proletariat was being forced into ever-increasing misery, but argued rather that the living standards of the working class were rising. Thus Bernstein concluded that the capitalist system would not collapse in revolution, that a violent overthrow of the prevailing system was in fact unlikely to occur, and that social changes should be gained by evolutionary and not revolutionary means. The strengthening of workers' parties and their unions, and the formation of consumer co-operatives and other kinds of mutual enterprises, would lead to a system of what he called 'municipal socialism'. This was more likely to bring real improvement than was revolutionary rhetoric.

The arguments of the 'revisionists', as Bernstein and like-minded Social Democrats were soon to be called, caused a heated and increasingly bitter debate in party periodicals and newspapers, and at annual conventions. The left wing of the party strongly attacked Bernstein's arguments. The comment by Rosa Luxemburg, who was establishing herself as one of the most prominent and outspoken members of the socialist left, that the work of the unions was the 'labour of Sisyphus', particularly angered the majority of party and union officials. The left did not see the growth of cartels as a stabilising economic factor, but as a sign that capitalism was nearing its final stage, in which vast properties were controlled by a few. Nor did a few years of economic growth, accompanied by a modest improvement in living conditions for the workers, mean that major convulsions of the capitalist system were necessarily a thing of the past.

The left wing of the SPD was also concerned about the party's coy stand on the ever-increasing militarisation, nationally and internationally. The Social-Imperialists (social democrats supporting Germany's policies of imperial expansion) were a minority before the war, but the domestic policy of the party leadership to avoid rocking the boat as much as possible caused growing concern. In the early twentieth century, there was a heated debate in the Socialist International about what action the proletariat should take in the event that war broke out. It was the German party leadership, in particular, that thwarted any attempt to commit national parties to the principle of international worker solidarity above the right of national self-determination.

Having suffered a major defeat in the so-called 'Hottentot election' of 1907, Social Democrat leader August Bebel gave a profoundly patriotic speech highlighting his party's sense of duty and its commitment to the German state. A number of other socialists re-iterated his stance, impressing some of their opponents. The National Liberal deputy Graf Du-Molin Eckhardt, for example, commented that in the last sitting of the Reichstag he had 'detected more German strength and national courage in the ironic laughter of the embittered Social Democrats than in the hollow phrases uttered by all speakers from the establishment parties'.[21]

The SPD deputies' reaction after the 1907 election was understandable: having refused to vote for further funds to enable the German government to continue its war of annihilation against the Herrero people in South-West Africa, the SPD was viciously targeted by the establishment for failing to support the fatherland. Their seats in parliament were reduced from 81 to 43.

More serious was the performance of Bebel and other party leaders at the 1907 congress of the Socialist International held in Stuttgart. At the centre of the debate was the principle of international socialist solidarity. Many speakers warned that acceptance by the international workers' movement of the right to national self-determination meant that the workers might properly be called upon to defend a nation's independence. Commenting on August Bebel's position on the need to defend the fatherland, Karl Kautsky made the cynical comment that 'one day the German government could succeed in persuading the German proletariat that they had become the victim of aggression, the French government could do the same to the French people, which means that there could be a war in which French and German proletarians would with great enthusiasm murder each other and cut each other's throats'.[22] Bebel replied that it would be a sorry business if men who had made politics their profession were not able to judge whether or not they were facing a war of aggression. Six years after Kautsky's grim prediction, the majority of the SPD voted for the vast increases in military spending demanded by a regime that the party had once sworn not to support with a single penny.

Signs that the German labour movement was heading towards a division were not confined to the party's theoreticians or to intellectual debates, but were also evident among the SPD's rank and file, and the workforce in Germany at large. Although huge industrial conglomerates had been formed by the beginning of the twentieth century—coal and steel empires, gigantic plants in the newer chemical and electrical industries—the majority of the German workforce was still employed in small-to-medium workshops, and factories in small-to-medium towns and cities. This meant that the industrial growth rate had not been too fast, and that large numbers of workers did not have to be recruited, accommodated, and incorporated into the workforce in the shortest possible time.

Houses for most workers were not slums. Some even owned their own small house, or rented a flat in a block with access to a square of garden to grow vegetables, and perhaps even a small shed for husbandry—important assets at a time when wages were never much above subsistence level. Unions aimed to gain gradual income rises, improve working conditions and working hours, and establish co-operative stores to provide cheaper goods—achievements far more significant than some distant workers' paradise. The memory of the difficult years under the anti-socialist laws had not altogether faded: why risk a new wave of suppression? And another factor was emerging:

with compulsory schooling, and with most German schoolteachers being ardent nationalists and imperialists, the message that Germany was being denied its proper place in the world was reaching schools in working-class districts as well. The daily propaganda in the conservative media of the day about Germany's world mission had its effect on workers. Although they still received rough treatment from Imperial Germany's economic, legal, and political establishment, the 'fellows without a fatherland' (*vaterlandslose Gesellen*), as Kaiser Wilhelm II had once labelled the SPD members, were starting to grow closer to the fatherland—a process that would have been even speedier had they not continued to receive rough treatment from the rest of society.

Karl Marx, however, did not have all his science wrong. In Berlin, Hamburg, Bremen, and other large cities, and many parts of the Rhenish-Westphalian region and centres in Thuringia and Saxony, industrialisation had advanced at such a rate that there was indeed proletarianisation. Housed in heartless tenement blocks (*Mietskasernen*), overcrowded and with poor or no sanitation, exploited by landlord and employer, and confronted with appalling working conditions, the workers here had nothing to lose but their chains, to quote another of Marx's famous dictums. Among them were Poles and other migrant labourers from eastern and south-eastern Europe—and German workers, like most other Germans, tended to think of the Slavic East as backward. There was little respect for ethnic minorities. Hence the real division in Germany as the twentieth century progressed lay not between the Social-Democratic movement and the rest of society, but within the workforce and the party itself. This split was not apparent until war broke out, but the origins of the division within the German labour movement date to the beginnings of the twentieth century. It was to become a bitter division that had fatal consequences for the Weimar Republic, which continued into the Cold War era, and which still influences German politics today.

'The spirit of 1870—71'

At the head of the kaiser's great pride, the imperial navy, stood Grand Admiral Alfred von Tirpitz. The son of a judge and the son-in-law of a doctor, he came from the professional middle class and, like so many of his contemporaries, had joined the navy rather than the army, whose upper hierarchy was preserved for the nobility. Tirpitz achieved a meteoric rise, resulting in his appointment as secretary of the navy in 1897. In his new position he managed, by tireless lobbying and constant intriguing, to increase the size of the German battle-fleet from seven capital ships in 1898 to 43 by the outbreak of war. Kaiser Wilhelm's ardent support for the construction of a powerful German navy greatly aided his cause. Tirpitz, a fanatical Social Darwinist, firmly believed in the superiority of German culture, and was convinced that the decisive battle for German world leadership had to be fought eventually against the decadent, materialist British empire. However, he attempted to conceal his intention not only from British leaders—without success—but also, because of the enormous costs of his program, from the Reichstag. He also concealed his plans from the army leaders, because his ambitions would rival their own plans and influence.

The admiral's assumption that sooner or later a Social Darwinist struggle for world domination would have to take place between the ageing, moribund, and essentially frivolous British civilisation and the spiritually superior German empire was shared by eminent history professors and theologians at German universities, who became outspoken exponents of *Weltpolitik* and its inevitable showdown with the United Kingdom:

> Quite consciously they were going to change established rules of international relations because of a commitment to a peculiar German philosophy of history and politics and, one could add, theology of state. There was hardly a pastor or theologian who did not believe Germany's God-given right to expand, by force if necessary, at the expense of the putatively inferior and moribund cultures of the other Great Powers, especially Britain's, because it was demonstrably the will of Almighty God.[23]

The idea that war was a kind of 'biological necessity', and that international politics amounted to a struggle between rival nations for supremacy and survival, was widely held in leading German military and political circles. The firm belief in German superiority was not directed towards Britain alone. Erich von Falkenhayn, the empire's war minister, Kurt Riezler, advisor to Reich chancellor Bethmann-Hollweg's, and Georg Alexander von Müller, the chief of the imperial navy cabinet, for example, all saw war as a means of preserving or asserting the German race against the Latins and Slavs.[24] Belief in the need of the German empire to expand was not confined to Social Darwinist disciples; voices in big business and industry also advocated the necessity for German economic hegemony (and, in its wake, political dominance) in Europe, a goal not likely to be achieved by peaceful penetration. However, the newer industries, the electrical and chemical conglomerates that had been witnessing a phenomenal rise in the pre-war years, shrank from the idea of major military conflict, as this would cause considerable harm to their flourishing trade. The chemical giants, in particular, that had outpaced all global rivals in the invention and manufacture of new pharmaceutical products, had nothing to gain from war. But as the excitement mounted, the leaders of German chemical companies could not escape the rekindling of the spirit of 1870–71. A short and decisively victorious war would cement the German empire's rightful place in this world, and (incidentally) facilitate further large-scale economic expansion. A study of Germany's chemical industries aptly summarises the situation:

> Patriotism, the sense that German aspirations were being stifled by its European rivals, and the expectation that the glorious triumphs of Sedan in 1870 could be repeated, were as openly expressed in the Rhineland boardrooms and laboratories of Bayer, Hoechst, Agfa and BASF as they were in the aristocratic salons of Potsdam, the bourgeois cafes of Berlin's *Unter den Linden*, and the working-class beer *Keller* of Essen and Hamburg.[25]

Heading for war

The German army had not grown as rapidly as the imperial navy. The army leadership was reluctant to expand, because this would have meant including middle-class rather than aristocratic officers, and working-class rather than peasant soldiers. Nevertheless the size of the army rose by almost one quarter from 480,000 to 588,000 between 1893 and 1905. By now, the Schlieffen Plan had become the preferred option in case of war, and it demanded a much larger army. Count Alfred von Schlieffen, chief of the German army from 1891 to 1906, had designed a two-pronged strategy should Germany find itself simultaneously at war with both France and Russia. The plan stipulated that almost all of the German army would invade the south-eastern Netherlands and Belgium, and then thrust into France from the north, defeating the French forces and capturing Paris. In Schlieffen's opinion, only a token force was needed to protect the border with the tsarist empire, because it was envisaged that Russia would not be able to conduct serious warfare for a number of years. Moreover, Russian mobilisation, it was believed, would take at least six weeks, by which time the capitulation of France would have ensured that an army at full strength would be able to achieve victory in the east as well.

The Schlieffen Plan was described by the German military, and later by apologists of the German action, as 'preventive warfare'. This concept dates back to the Prussian King Frederick II (the so-called Great), who in 1756 had faced a coalition of continental Europe's three main powers, France, the Habsburg empire, and tsarist Russia.

In a preventive strike, he invaded the small German state of Saxony to launch an attack on the Austrian empire—the event that started the Seven Years War of the eighteenth century. In reality, the execution of the Schlieffen Plan would be an unquestionable act of offensive warfare. The elder Moltke, the German war hero who led the army to victory over France in 1870–71, had also planned for a possible war on two fronts. He would hold the German forces behind the frontiers. In the west, the German army would wait until the French invaded the disputed provinces of Alsace and Lorraine and then attack. In the east, superiority of German road and rail communications lines meant that wherever the Russians attacked, German forces could move to await and crush them. If this did not cause a complete Russian collapse it would eventually drive the tsar to sue for peace.

Moltke's plan was a defensive one. Schlieffen's Plan, regarded by the military and political leadership as a certain recipe for victory, was not. By the time the plan was in place, the German military had made it clear that they had no interest in the two conferences at the Dutch capital, The Hague, aimed at preventing a repetition of the savagery that had featured in both the Franco-Prussian War of 1870–71 and the American Civil War.[26] The German empire was among the signatories of the Hague Convention IV 'Respecting the Laws and Customs of War on Land', which forbade pillage and the punishment of innocent civilians, including the taking of hostages and the use of human shields, as well as assault or bombardment 'by whatever means' of towns, villages, dwellings, or buildings that were undefended. Convention IV further stipulated that armed corps had to be under responsible command and observe the laws of war, and that there must be no destruction of the property of municipalities or institutions of a religious, charitable, or educational character, nor of historic monuments and works of art and science.

Although Germany signed, it soon became clear that the German army had no intention of observing these provisions, either in spirit or in letter. Senior military figures dismissed the convention as hypocrisy, signed by nations that 'behave as if they were serious about the silly negotiations and agreements', but in reality had no intention of sticking to them. Aspirations to peace 'were simply evidence of these nations' moral and military decay'.[27] Not surprisingly, field-service regulations issued in 1908 clearly stated that 'preventive' measures against civilians were justified.

The Schlieffen Plan demanded many more soldiers than were available in 1905. The German army leadership, for the reasons stated above, resisted any significant enlargement, but after new crises in North Africa and the Balkans, in particular after the first Balkan War of 1912, there was a decisive change in attitude. Germany had suffered a further international diplomatic setback in this conflict, which led Kaiser Wilhelm to meet with military leaders in December 1912, where he called for immediate war against France and tsarist Russia. He was strongly supported by the chief of the army's general staff, Count Helmuth Johann Ludwig von Moltke (commonly referred to as the younger Moltke), who was a particular enthusiast for the Schlieffen Plan. He stated that war had become inevitable, and that the sooner the showdown with the rival European powers could start, the better. This view was supported by the army's leaders, but opposed by Grand Admiral von Tirpitz, because the navy was as yet not ready for warfare against Britain. Other than ordering an increase of the German army (eventually to 800,000), no concrete decision was taken at this 'War Council Meeting'. The continental Entente powers responded by also sharply raising the size of their military.

As war clouds were gathering, the majority of Germans had become convinced that the empire was facing a deadly challenge from its rivals. This scenario was fostered no doubt by commentary from the government and much of the media, but the image of revanche-lusting French, Russian Slavonic expansionists, and trade-jealous Britons found an eager audience. The signs were ominous, should things go wrong.

And things did go wrong. The assassination of the Austrian Crown Prince Franz Ferdinand and his wife at Sarajevo on 28 June 1914 triggered a chain of events. Supported by assurances of German support in case of conflict, the Austro-Hungarian empire on 23 July presented the Kingdom of Serbia with a ten-point ultimatum to cease all activities directed against the Habsburg empire, to outlaw all organisations involved in such activities, and to allow police officials from Vienna to participate in a full investigation into the couple's murder. The Serbian government accepted nine of the demands, but rejected Point Six, empowering Austro-Hungarian officers to participate in the investigation, as this was an insult that no independent state could tolerate. This led the Habsburg empire to declare war on Serbia on 28 July. Tsarist Russia ordered a partial mobilisation the same day and, after the Austrian bombardment of Belgrade, as a precautionary step but not as a war-declaration, it ordered a full mobilisation on 30 July. Although the German chancellor, Bethmann-Hollweg, agreed that the tsar's mobilisation measure did not mean that Russia was intent on waging war,[28] this step was used to rally the German people behind what was claimed to be a defence against aggression from the barbarian east. On 1 August, the German government declared war on tsarist Russia, followed by a declaration of war on France on 3 August. On 4 August, the German army, in accord with the Schlieffen Plan, invaded Belgium. As this was a violation of Belgian neutrality, the British government presented Berlin with an ultimatum to stop the invasion immediately. When this was not forthcoming, the British empire declared war on Germany at midnight on 4 August.

Austria-Hungary's declaration on 28 July marked the outbreak of war. Germany's subsequent policies turned what was a localised conflict into a global conflagration.

CHAPTER TWO

The Great War

The German Supreme Army Command (OHL) fought the war from the outset with the utmost brutality, both in regard to the waste of their own human resources and the treatment of the civilian population in the occupied countries. Convinced that the war on the Western Front would take five, or at most six, weeks — 'You will be home before the leaves have fallen from the trees', Kaiser Wilhelm II had promised — the armies proceeded in their task without mercy.

The storming of the Belgian bastion-city of Liège was a grim foretaste of the kind of warfare that lay ahead. The OHL had expected that the occupation of Belgium would not involve serious military action, but their brigades got stuck at the four easternmost forts of the city. The shells they used were too light to penetrate the fortifications, and the Belgians had little difficulty in pouring fire into the German troops, slaughtering row upon row. The dead piled up in ridges a metre high, but the assault continued. Lives were spent like bullets in the knowledge that there were plentiful reserves to make up the losses.

American historian Barbara Tuchman, in her acclaimed *August 1914*, quotes a Belgian officer's account of the bloodbath. He watched stunned as the German soldiers marched wave after wave into the machine-guns. The wall of dead and wounded grew so high that the Belgians did not know whether to fire through it or crawl out to clear openings with their hands. Unbelievably, the Pickelhaubens kept coming, sheltering behind the barricade of their own dead and dying to charge up the glacis, only to be mowed down.[1] Tuchman makes the point that the over-lavish waste of human lives by all sides throughout the war began at Liège on the war's second day. It was a grim portent of the Somme, where hundreds of thousands fell, and of the apocalypse at Verdun.[2]

Belgian forts were not taken until ten days after the Germans had moved in a number of huge artillery pieces produced by arms manufacturer Krupp in Essen and the Austrian firm Skoda. Krupp's 420mm howitzer was the largest siege weapon ever produced: eight metres long, weighing 98 tons, needing a crew of 200 to operate. Equipped with a 42-centimetre calibre barrel, 'Big Bertha', as the gun was nicknamed, could fire a shell weighing 800 kilograms over a distance of 15 kilometres. One Krupp 420mm and several Skoda 305mm guns blasted the Belgians into submission within several hours.

The advance into France was marked by a wave of atrocities directed against alleged *francs-tireurs* that resulted in the massacre of thousands of civilians in both Belgium and France.[3] For Belgium, German occupation meant that for the next four years the country was stripped barer than by a plague of locusts.[4]

Appalled by the viciousness of the German attack, the Allies, by the end of August 1914, were convinced that they faced an enemy that had to be beaten, a regime that had to be finished off, and a war that had to be fought to the end. On 4 September, the Russian, French, and British governments signed the Pact of London, which stipulated that they would not conclude a peace separately.

Although contemporaries believed that the German advance had been held up for two weeks by Belgian resistance, in reality the timetable to take Paris was delayed by only four days. Still, this was sufficient for almost 200,000 British soldiers to join the French in their efforts to halt the invasion. The inadequacy of the Supreme Army Command's planning became obvious, however, when only two weeks after the outbreak of war, two tsarist armies invaded East Prussia. The OHL's perception that it would take six weeks for the Russian military to reach combat strength was now disproved.

Immediately, retired General Paul von Hindenburg and his assistant, Erich Ludendorff, were dispatched to the east to take command of the Eighth German Army, the only force not involved in the west. The ensuing battles at Allenstein (today's Olszlyn, Poland) and the Masurian Lakes saw the slaughter of tsarist soldiers; 40,000 were left dead or wounded, four times the German casualty list. This decisive victory, however, was to have fatal consequences. The popularity of Hindenburg and Ludendorff rocketed sky-high, further enhancing the prestige of the army. As the political power-base in Germany was soon to shift from the civilian administration to the military, Germany's fate was eventually to end up in the hands of a military die-hard and an ambitious careerist and unscrupulous warmonger.

In the west, the Germans had speedily advanced to the River Marne, where they were halted and pushed back to the River Aisne by the British and French. The Schlieffen Plan had failed. By the end of the year, the Western Front had stabilised into a line stretching from Ypres in Belgium to the south of Alsace, marking the start of four years of trench warfare that would take the lives of four million soldiers. The chief of the general staff, Helmuth Johann Ludwig von Moltke, was blamed for the plan's failure because of the alterations he had made. As stated above, the plan's designer, Count Alfred von Schlieffen, had envisaged a decisive strike through the Netherlands and Belgium to encircle Paris. Cut off from the capital and from its source of supplies, the French army would have to surrender, after which Germany could turn its entire military might on tsarist Russia. It was said that Moltke's alterations weakened the force of the onslaught by confining the attack to Belgium. Furthermore, by withdrawing divisions from the invading armies to protect south-western Germany, and by placing one army on the Russian border, a rapid defeat of the French had been frustrated. The result was trench warfare, with Germany committed to fight in both east and west.

German mythology is one side of the story; the reality of the situation is another. The truth is that the Schlieffen Plan was mistake-ridden and bound to fail from the outset. As had become immediately clear, the assumption that the tsarist war machinery would take weeks if not months to get into action was based on unsound speculation. An invasion of the Netherlands would not only have further outraged neutral countries—in particular, the United States—but would also have demanded additional army units that were not available. In this respect, Moltke had judged the situation correctly, and his decisions were justified. Nevertheless, it was he who was blamed for the failure of the Schlieffen Plan, and he was subsequently removed from the army leadership. A bitter and broken man, he died in June 1916.

It was irrelevant that troops were diverted to the east and south-west. The German plan to paralyse Paris and finish the war in the west was unrealistic. There was a discrepancy between the strategies of the military leaders and the reality of twentieth-century warfare. The military, and not only in Germany, was still thinking in terms of nineteenth-century warfare: quick movements and speedy actions made possible by brisk cavalry charges and the deployment of light artillery and relatively small armies. Their plans failed to take account of transport infrastructure. Over a million troops had to be shifted, and many artillery weapons could not be carried by men or horses, at least not over long distances. Railways were important but geographically limited, and could be destroyed by the retreating enemy.

As the German armies moved deeper into France, men scheduled by the plan to advance over 40 kilometres a day began to tire, and supplying them chiefly by horse-drawn transport became more difficult. The design of motorcars and trucks had not advanced far enough to provide a more flexible and efficient means of transport; nor was there capacity to produce such vehicles in large numbers. Tanks entered the war in its later stages and, indeed, played a key part in the outcome — but on the wrong side, from the German point of view.

Frustration with the failure of the Schlieffen Plan to provide the expected speedy defeat of the French led the German army to look for other means to win the war. Military action resumed after the winter of 1914–15, when the commander-in-chief of the British army, Field Marshal Sir John French, sent this disturbing cable to London:

> Following a heavy bombardment the enemy attacked the French Division at about 5pm ... Aircraft reported that thick yellow smoke had been seen issuing from the German trenches between Langemarck and Bixschoote ... What follows almost defies description. The effect of these poisonous gases was so virulent as to render the whole of the line held by the French Division ... practically incapable of any action at all. It was at first impossible for anyone to realise what had actually happened. The smoke and fumes hid everything from sight, and hundreds of men were thrown into a comatose or dying condition ...[5]

The instigator of poison gas and its use in warfare was Fritz Haber, a German chemical scientist who had garnered an international reputation through his development of synthetic ammonia. Aged 46, he could not be called up for military service at the front and, as a Jew, he would not qualify for a home-front commission. Nevertheless he was a deeply patriotic fatherland supporter, and most keen to play his part in the war effort. He was one of the signatories to the Fulda Manifesto, an imperious statement signed by many intellectuals that denied any German responsibility for the outbreak of war, and which claimed that the country's military stance prevented the destruction of its entire civilisation. When approached by the chief of the German War Raw Materials Office, Walther Rathenau, to look for possible solutions to break the stalemate at the front, he set keenly to work. Poisonous chlorine gas was the outcome.

The use of poison gas had been forbidden under the Hague Convention of 1907, which stipulated that warring nations 'agree to abstain from the use of projectiles the objective of which is the diffusion of asphyxiating or deleterious gases'. The treaty had been signed by Germany, although, as stated above, the German signature had always been a half-hearted one. There was little subsequent hesitation when it came to subordinating ethical principles to military necessity. On 22 April 1915, the first gas attack was launched. The result was devastating:

> Within a few seconds the throats, noses and eyes of the unprotected soldiers in the Allied trenches were smarting agonisingly. Shortly thereafter the men began to cough and vomit blood, their chests heaving as they tried to draw breath, but only managing as they did so to suck more of the deadly poison down into their lungs ... By sunset an estimated five thousand Allied troops had died and another ten thousand or so were barely hanging on to life in field medical stations.[6]

The panic brought about by this gas attack allowed the Germans to breach Allied defences, but—much to Haber's disgust—they had not assembled sufficient troops to drive the advantage home. A counterattack by Canadian forces closed the gap again. The dilettantism that surrounded so much of Germany's military planning soon marked its efforts to change the course of the war by the use of poison gas. The French and British speedily developed their own gas and, as the wind in Western Europe blows mainly from the west, German soldiers copped much more gas than did their counterparts, and they had no hesitation in voicing their anger.

When confronted in later years with questions about the ethics and morality of his wartime conduct, Haber claimed that to be killed by gas was no worse—in some cases, it might be even better—than being blown up and mutilated by explosives, or mowed down by machine guns. He had only done his patriotic duty. He was at odds with his wife, Clara Immerwahr (the first woman to graduate with a Ph.D. in physical chemistry at Breslau University), who committed suicide after the gas attacks of spring 1915. The Allies attempted to try him for war crimes, but he escaped to Switzerland, where he was able to hide until he could safely return to Germany. Much to the disgust of British and French scientists, he was awarded the Nobel Prize for his discovery of synthetic ammonia in late 1918. During the 1920s he participated in the reconstruction of the nation's chemical industries, but his luck ran out in 1933 when the Nazis took power. They had no interest in his achievements for the fatherland, and because of his Jewish background he was forced to flee to England. Not surprisingly, given his role in the development of poison gas, the British scientific community gave him a rather hostile reception. He took up a position at the Hebrew University in Palestine, but died unexpectedly in January 1934 while visiting his family in Basel, Switzerland.

Germany's inability to defeat the Allies on land was paralleled by their lack of success at sea. With the outbreak of war, both Germany and the United Kingdom instituted blockades, but with the superiority of the British fleet the German declaration was an empty gesture. The consequences of the *Kaiserreich*'s naval inferiority were clear by the beginning of 1915. The nation had depended heavily upon international trade. Half of its raw materials and about one-third of its food were imported before the war; almost two-thirds of its manufactured goods were sold abroad. The imposition of the British blockade deprived Germany of all but 20 per cent of its export market. Although there was initially strong opposition from the civilian government—the torpedoing of merchant vessels without prior warning was a further violation of the Hague Convention—the ever-deteriorating military situation soon removed all opposition to moving maritime warfare below the surface. The unlimited U-boat warfare that began in February 1915 soon proved another nail in the coffin of the German empire. The damage done to Allied shipping by U-boat warfare was limited, but that done to Germany's international reputation was huge.[7] In particular, the sinking of the British passenger liner *Lusitania* on 7 May 1915 led to outrage in neutral countries—above all in the United States, as 120 of the 1,200 dead were U.S. citizens.

Public opinion in the United States had largely supported the Allies after the outbreak of war. Since the abortive attempt by the British empire to bring the disloyal North American colonies back into the camp in 1814, British-American relations had been cordial. In particular, trade between the two states had flourished for a century, and the bulk of the States' population was of British descent. In addition, most politicians and media commentators believed that the responsibility for the slaughter that had broken out in Europe had to be borne by the Central Powers.

The sinking of the *Lusitania* raised, for the first time, the real spectre of America entering the war. After the sinking of the British vessel *Arabic* in August 1915, when again a number of U.S. citizens lost their lives, submarine warfare was halted temporarily. It was resumed at the beginning of 1916, the German war leadership hoping perhaps that there had been a softening of American attitudes. When this proved a miscalculation after the sinking of the cross-channel steamer *Sussex* (which caused another massive outcry in the United States), unlimited submarine warfare was again called off in May 1916.

On 31 May 1916, the German navy challenged the British in a massive encounter off Jutland, which ended in a decisive defeat. The father of the German navy, Admiral von Tirpitz, had been forced to resign two months earlier. His grandiose design to achieve German global hegemony by building a huge battle fleet had proven a huge failure and a waste of money. For the German empire at sea and on land, the writing was on the wall.

War aims

From the beginning, German war aims lacked moderation. This was in part because the Germans had persuaded themselves that they were victims of Allied aggression, and consequently would gain generous compensation for having been forced to fight, and in part because they needed to secure their empire's future military position. With their armies advancing on Paris in the second half of August, and the capitulation of France seemingly only weeks away, key sections of the German economic, political, and military establishment saw the alleged injustice done to the German nation as a licence to rob and plunder. As the Reichstag deputy of the Catholic Centre Party, Matthias Erzberger, put it in a three-point program to the German chancellor on 2 September:

> The slaughterous struggle ... makes it an obligatory duty to take advantage of victory ... Germany's military supremacy on the [European] continent has to be secured for all time so the German people are able for at least the next 100 years to enjoy unmolested peaceful development ... the second goal is the removal of Germany's unbearable subordination to England's perpetual domination in all matters of world policy, the third the break-up of the Russian colossus. It is for this price that the German people went into the war.[8]

In this spirit, the leading Rhenish-Westphalian industrialist August Thyssen developed his plan for the future shape of Europe in late August 1914. In the west, Germany would incorporate Belgium and the French departments of Nord, Pas-de-Calais (including Dunkirk and Boulogne), Meurthe-et-Moselle with its belt of fortresses, and, in the south, Vosges and Haute-Saône. France would have lost virtually all of her iron-ore regions. In the east, Russia would have had to cede her possessions in Poland, all the Baltic provinces, the Don region with its capital, Odessa, the Crimea, and a large part of the Caucasus, which would enable Germany to spread her sphere of influence into Asia Minor and Persia. The realisation of these aims would lift Germany to the rank of a world power equal to the British empire.

With minor variations, these views were widely shared by other influential members of heavy industry, East-Elbian conservatives, and the Pan-German League. The leaders of the banking sector, the shipbuilding industry, and the newer electrical and chemical industries refrained from demanding large-scale outright annexations, preferring an economic and political European union under German military leadership.

Chancellor Bethmann-Hollweg also saw as an aim of the war '... not to restore the European balance of power, but precisely to eliminate for all time that which has been termed the balance of power and to lay the foundation for German predominance in Europe'.[9] He ordered his secretary, Kurt Riezler, to streamline the various demands into a provisional outline of German war aims. Known as the 'September Program', its chief demand was the establishment of German hegemony in Europe. France was to be weakened to such an extent that it would cease to be a leading power. In addition to its territorial losses (the annexation of Belfort, the western Vosges, the coastal region from Dunkirk to Boulogne, and the iron-ore region of Briey being the minimum demands) France was to pay an indemnity large enough to cripple its armament production for the next 18 to 20 years. This was part of the overall goal to make the country economically dependent on Germany. Luxembourg was to become a federal state within the empire, and Belgium to be given the status of a vassal state. In the east, the non-Russian nationalities were to be liberated from 'Russian oppression'. Instead there was to be a 'cordon sanitaire' of small states under direct or indirect German rule.

The chief aim of the September Program, however, was the foundation of a central European customs union (*Mitteleuropa*) incorporating Austria-Hungary, France, the Netherlands, Denmark, Norway, Sweden, and Poland. Although the union was to have no constitutional government, and although the principle of equality among members was to be presented to the outside world, the intention was that *Mitteleuropa* would secure German economic (and hence political) predominance in Europe. Overseas, there was to be the creation of a German empire in Central Africa.

The halting of the German advance at the River Marne and the subsequent failure to break through Allied defences at Ypern led to a moderation of war aims. This was temporary. Because the government and the military leadership had concealed from the public the consequences of the failure of the Schlieffen Plan, and as German losses by the end of 1914 already amounted to hundreds of thousands, demands for massive compensation from France and other enemy countries were soon being voiced again with renewed vigour. In fact, rather than weakening as the war progressed, they became ever more radical.[10] In the later debate about German war guilt and German expansionism, these war aims were dismissed by apologists of the *Kaiserreich*'s role in the disaster of 1914–18 as the fantasies of 'expansionist dreamers', and not to be given any credibility,[11] or seen as the last utterings of reactionaries who were wedded to a moribund political system and who thus could not be taken seriously.

German peacemaking in 1917 and 1918 was to show there could be no more serious misinterpretation of the reality of the situation.[12] In fact, when chancellor Bethmann-Hollweg urged moderation because of the need to secure the continuous support of the German labour movement, he soon lost his position.

The German Social Democratic Party

The outbreak of war in 1914 took the Social Democratic German labour movement by complete surprise. The assassination of the Austrian crown prince and his wife at Sarajevo on 28 June was condemned by the party and its media as a mindless act orchestrated by fanatical supporters of a Greater Serbia. No one foresaw a danger to international peace in the action. This view changed on 24 July when the outside world heard the news of the Austro-Hungarian ultimatum to Serbia, and its insistence that the government in Vienna carry out the investigation into the assassination.

After this, the party called mass demonstrations against the impending war, in which hundred thousands of workers participated. Leadership and newspapers protested against the policies of the Vienna government towards Serbia, which seemed bent on bringing about war. They also lodged an appeal with the German government to refrain from any military intervention and to put pressure on Vienna to maintain peace. A meeting held at the office of the Socialist International at Brussels on 29 July, in which Rosa Luxemburg, Hugo Haase, Karl Kautsky, Jean Jaurès, and other leading socialists participated, merely asked for further peace demonstrations and for renewed demands upon the governments in Berlin and Paris to pressure tsarist Russia and the Habsburg empire to de-escalate the worsening international situation.

The SPD's attitude to the situation changed completely with the declaration of tsarist Russia's partial mobilisation later that day, widely seen as an act of imminent war against the German empire. Behind the decision of the party to unanimously vote for the granting of war credits on 4 August stood the perceived need to defend the nation against attack from Russia, always viewed by German Socialists as the symbol of reaction and the arch-opponent of democracy and social progress.

The bulk of the party leadership and the rank and file accepted the state of 'civic truce' (Burgfrieden) declared by the kaiser—that all citizens, regardless of their political leanings, should now fully support the German war effort—without any qualification, and they supported the war until the end. This is in part explained by the fact that most members were content with the reformist approach the party and union leadership had been pursuing since the abolition of the Anti-Socialist Laws in 1890. Progress in bettering workers' wages and conditions was slow, but progress there had been.

The year 1912 saw the SPD emerge as the largest party in the Reichstag, and membership and voters' support continued to rise. By the outbreak of war, the party could count on over one million members, and the affiliated Free Union movement over two-and-a-half million members. Policies that might endanger the organisations through confrontations with the state, or other radical actions such as general strikes, were not popular. The workers themselves, notwithstanding their humble social and political status, felt greater loyalty to the Wilhelmine state than they did to their fellow workers in other countries. The party still maintained its Marxist theoretical program of aiming to establish a socialist order, but the advocacy of radical policies before the Great War was confined to a small left wing made up chiefly of intellectuals.

There was another reason why gradualism and moderation, and not class warfare or confrontation, determined party and union policies. Because of their organisations' growth, salaried officials had to be appointed to run and administer the enterprises. These officials, who were chosen for their presumed administrative skills rather than their political views, soon dominated key positions at local, regional, and national levels. This meant that a great deal of power and influence was in the hands of professional administrators—bureaucrats who were bent on avoiding risk and accommodating the powers that be. Managing finances, improving the efficiency of agitation, and conducting election campaigns became the sole occupation of many administrators. So the growth of a major bureaucracy had a very conservative impact upon the German socialist movement in the years before 1914.

It was not only for altruistic reasons — love for the fatherland, and duty to the kaiser in times of crisis — that influenced many party and union leaders to support the war unswervingly. If Germany's workers helped in the successful defence of the nation, surely there could be no more obstacles in the path to major political reform that would make the country more democratic and allow the working class, too, to participate in governing. Chancellor Bethmann-Hollweg told party and union officials repeatedly that their part in the nation's war effort would be rewarded. So whether by unqualified conviction, or by pragmatism, the majority of the leadership viewed as a luxury any discussion about who had started the war or what the aims of the imperial government might have been. Germany had to avoid defeat at all costs; their contribution must be to keep the workers attached to the national cause, and partisan political activity had to be suspended. To deviate from this position was heresy.

It did not take very long, however, before the official position of the party and union leadership in support of the German war effort was challenged by an initially small but rapidly growing opposition. Although the party had voted unanimously for the granting of war credits on 4 August, there had been dissent in the SPD's Reichstag caucus the night before, when 14 of the 92 members implied that they would vote against it. This was not because they refused to believe the official explanation for the declaration of war—that a Russian attack was imminent—but because they wanted to uphold the traditional Social Democratic principle of not supporting the imperial system with a single penny. In the end they buckled, and for the last time the SPD's vote was unanimous.

The reason given for the outbreak of war was first challenged by an outspoken member of the SPD's left, Karl Liebknecht. He had gone to Belgium in the autumn of 1914, returning convinced that Germany was waging an aggressive war—a view that was hardened by his growing realisation that German war aims envisaged that, in the event of a victorious war, continental Europe would become, more or less, a greater Germany. In a rare act of civil courage, Liebknecht was the sole Reichstag member who in December 1914 voted against the further granting of war credits.

During 1915, opposition to the war within the workers' movement grew rapidly. As the German armies advanced far into enemy territory, and the threat to the fatherland diminished, the question was raised why no attempts were being made to bring the war to an end. When a third vote for war credits was taken in March 1915, 30 SPD deputies left the chamber, and Otto Rühle joined Liebknecht in voting against the bill. Two months later, a resolution drafted by Liebknecht proclaiming that the policies pursued by the party since August 1914 were violating party principles was signed by close to 1,000 officials. On 19 June 1915, the oppositionists published an article in the *Leipziger Volkszeitung* entitled 'The Command of the Hour', which maintained that Germany was pursuing expansionist aims, and asked all members to demand an end to the

Burgfrieden and to refuse further support for the war effort. On 21 December, the number of SPD deputies voting against new credits rose to 20; 22 had left the chamber beforehand, and the pro-war faction was thus reduced to 50. Three months later, those who again defied discipline by voting against war credits were expelled from the party. The dissidents responded by forming a Socialist Working Alliance (*Sozialistische Arbeitsgemeinschaft*, or SAG). Throughout 1916, the conflict spread to regional and local branches, reaching an initial peak on 28 June when 55,000 workers in Berlin staged the first political strike of the war in protest against the trial of Karl Liebknecht. With harshly worded attacks on the party's stance pouring in from many influential district executives, the confrontation between the majority and the dissidents became ever more embittered. This was particularly obvious in the struggle for control of the party press. Supported by the strong arm of the law, supporters of the war wrested many affiliated newspapers from opposition editors, and ousted party functionaries. The majority of the leadership stuck to their guns. As the losses at the front reached staggering proportions, it took courage and conviction to admit that the death toll was due not to the need to defend the home-country, but to the expansionist aims of Germany's leaders. Most lacked this courage. To doubt the defensive nature of Germany's war effort was a mortal sin.

A last bitter confrontation within the party occurred over the Auxiliary Service Law (ASL), which was introduced in December 1916 to solve Germany's severe labour shortage. Neither the movement of soldiers from the front nor the employment of prisoners of war or foreign workers brought into Germany achieved the numbers of labourers needed to meet the industrial requirements of the war. The result was increasing job mobility, as most workers naturally preferred higher-paid work, especially in ammunition plants. This endangered production in other industries where pay was lower, and threatened important public services such as the railways. The ASL placed restrictions upon the movement of workers for the duration of the war, but employees were still able to change jobs, provided they could prove to an arbitration committee that their new employment would constitute a marked improvement on their previous position. These arbitration committees were made up of representatives from labour and the employers. The pro-war SPD leaders and the unions were satisfied with the ASL because, for the first time, German industrialists were compelled to sit down in joint meetings with them. On the other hand, the ASL met considerable resistance from employers who participated reluctantly and often only after pressure from government authorities.

The oppositionists in the SPD feared that the ASL would be a means of coercing the workforce into unconditional support for the war. When they held a separate meeting on 7 January 1917, all who attended were suspended from the party. In response, on 6 March 1917, the day the United States declared war on Germany, the dissident party members founded the Independent Social Democratic Party (USP). The spirit of the Russian March Revolution, which broke out two days later, on 8 March, greatly influenced the gathering. Hugo Haase, one of the two party leaders, opened the conference:

> The storms of March roar through the world. The
> red dawn shines across the Russian borders into this
> hall. All who have gathered are filled with admiration
> for the Russian brothers' fight for feedom and peace.
> They also feel solidarity with all like-minded in the
> International.[13]

The newly founded party was not an homogenous organisation. USP membership ranged from the chiefly intellectual left, centred around Rosa Luxemburg and Karl Liebknecht (who were demanding revolutionary proletarian action to change the imperialists' war into a class war), to leading reformists such as the party's chief revisionist theorist, Eduard Bernstein, and the Neo-Kantian journalist and party editor, Kurt Eisner. These various factions came together for the duration of the war in their desire for peace and their opposition to the continuation of the mass slaughter. They protested against the ever-worsening living conditions suffered by the bulk of the population, against the shameless annexation demands, against the failure to achieve any social or political reforms, and against the remorseless oppression of the workers and their leaders under the state of siege imposed at the outbreak of war and subsequently by the Auxiliary Service Law. Their membership increased rapidly: 120,000 members had gone over to the USP by the end of 1917, and the SPD's membership had fallen from almost one million to 240,000.

Dwindling numbers notwithstanding, the SPD did not waiver in its loyalty. The party continued to remind members of their duty to support the defence of the fatherland, and they promised that there would be rich rewards in the end. Not that they had grounds for optimism as far as political or social reforms were concerned: as prominent German historians have argued persuasively, German victory in war would have meant the consolidation of the existing political, economic, and social order, not its demise.[14] Whether gains made by the unions under the ASL would have survived once the pressures of war had disappeared is equally doubtful.

Without the untiring efforts of the SPD and affiliated union leaders to keep production going, Germany's war effort would have collapsed much sooner. This was to have two fatal consequences. In the short term, it ensured that the slaughter continued until, bled dry by the Allied advances in the west, the front finally collapsed—though not before hundreds of thousands more soldiers had fallen. In the long run, the SPD joined the bulk of German society in its conviction that the acceptance of peace terms that did not specifically free Germany of responsibility for the outbreak of war, and make an adequate allowance for the suffering of the German people, would amount to a mortal sin.

The changing fortunes of war

It would be wrong to suggest that the military blundering and the massive waste of human lives due to arrogant, careless, and incompetent planning was confined to the German side. The British secretary of state for war over the first two years, Lord Herbert Kitchener, was not up to the task of providing effective military leadership. He was uncertain about Britain's role in the war, and he was perplexed by the trench warfare that had developed on the Western Front after the battle of the Marne. 'I don't know what is to be done' he is often quoted as remarking, 'this isn't war'.[15] Nor were the British army commanders much more competent. An Australian officer summed it up when he observed that the training manuals of the British army were as much use for the conduct of war as were the 'cuneiform inscriptions of a Babylonian brick'.[16] In a war that soon depended on engineers and artillery officers, the British army was dominated by horse soldiers: five of the nine army commanders were cavalrymen. In particular, General Sir Douglas Haig, who together with Sir William Robertson had taken command of Britain's war effort by the beginning of 1916, continued against all advice (and all evidence) to maintain that the cavalry had a vital role to play in modern warfare.

The Entente's blunders began in the spring of 1915 with the decision to attack the Turkish empire (which had entered the war on the Central Powers' side on 29 October 1914) at the Dardanelles. With the war in Western Europe at a stalemate, a group of ministers—including David Lloyd George, the chancellor of the exchequer; Winston Churchill, the First Lord of the Admiralty; and Maurice Hankey, the secretary of the War Council—had started to argue that a successful Dardanelles attack would bring decisive advantages to the Entente. The opening of the Dardanelles Straits and subsequent capture of the Turkish capital Constantinople would enable shipping to assist the Russian war effort, Serbia might be saved, and the Balkan countries might be mobilised against the Habsburg empire's southern flank. Without any scrutiny as to the military and strategic feasibility of the plan, a naval onslaught was launched in mid-March 1915.

When this was easily rebuffed by the Turks, it was decided to launch an amphibious landing of British, Indian, French, Australian, and New Zealand divisions—amounting initially to 75,000 soldiers—at the Gallipoli peninsula. The commander-in-chief of this operation, British General Sir Ian Hamilton, had little knowledge of the peninsula's geography, which, marked by a continuous succession of steep hills along the entire coast, was a defender's dream. Virtually all beaches were exposed to fire from surrounding cliffs and hills that provided ideal cover for the Turks to inflict heavy casualties upon the invaders.

The difficulty had become obvious by the first day of the campaign, on 25 April 1915, when Australian and New Zealand forces landed at a small beach near Gaba Tepe in the north of the peninsula. They managed to dig in and establish trenches at a number of beachheads over the next weeks, but it was soon apparent that attempts to break through the well-fortified Turkish lines were bound to fail. The attempt to invade the Ottoman empire from the Dardanelles was a waste of men and money. Ships needed to carry war supplies to Russia were not available, Serbia had already been defeated by Austria-Hungary and, with the exception of Romania, no Balkan country showed any inclination to join the Entente powers. Even so, the Gallipoli campaign was prosecuted until January 1916, leaving 200,000 casualties on both sides.

The campaign was the only major victory for the Turks

in the 1914–18 war, and is regarded as a defining moment in the nation's struggle to transform itself from Ottoman empire to Turkish Republic. The date of the first landing at Gallipoli became one of major importance to Australia and New Zealand. Anzac Day, as it was soon named, was to stand as a national symbol, not only for the commemoration of the fallen and the veterans in these two countries but also as one important step towards the birth of a national consciousness — a move away from rule by Britannia.

But in terms of military casualties, the battle for the Dardanelles ranks among the also-rans. Leading these sad statistics is the battle of Gorlice-Tarnow in Galicia in May 1915, where Russian troops had managed to invade the Polish part of the Habsburg empire. The army command of the latter was forced to ask for German assistance, and the ensuing offensive saw the Central Powers' largest victory. The Russian front collapsed under the enormous losses: 743,000 casualties, and 895,000 soldiers taken prisoner.

Frustrated by the continuous failure to break through Allied lines in the west, the German army leadership decided to attack the French fortress of Verdun in late February 1916. The declared purpose of this enterprise was to bleed the French forces to death. Relentless fighting raged for five months, with every metre of ground fought for. The French withstood all attacks, and the OHL had to call off the battle in July. French casualties amounted to 317,000 soldiers; German casualties, to 280,000. For the Germans, Verdun became a symbol of senseless slaughter, undermining the nation's fighting spirit.

In the second half of June 1916, the British and French launched an attack on the Somme. For one week, their artillery pounded each square metre of the German positions with a ton of shells. Then the infantry divisions attacked and pushed back the 50 kilometre-long German front line by two kilometres. The cost of this meagre gain amounted to 400,000 dead and injured for Britain, and 200,000 for France. The German defenders lost 400,000 soldiers. When the campaign was called off by the Allies in November, the battle of the Somme had consumed over one million lives.

Notwithstanding their defeat in Galicia the year before, the Brusilov Offensive, launched in June 1916, brought tsarist Russia's largest success. Austria-Hungary's losses amounted to 250,000 casualties, while 370,000 of their soldiers were either taken prisoner or deserted. The disaster of the Brusilov Offensive greatly strengthened the position of the forces working towards the destruction of the Austro-Hungarian empire, and marked the beginning of the end for the Habsburg monarchy, which for nearly half a millennium had provided stability in Europe's most unstable region.

Although time should have been on the side of the Allies because of their superior resources in manpower and ammunition, poor military planning meant that by the beginning of spring 1917, the Entente powers were in strife. Failure to achieve success on the battlefield was matched by dire economic conditions.

A great deal of hope now rested on the United States entering the war. There was widespread support in leading U.S. political and military circles to go to the aid of the Allies, but one person steadily resisted all efforts to abandon American neutrality. Unfortunately for the Allies, that person was the only one who could make the decision: the U.S. president, Thomas Woodrow Wilson.

Woodrow Wilson

This man, on whom so many hopes and expectations rested, and on whom so much responsibility was to fall, was born on 28 December 1856 in Staunton, Virginia, the son of Presbyterian Minister Joseph Ruggles Wilson and his wife, Jessie Janet. During the Civil War, his father was a pastor in Augusta, Georgia. Woodrow graduated from Princeton and the University of Virginia Law School, gaining his doctorate at Johns Hopkins University. Thereafter he pursued an academic career, becoming professor of political science at Princeton, where in 1902 he was appointed as the University's president. In 1910, he was persuaded by the Democrats to contest the governorship of New Jersey, which he did successfully.

In 1912, he was nominated as the presidential candidate for the Democrats, scored a convincing victory in the election, and introduced a number of economic and social reforms in his first term of office. A person of firm moral convictions, a staunch believer in American principles of freedom and democracy, Wilson held deeply religious beliefs. Gossip had it that his greatest regret was that there had been room for only one on the Cross. These elements combined in the foreign policies Wilson formulated and pursued following the outbreak of the European war in 1914. If disorder and usurpation of rights provoked war, then ordered relationships and obligations fostered a moral sense of community among nations; if Christianity brought about the brotherhood of men, then there should also be brotherhood among nations; if the weight of popular opinion and institutions of free debate and representation were allowed to prevail, then human progress would triumph over autocratic destructiveness and repression. The establishment of a community of free nations with free citizens at the end of the war was to become Wilson's great goal.

In January 1915, Wilson sent his closest confidant, Edward Mandel House, commonly referred to as Colonel House, to London in a six-month attempt to persuade the French and British governments to accept U.S. mediation. Colonel House was not successful, but he developed sympathies for the cause of the Entente during that time, almost costing him his influential position in the president's team. On a second mission to Europe in January 1916, he brokered with the British foreign secretary, Sir Edward Grey, what virtually amounted to an ultimatum to Germany: submit to American mediation, or face U.S. military intervention. This went far beyond anything the president wanted, and House was spared a breach with Wilson only because the British government itself disavowed what became known as the 'House-Grey Memorandum'.

In May 1916, the president for the first time outlined officially a scheme for the creation of a League of Nations in a speech given to the United States 'League to Enforce Peace'. Such an organisation was to be based on a model of collective security aimed at preventing a future renewal of war. His suggestion failed to make an impact anywhere, but this did little to dissuade the president from embarking on more serious efforts to stop the slaughter.

On 19 December 1916, the belligerents, in a so-called 'Appeal for Peace', received a note from president Wilson setting out the terms upon which war might be concluded. Wilson presumably felt that once they had committed themselves to moderate terms, negotiations could begin. The note stressed that he was not offering to mediate, and he certainly wanted to maintain an impartial position. In Wilson's opinion, the objectives of both sides as stated by their leaders seemed virtually identical: to secure the rights and privileges of weak peoples and small states, and to put in place a lasting peace and security against aggression or selfish interference. In claiming that the objectives of both sides were virtually the same, the president obviously hoped that the peace terms put forward by the warring nations would not be excessive.

The president's move was as ill-timed as it was ill-conceived. Wilson's assumption about each side's objectives aroused London, Paris, and Petrograd, and in all three places his action was received with anger and consternation. The note had been sent out only one week after German chancellor Bethmann-Hollweg had offered a peace note on behalf of the Central Powers, and consequently the Allies suspected the U.S.A. of acting in co-operation with Germany. The French ambassador in Washington expressed Allied vexation at a meeting with U.S. secretary of state Robert Lansing. Lloyd George called the American note an insult, and the Foreign Office tried its best to calm an angry press.

Nevertheless, the Allies had to step carefully. The British war effort depended greatly on American supplies. The country still had enough general resources for a further six months, but any cut-off of American nitro-cellulose after June 1917 might have been catastrophic. The Food Controller estimated that Britain depended upon America for 40 per cent of its flour supplies. The director of army contracts admitted that there was no alternative source for the supply of lubricating oil, without which Britain's war machinery could not keep running. He also indicated that Britain's war effort was almost as dependent on the U.S. for petrol. Beyond these essentials, there was a large range of important commodities that it would be difficult to obtain outside America in sufficient quantities.[17] Finally, the Allies' war effort was heavily dependent on U.S. loans.

The German peace proposal was easily dealt with. It had been drafted a few days after the psychologically important capture of the Romanian capital, Bucharest, on 6 December 1916. Hindenburg and Ludendorff had insisted on the boastful tone; but, as far as its content was concerned, the proposal amounted to little more than empty rhetoric. In a conglomeration of commonplace and non-committal phrases, the Central Powers announced a 'candid and loyal endeavour to enter into discussion'. They proclaimed their 'love of peace', and asked the Entente to disclose its terms—although they failed to state any terms themselves. The peace note lacked sincerity, and constituted a diversionary manoeuvre; it had probably been intended mainly for domestic consumption. There might also have been hopes that the move would favourably influence world opinion, particularly among the neutrals.

It was on the basis of the absence of any terms that the Allies dismissed the German proposal. Lloyd George gave the official rejection in a House of Commons speech on 19 December. He stated that Britain would not negotiate without hearing Germany's terms, that Germany was dangerous and could not be trusted, and that any terms would have to be more unfavourable to Germany than the *status quo ante bellum.*

To deal with Wilson's note, however, was not so easy. Although the Allies must have been tempted to return a negative reply because they felt angry and insulted, it would have been dangerous to offend Wilson and endanger neutral opinion. After much discussion, they finally agreed on a mutual response, which they handed to the American ambassador in Paris on 10 January 1917. They recognised the plight of neutrals, for which the Allies were not to blame, having in no way provoked the war, and they stressed that Allied governments were trying to minimise neutral losses to the extent their defence against the enemy allowed. Then followed an expression of satisfaction that the president's note was not associated with that of the Central Powers. Again the Allies protested at Wilson's implication that the aims of the belligerents were the same.

Listing the many misdemeanours committed by the Central Powers, the Allies stated their terms. There was to be restoration and reparation for Belgium, Serbia, and Montenegro. France, Russia, and Romania were to be evacuated, with reparations. Moreover there was to be liberation of the Italians and Slavs, and the creation of a free and united Poland. The terms ended with the declaration that the Allies did not seek the 'extermination or political extinction of German peoples',[18] but that they were determined to seek victory to ensure a safe and prosperous future for civilisation in the post-war era.

To the Entente, the president's note had clearly shown how little the American public was aware of the nature of the war, its causes, and its likely consequences. Hence the British government decided to give the Allies' reply plenty of publicity: there was to be widespread publication not only in the principal cities of the United States, but also in the provincial press, including the Sunday and local 'boilerplate' newspapers, resulting (it was hoped) in greater understanding by the American public. The British government was able to use Wilson's 'peace note' for effective propaganda against peace without victory, and the president's initiative had to be ranked a flop. The German government replied evasively, still refraining from stating any terms, and there were no signs that the OHL would accept a return to the *status quo ante bellum*. Under these circumstances, to threaten the Allies with cutting off supplies was unwise, as his advisers told Wilson.

Yet the president's peace efforts were not to be derailed so easily. On 22 January, he gave his famous 'Peace without Victory' speech to the U.S. Senate, largely a repeat of his note of 19 December. Before the Allied governments could recover from a wave of consternation and frustration caused by this renewed mediation attempt, they received vital and decisive assistance from the enemy's military leadership. On 1 February, chancellor Bethmann-Hollweg, at the demand of the OHL, announced the recommencement of unlimited submarine warfare. It was the first of two acts of great folly. On 3 February, the United States broke off diplomatic relations with Germany.

1917

If the United Kingdom was facing a host of difficulties by the beginning of 1917, Germany's situation was worse. Admittedly, they had had the better of it on the battlefield in the preceding year. They had gained control of the Balkans, pushed the tsarist forces back on the eastern front, and had withstood Allied attempts to achieve a breakthrough on the Western Front. On the other hand, their own attempts to gain the upper hand in the west had failed as miserably as had those of the Allies, and the British blockade was having an ever more serious impact.

Particularly hard hit was the food supply. German agriculture was not prepared to withstand the effects of prolonged warfare. In pre-war years meat, wheat, poultry, eggs, fish, and various vegetables had to be bought on a large scale from abroad, predominantly from nations that had now been cut off by the blockade. This was also the case with concentrated fodder and artificial manures, especially Chilean saltpetre and raw phosphates. German agriculture was also severely handicapped by the lack of labour. Rural districts had lost as much as 40 per cent of their population through call-up, a loss that could not be compensated for by the labour of women or prisoners of war. The civilian population had also suffered from the priority given the military in food distribution. Partial failure of the potato crop led to the notorious 'turnip winter' of 1916–17, when the weekly potato ration declined to 500 grams, supplemented by 1 kilograms of turnip. Meat had fallen to 400 grams, and butter was replaced by margarine.

Other problems were caused by the lack of raw materials.

Thus civilians faced a severe shortage of heating, clothing, fuel, and hygiene products, and in its wake came physical exhaustion, mental fatigue, and lack of concentration caused by undernourishment. As all industries associated with war production had to rely on a large intake of unskilled women and juveniles, the rate of accidents caused by negligence and inexperience soared, rising by ten times between 1914 and 1917. The number of strikes was increasing. In addition, all the forced measures introduced to overcome the shortage of labour failed. Neither the Auxiliary Service Law, nor the employment of POWs, nor the forced recruitment of labour in occupied countries could prevent the German war effort from running out of manpower by the beginning of 1917. If the war was to be won it had to be soon, and this meant the British blockade had to be broken—by hook or by crook.

The resumption of unlimited submarine warfare was almost certain to bring the United States into the war—a disastrous prospect, as a number of military and political leaders (including the chancellor) warned. But the proponents of renewed total submarine aggression won the day. They argued—correctly—that it would take the best part of a year before the U.S. would be able to put sufficient troops into the field; by then, they said, Britain would have been brought to its knees. They also doubted—incorrectly—that American soldiers would make a significant military contribution.[19] Initially, all seemed to go well for the OHL. Although Wilson had indeed broken off diplomatic relations with the German empire on 3 February, and although the recommencement of unlimited submarine warfare had put an end to Wilson's rhetoric about peace without victory, as yet there had been no American declaration of war.

A month later, the March Revolution of 1917 disposed of the tsar. Although the Russians remained in the war, the chief force that drove the uprising—the extreme war-weariness of both soldiers and civilian population—was not eased. The German war leaders were already designing schemes aimed at finishing off the Russian empire.[20]

In the submarine war, German U-boats were inflicting massive damage: 840,000 tons of Allied shipping were sunk in April 1917 alone. A continuation of such losses might indeed have forced the Allies to sue for peace. This did not eventuate, because the German leadership obliged with a second disastrous decision.

On 17 January 1917, in Whitehall's Room 40—the most secret chamber of the British Secret Service—two cryptographers, the Reverend William Montgomery and Nigel de Grey, a young publisher the service had borrowed from William Heinemann—were routinely working through intercepted telegrams when Grey noticed an unusually long message comprising more than a thousand row of numerals. Because Britain already knew how to decipher German diplomatic codes, the pair realised, after hours of painstaking work, that they were looking at telegrams sent by the state secretary of the German foreign office, Arthur Zimmermann, to the German ambassador in Washington, Count Johann von Bernstorf.

In what could easily have been a routine message, the decoders were struck by the word 'Mexico' and later by the word 'alliance'. They worked out that the message fell into two parts. The first announced that German submarine warfare was to recommence on 1 February, a decision the

Allies had long been expecting (and dreading). The second, which was to be passed on to the resident minister for the German empire in Mexico, Heinrich von Eckhardt, was much harder to understand. They made out words proposing an alliance, joint conduct of war, and joint conclusion of peace, but it was only after days of work that they understood the full implications of the telegram: Germany was promising to assist Mexico 'to regain by conquest her lost territories in Texas, Arizona, and New Mexico'.[21]

The cryptographers were aware of the great importance of their discovery: here at last was the instrument to puncture U.S. neutrality. They informed their superior, the director of naval intelligence, Admiral Sir William Reginald Hall, who also realised the complexity of the problem. How could the Zimmermann telegram be revealed to the Americans, and above all to president Wilson, without revealing how it had been obtained? The U.S. would not believe it to be genuine if it came from a British source, but Hall was fearful about the risk of disclosure. If the Germans realised that British security had cracked their code, the British advantage would be ended.

Admiral Hall waited until 1 February, the date the Germans proposed for the recommencement of unrestricted submarine warfare. He had assumed, like almost everyone else in the United States and among the Allies, that such resumption would inevitably mean the U.S. declaration of war against Germany. Alas, having broken off diplomatic relations with Germany, president Wilson gave no hint that he intended to go further. Hall decided to act. On 5 February, he informed the secretary of state for foreign affairs, Arthur Balfour, of the telegram. By now he had also worked out how to make the telegram's existence public without revealing that the British had deciphered the German code. What was needed was to obtain a copy of the telegram that had been sent by von Bernstorf to Mexico. The von Bernstorf telegram would have small but vital differences in date, address, and signature from the original. This copy, when published, would lead the Germans to believe that the interception had been accomplished somewhere on the American continent. Convinced of the inviolability of their code, they would assume that an already decoded copy of the telegram had been stolen or leaked *after* reaching Mexico, and that there must have been spies or betrayers in Washington or in Mexico. Hall proved right in all of his assumptions.

It was several days before the British contact in the Mexican Telegraph Office managed to secure the desired copy. When obtained, it was found to differ in the essential points that Hall had hoped for. It took a further fortnight to complete the decryption of the Zimmermann telegram. Balfour and Hall decided that the admiral should reveal the telegram to Mr. Edward Bell, the U.S. chief intelligence officer, on 22 February. Bell's reaction was the same as that of many Americans who subsequently saw the telegram—it was a fraud. How could anyone in his right mind plan to dispossess the United States of a huge part of its territory? However, after Hall had convinced Bell of the authenticity of the document, his doubts were settled, and he assured Hall that publication of the telegram would certainly mean war. At 1.00 p.m. on 24 February, Balfour formally sent the full text of the telegram to Walter Hines Page, American ambassador to the United Kingdom, who forwarded it to the White House, along with a note explaining how the document had been obtained.[22]

Realising he had been deceived by the Germans, the president was outraged, as was the majority of the American public when the text was passed to the media on 28 February. At the same time, both Houses in Washington were considering the so-called 'Armed Ship Bill'—a bill to equip merchant ships with navy gunners who were empowered to shoot on sight. The bill was widely seen as a last warning to Germany that U.S. entry into the war was imminent if submarine warfare were resumed, and it had thus met hefty opposition from pro-German and pacifist organisations. The House of Representatives was so outraged by the newspaper reports about German perfidy that it passed the bill virtually unanimously. Not so the Senate, where a small but vociferous section of pro-German senators and a group of equally vociferous pacifist members questioned the authenticity of the telegram and demanded convincing evidence that the document was not a hoax.

This meant that state secretary Robert Lansing, who was officially in charge of handling the affair, faced the difficulty that had earlier hampered Page and Hall—how to make it public enough to convince, but not so much as to give away the source. The attack upon the genuineness of the telegram gathered momentum inside and outside the Senate over the next 24 hours, and the State Department was expecting that the situation would be further complicated should Zimmermann deny sending it. To the stunned amazement of all involved, however, the problem was solved the next day when the German foreign secretary, for reasons known only to himself, admitted sending the telegram. This effectively ended pro-Germanism in the United States, although the Senate still refused to pass the Armed Ship Bill. On 9 March, using his executive authority, Wilson gave the order to arm the ships anyway. On 18 March, three American vessels were sunk without warning by German submarines. Two days later, Wilson reconvened Congress for 2 April to hear a matter of grave national importance. On 6 April, the United States entered the war. On that day, Zimmermann was dismissed.

As Hindenburg and Ludendorff had correctly predicted, U.S. entry into the war was not followed by the speedy arrival of large numbers of American troops, but it did give the Allies an immediate boost in morale, and it meant that there was no longer a threat that the president would cut off supply or loans. By May 1917, the British had also found ways to blunt the German submarine attacks. The re-introduction of the convoy system—a group of merchant or troopships travelling together with a naval escort—had immediate results. Convoys had been widely used in the age of sailing vessels, but had been discarded in the age of steam. Now, aircraft helped to make the new convoy system particularly effective: from June 1917 until the end of the war, only 138 of 16,539 vessels convoyed across the Atlantic were sunk, 36 of these because they were stragglers.[23]

Under these circumstances, and in the light of the disastrous battles of 1916, the Allies' best strategy would obviously have been to wait and see, avoiding further massive loss of human lives, as time was on their side. This time, however, the French army leadership felt sure that the German war effort in the west could be broken without too many losses. Robert George Nivelle, head of the French military since December 1916, designed an attempt to break through German defences on the River Aisne in the spring of 1917. The British leadership initially held great reservations about Nivelle's plan, but as the bulk of the attack was to be carried out by French forces, they consented. Nivelle launched his offensive in mid-April. Within a month, the French had suffered such heavy losses that parts of the French armies began to mutiny, and his campaign collapsed. In the end, it was not the German but the French war effort that had been brought to the brink of collapse.

By now, one might have expected even the thickest of army commanders to have realised that trench warfare created serious disadvantages for attacking forces seeking to overcome entrenched defending troops — but not so the commander-in-chief of the British army, Sir Douglas Haig. Haig ordered a renewed attempted to break the German lines in Flanders in August 1917, against considerable opposition — in particular from Lloyd George, who had replaced Herbert Henry Asquith as prime minister in December 1916 (and who regarded Field Marshal Haig as 'dull witted').[24] The ill-fated enterprise, which reached its nadir in the bloodbath at Passchendaele in November 1917, left the U.K.'s war effort, as the year drew to its close, once more in a dire position. The French were still licking their wounds after the failure of the Nivelle offensive, and the Italians had been repeatedly mauled in their unsuccessful and costly attempts to invade Austria. Then came the news from St. Petersburg that Russia was pulling out of the war.

The March Revolution had sent a clear message that the Russian war effort was not likely to survive much longer. The provisional government tried its best to avoid the collapse, but opposition to the war was increasing by the day. The most outspoken radicals in the anti-war movements were the Bolsheviks, but virtually all of their leaders were in exile, mainly in Switzerland. If the exiles, particularly their chief theoretician, Vladimir Ilyich Lenin, could be brought back to Russia, they would surely hasten the process of disintegration. With the aid of the Social Democrats, the German government struck a deal: on 9 April 1917, Lenin and all of the Bolshevik exiles in Switzerland were put onto a sealed train at Zurich and carried through Germany to the Baltic port of Sassnitz, where they boarded a ship to Sweden. From there they made their way by train to Petrograd's Finland Station, where they arrived at midnight on 16 April. They were greeted by crowds of workers, sailors, and soldiers singing 'La Marseillaise' and waving red flags. Lenin gave a short speech heavily criticising the Petrograd Soviet, which he described as a stinking corpse. He demanded that the Petrograd government and capitalism be overthrown, that Russia withdraw from the war, and that all lands be given to the peasants; in short: peace, bread, land—all power to the Soviets. It took the Bolsheviks all of six months to take government in the October Revolution of 1917. They immediately withdrew from the war.

The showdown

As the year 1917 drew to its close, the Allied war effort rested almost solely on the shoulders of the United Kingdom and its empire—a situation serious enough to persuade the

British prime minister to once again address the question of peace negotiations. His speech to the British Trade Union Congress of 5 January 1918 followed a peace feeler by the German secretary of state, Richard Kühlmann. Under what came to be known as the 'Kühlmann Peace Kite', the Berlin government was willing to accept terms favourable to Britain. Belgium and Serbia were to be restored, Alsace-Lorraine to be returned to France, and there would be colonial concessions to Britain. As there was no reference to Russia, the Germans obviously expected compensation at Russia's expense. The Kühlmann Peace Kite soon turned out to be another diversionary manoeuvre, like the German peace talk a year earlier, but the possibility of peace in the east offered a way out of Britain's difficulty.[25]

Referring to the German-Bolshevik peace negotiations at Brest-Litovsk, Lloyd George expressed his regret that the current Russian rulers had withdrawn from the war and had commenced negotiations with the enemy without consulting the Allies. Thus the latter had 'no means of intervening to arrest the catastrophe which is assuredly befalling their country. Russia can only be saved by her own people'.[26] Lloyd George did not call for the destruction of Germany or Austria-Hungary; nor did he want Germany to lose her former position in the world. Only her quest for world domination was to be abandoned. The demand for a democratic order in Germany, it was hoped, would strengthen the position of moderate elements in German politics against the OHL. The independence of Belgium, of course, had to be restored, and Alsace-Lorraine returned, but his reference to Russia offered Germany a chance of peace with gains in the east.

Lloyd George's speech, which also aimed at securing the support of the British workforce for a further year of war, was almost immediately overshadowed by a move that was to have enormous consequences for the peacemaking of 1918–19 and the rest of the century: president Wilson's Fourteen Points. Announced by the president on 8 January 1918, they played a key part in the evaluation of the post-war peace treaties, and in particular the Treaty of Versailles. Since the signing of the treaty, accusations have been made that international guarantees allegedly made by the president in the Fourteen Points were not honoured. The losers were deceived and treated in a dishonest manner. As will be shown below, according to post-war German political and historical accounts, this failure to follow 'Wilsonian principles' was the chief injustice imposed on the German nation in 1918–19. Over the years, this interpretation has also gained considerable support in some in the former Allied nations. The importance of this issue for the subsequent discussion in this book calls for a brief analysis of the Fourteen Points.

Wilson made his proposals in January 1918, at a time when U.S. troops were still to arrive in Europe in significant numbers. They were another attempt by the president to stop the slaughter and to establish peace. No doubt he also hoped that the success of his initiative would spare the Americans major combat and loss of life. That some of his points later became part of the peace treaties, and were incorporated into the charter of the League of Nations, did not make them *post facto* into a binding legal document or a set of immutable laws for the peacemaking process. They did not and could not constitute more than another step on the part of the president towards finding a way to end the war; nor were they meant to. Any serious peace negotiations could only commence in collaboration with the Allies—above all, Britain and its empire, France, and Italy, who had borne the brunt of the war on various fronts for three-and-a-half years.

The first five of Wilson's points dealt with general issues: (1) open covenants and abandonment of secret diplomacy; (2) freedom of the seas in times of war and peace; (3) freedom of trade; (4) reduction of armaments; and (5) a fair settlement of colonial issues.

Of these, the first two had a short life. Article 2 was not accepted by Britain. The first demand, to establish open covenants, was also abandoned before the peacemaking process proper commenced. Wilson himself acknowledged that open diplomacy, which would involve media access to the negotiations, would allow the deleterious effect of public opinion to influence the proceedings, rendering meaningful negotiations impossible.[27] As the subsequent century has shown, noble as are the goals of abandoning secret diplomacy, no government lays bare its security and surveillance policies.

Articles 6 to 13 contained demands affecting specific countries involved in the war. There was to be withdrawal of foreign troops from Russia (Article 6); from Belgium (Article 7); from France, which included Alsace-Lorraine (Article 8); and from Romania, Serbia, and Montenegro (Article 11). The peoples of the multinational empires of Austria-Hungary and Turkey were to be given the freest opportunity for autonomous development (Articles 10 and 12), the frontiers of Italy were to be adjusted along recognisable lines of nationality (Article 9), and there was to be an independent Polish state with free and secure access to the sea (Article 13). Last but not least was the formation of an association of nations to secure international stability and order (Article 14).

The Allies' enthusiasm for Wilson's latest peace initiative was lukewarm. Officially, the British, French, and Italian governments backed his proposals. After all, they included some of the Allies' key demands — withdrawal of German troops from France, Belgium, and large parts of south-eastern Europe, free access to the sea for Poland, and adjustment of Italian frontiers — and, of course, the last thing they could afford at the beginning of 1918 was to put off the U.S. Behind the scenes, however, they held fears that the 'holier than thou' president Wilson, with his Presbyterian idealism and his belief that it was his God-given task to secure world peace and democracy, would monopolise the peacemaking process and might give away at the peace table what the soldiers had been fighting for so bitterly — a settlement that would put an end to future German aggression.

Their concerns were soon laid to rest. Little more than two weeks after Wilson's proposal of the Fourteen Points, the new German chancellor, Georg Friedrich von Hertling, who had succeeded the ousted Bethmann-Hollweg in November 1917, rejected both peace moves on behalf of the German government and military. Germany's military leaders remained firmly committed to the fight for realisation of their maximalist war aims, and all political parties with the exception of the Independent Socialists rejected the Allies' proposals outright, despite the fact that acceptance would have left the German empire in a far stronger position in the peacemaking process than was the case at the year's end.

The OHL, and in particular Ludendorff, obviously buoyed by their victory in the east, would ensure that there were rich pickings. Negotiations with the new Bolshevik government started on 22 December in the Belo-Russian city of Brest-Litovsk. Trotsky, who led the Soviet delegation, tried his best to avoid a catastrophe for Russia. In mid-January, the chief German negotiator, Max Hoffman, presented the German demands. These included the establishment of independent states in the Polish and Baltic regions formerly belonging to the Russian empire, and in the Ukraine.

For a month, Trotsky tried various tactics to stall the negotiations, in the hope that the revolution would spread to Germany or that Germany might be defeated in the west. But when the Germans, tiring of his efforts, resumed their military offensive on 18 February, the Soviets had no alternative but to surrender. This time, the terms were much harsher. Russia ceded more than 290,000 square miles of land and around a quarter of its population. This territory effectively contained the countries of Finland, Latvia, Lithuania, Estonia, Poland, and Belarus, where the Germans immediately set out to establish client states. Russia, in addition to its population losses, lost half of its industries, nine-tenths of its coal deposits, one-third of its railway network, one-third of its agrarian lands, and its complete oil and cotton production. The treaty, which achieved the maximalist war aims spelt out by the German establishment as from September 1914, aroused the sort of popular euphoria that had greeted the outbreak of war, and was supported with great enthusiasm by the middle-class parties in the Reichstag. As the SPD had always maintained that Germany was fighting a defensive war and was not bent on achieving territorial gains, its caucus members officially abstained from voting. Again, only the Independent Socialists voted against Brest-Litovsk.

To most Germans, the Treaty of Brest-Litovsk seemed to confirm that the stand taken by the war leadership was the correct one, further enhancing the prestige of Hindenburg and Ludendorff. The German victory in the east had the effect of consolidating the social, economic, and political system of Wilhelmine Germany, rather than hastening its demise.

The Treaty of Brest-Litovsk did not end German expansion in the east. Their forces continued to push into southern Russia, occupied the Crimea, and, after reaching the Black Sea, advanced into Trans-Caucasia. In August 1918, the Soviets signed a further treaty that forced them to cede Georgia, surrender all of Russia's gold to Berlin, pay six billion marks in reparations, and leave the full exploitation of the Donetz Basin coal-fields to Germany. As German historian Hans-Ulrich Wehler aptly comments, '[T]he constellation in the East in the summer of 1918 make the goals of Hitler's Russian politics in no way appear as the megalomaniac visions of a fantasist, a foreigner who imposed himself on German history, but as the concrete continuation of the state of affairs already established a generation earlier'.[28] The jubilation of the OHL over their conquests in the east was to be ephemeral: dark clouds had massed in the west.

Imperial Germany's final attempt to defeat the Western Allies began on 21 March 1918. Backed up by artillery fire from 2,800 guns and 1,400 heavy mortars, a force of close to four million men, attacking on a front of 50 kilometres, managed to penetrate 60 kilometres into enemy territory. It was Ludendorff's last hoorah. 'Operation Michael' ran out of steam on the second day. As in the summer of 1914, inadequate transport ensured that the advancing troops could not be properly supplied with reinforcements, ammunition, and, this time in particular, food. Allied forces were able to regroup, and managed to push back all subsequent attempts to break through. At the end of April, Ludendorff had to admit that the attack had failed. He continued for another two months with various efforts ('hammer-blows') to bring about a change in the fortunes of war, but 1.5 million casualties had brought Germany's fighting capacity close to its end. In mid-July, the Allies started their counter-offensive. Because of the losses Germany had incurred in Operation Michael, the Allies had the advantage in manpower. Moreover, 100,000 motor trucks ensured that there would be no supply problem (the German army at its peak could boast only 20,000 motor cars). The Allied advance was supported by 1,500 British and French tanks, while the sum total of German tanks was 80, most of them out of action. France and Britain had also gained control of the air: France alone was able to put 3,440 aircraft into the sky.

The French commenced the offensive, and succeeded in pushing back the Germans at a rapid rate. They were joined at the beginning of August by British, Australian, and Canadian forces who, on 8 August at Amiens, broke decisively through the trench-line for the first time in the war. The breakthrough was supported by 500 tanks, which this time made easy work of the barbed wire. Now there was no halting the advance. On 29 September, British and Australian troops broke through the well-fortified Hindenburg Line, which rapidly collapsed, and the German war effort was suddenly in free fall. The soldiers, undernourished, and physically and mentally exhausted, deserted in droves. The OHL was forced to admit that the war had been lost and that the government should seek armistice negotiations.

It speaks to the moral and ethical bankruptcy of the supreme command that they blamed everyone but themselves for Germany's defeat. On 1 October, Ludendorff, who more than anyone had been responsible for the mindless prolongation of the slaughter, instructed the Kaiser 'to bring those people into the government [the Reichstag members—in particular, the Social Democrats] who are largely responsible for things having turned out as they have. We shall therefore see these gentlemen enter the ministries, and they must now make the peace that has to be made. They must now eat the soup that they have served us'.

The view that the German military had fought bravely and well to the end, and would not have faced defeat but for the civilian government and the political left, was widely shared by the German officer corps. They were to despise the Republic that emerged from the war. Ludendorff's shifting of responsibility was the beginning of a legend that was to bedevil Weimar democracy from the beginning. The alleged breaking of the Wilsonian promises and the 'stab in the back' legend would play a key role in the rise of National Socialism.

Götterdämmerung (The End)

The news that Germany's war effort had collapsed was received by the Reichstag, politicians, the media, the civilian administrators, and the public at large with the greatest incredulity. The OHL had continued to maintain that Germany's victory was imminent until they stared defeat in the face. However, there was no time to procrastinate about the responsibility and the reasons for defeat. The Supreme Army Command had insisted that armistice negotiations commence immediately. A hastily convened new government under Prince Max of Baden, to date an unknown political quantity, which included Reichstag members and even Majority Socialists, approached the U.S. president on 4 October to commence negotiations based on his Fourteen Points. It must be pointed out, however, that the formation of this government was seen by the OHL and its political and economic backers as a temporary measure intended to solve Germany's hopeless military situation. With peace established, the generals were confident and determined that there would be a return to—what was to them—the state of political normality: the traditional Kaiser system with its inequality, class system, and social discrimination.

On 5 October 1918, French intelligence detected that the newly formed government had secretly approached Wilson for an armistice. The realisation that the president was considering a response to the German request without consulting his Allies stung the Entente leaders, who angrily informed Wilson that they would not negotiate an armistice agreement on the basis of the Fourteen Points. Wilson's note of 15 October to the German government, which stressed that armistice conditions could only be worked out in full consultation and co-operation with his Allies, and that they would commence only after serious constitutional changes had been implemented (which included the abdication of the kaiser), did little to pacify the governments in London and Paris.

Wilson's note immediately brought cries of foul play from the German establishment. They claimed that, by attempting to dictate the peace (*Friedensdiktat*), the Allies were playing a cheating game. In the meantime, the conflict between those who tried to save as much as possible of the old imperial system and proponents of a constitutional monarchy dragged on until the end of October, when the latter carried the day. All attempts to establish a workable political solution were cut short by the consequences of the decision of the German admirals to sail their ships from their anchorage at Kiel to challenge the Royal Navy. Apparently it was more important to save their honour and that of the German navy than to go on living since, given the vast superiority of the British battleships, it would have been nothing more than a suicide mission. The sailors, on hearing the news, decided that they preferred life, and mutinied. They were joined within a day by workers in the city, where on 2 November a Soldiers and Workers Council was formed. This had a snowball effect throughout Germany, and little more than a week later the once mighty Imperial Germany was overthrown by revolution.

In the midst of this revolutionary turmoil, the Allies finally agreed on a reply to the German request for an armistice. Following three weeks of acrimonious confrontation—at one point, Lloyd George angrily announced that if the Americans wanted to make peace with the Germans, they should do so, but that the British nation would then continue the war itself—the victorious powers drafted the armistice conditions, which they handed to a German delegation on 8 November at Rethondes in the forest of Compiègne. Peace was to be based on president Wilson's Fourteen Points, with the following addendum, drawn up by U.S. secretary of state Robert Lansing on the insistence of Lloyd George, and since referred to as 'Pre-Armistice Agreement' or the 'Lansing Note':

> Further, in the conditions of peace laid down in his address to the Congress of January 8, 1918, the President declared that invaded territories must be restored as well as evacuated and freed. The Allied Governments feel that no doubt ought to be allowed to exist as to what this provision implies. By it they understand that compensation will be made by Germany for all damage done to the civilian population of the Allies and their property by the aggression of Germany by land, by sea and from the air.[29]

The public was not made aware of this addition, and one of the many stratagems used by the subsequent German government to undermine the Versailles Peace Treaty was to claim that they had been made to believe that peace was to be based on what were to be called Wilson's 'original points'.

Then followed the other armistice conditions (also largely concealed from the public eye): German armies were to withdraw to the right bank of the Rhine, and three military bridgeheads were to be established by the Allies at Cologne, Mainz, and Koblenz, extending 30 kilometres to the east of the river. There was to be the surrender of huge quantities of military material and transport equipment, the immediate release of prisoners of war without reciprocity, the destruction of Germany's U-boats and the internment of the bulk of the German naval assets, and the renunciation of the treaties of Brest-Litovsk and Bucharest.[30] The Fourteen Points, along with the Lansing Note and the armistice conditions, were to be binding—that is, there were to be no negotiations. There was no alternative to acceptance of the armistice conditions. At 5.40 a.m. on 11 November, the armistice was signed at Rethondes.

Two days before the signing, Kaiser Wilhelm II left Berlin for the Netherlands to seek political asylum, which was granted by the Dutch royal family. On 9 November, a revolutionary government was formed in Germany, which immediately announced Wilhelm's abdication as German Kaiser and King of Prussia.

To summarise, the signing of the armistice was not an act of preparation for a mutually negotiated peace agreement. It was an unconditional capitulation on the part of the German empire. But this was not how the events of 11 November were presented to the German people—nor, if it had been, would they have believed it.

CHAPTER THREE

Paris

The retreat of the German armies through France and Belgium in November 1918 can only be described as a scorched-earth policy. The devastation was deliberate and systematic. Towns, villages, and farmsteads — already battered by four years of war — were looted and razed mercilessly, by order of the High Command. Industrial plants were removed to Germany, and factories that could not be transferred were blown up. Railway tracks were torn up, and the coalmines of north-western France were flooded. Returning POWs and people pressed to work in mines and factories painted a stark picture of the horrors.

Even as the German government sought an urgent armistice from president Wilson, the British mail-boat *Leinster* was sunk by a torpedo, killing 400 civilians. Not surprisingly, the term 'the Huns' once more abounded in the Allied media. British foreign minister Arthur Balfour, not known for his passionate speeches, summed up the prevailing spirit of the time in the House of Commons when he commented that the Germans 'were brutes when they began the war, and, as far we can judge, brutes they remain'.[1] This was not to assist Germany's cause as the peace negotiations were drawing near.

The Allies started proceedings in Paris, which, after brief consultation, had been chosen as the site for the negotiations that would shape the post-war world. President Wilson took only three weeks to arrange his departure for Europe, and on 4 December sailed on the *George Washington* for the French port of Brest. He was accompanied by what one historian described as 'as high-minded a company as can ever have crossed the Atlantic since the voyage of the *Mayflower*'.[2] They were mainly young and idealistic scholars. The delegation in the end would number 1,300 civilian and military members—probably the largest national contingent ever to attend an international conference.[3] During the journey, they were privileged to hear lectures from the president about his plans for the reconstruction of a better world.

He reiterated the chief ideas he had stated in his 'Fourteen Points', his 'Four Principles', his 'Four Ends', and his 'Five Particulars', and he demanded that the old system of peoples' oppression be dismantled. Secret alliances and warfare must be discontinued. Instead, forward-looking men and women, modern nations, and enlightened communities would aim for higher principles. The United States had entered the war because gross violations of rights had occurred; these had to be corrected, and steps had to be taken to prevent their recurrence. As he had stated in introducing the Fourteen Points, the peace should be so constructed 'that the world be made fit and safe to live in; and particularly that it be made safe for every peace-loving nation which, like our own, wishes to live its own life, determine its own institutions, be assured of justice and fair dealing by other peoples of the world, as against force and selfish aggression'.[4]

The principle of national self-determination was the one point in the president's statements that was to most influence the peacemaking process and, in its wake, Europe's and the world's history.

Nationalism can be described as a state of mind in which the supreme loyalty of the individual is felt to be due to the nation state. It was a relatively new concept in Europe. The idea of *the* French nation, *the* German nation, or *the* Italian nation was less than a hundred years old. Previously, the loyalty of subjects was to other forms of authority—to dynasties (the emperor, king, or duke), or to the Church, or to local oligarchies. Thus the term 'German' implied an ethnic or, at best, a cultural reference. A 'German' was a person living in an area bordered by the North and Baltic Seas and the Alps, who spoke one of several dialects. There were no political connotations. Larger states, such as the Austrian and Russian empires, or the kingdoms of France, Spain, or Prussia, were made up of many ethnic groups speaking different languages.

In the eighteenth century, enlightened thinkers— literati, intellectuals, and philosophers—began to advance ideas about reconstructing the state along more liberal and rational lines, and expanding government beyond the rule of a small section of society. Their ideas gained momentum after the French Revolution of 1789 when the revolutionaries, having cut off their king's head, faced a crisis of legitimacy. If government was no longer to be by divine or hereditary right, new forms of authority were needed. In France, the slogan *liberté, egalité, fraternité* aroused the loyalty of erstwhile subjects—now citizens. The newly formed French Republic demanded that the French give their loyalty to the nation state instead of the dynasty—to *la patrie*, not to the ousted Louis Capet.

Anti-French feeling in the wake of the Napoleonic Wars added to the growth of nationalism in central Europe. If France was a nation, then the German lands that had an equally proud cultural tradition should become a nation also. The 1848 Revolution was an attempt by sections of the educated European middle classes to establish nation states under a system of parliamentary democracy. When it failed, modern nationalism took a turn for the worse.

With hindsight, it can be argued that in the slow and difficult progress of European (or, indeed, Western) civilisation towards what is today called 'civil society', the concept of nationalism and the idea of 'the nation state' contributed little. Rather, it has hindered humanity in its search for a better and fairer society by channelling resources into petty and mediocre political ideologies. These ideologies at best glorified the trivial and, at worst, led many Europeans into xenophobia, racial hatred, and, finally, ethnic cleansing and genocide.

The challenge to dynasticism had a negative impact on Europe almost from its inception. It was originally designed to help replace absolutist inefficiency with liberal concepts, and to establish a stable and equitable civil and international order, but nationalism soon deteriorated into a doctrine that promulgated little more than crude populism. Moreover, in eastern Europe, nationalist aspirations were espoused chiefly by a small privileged elite in order to foster its vested political and/or economic ambitions. The majority of the chiefly rural population remained largely indifferent to concepts of national identity, and stayed wedded to traditional forms of loyalty.

President Wilson first raised the principle of self-determination in his answer to German chancellor von Hertling's reply to his Fourteen Points. There was no reference to national self-determination in those points. They stated merely that the peoples of Austria-Hungary should be accorded the 'freest opportunity of autonomous development', and that the nationalities under Turkish rule should be assured 'an undoubted security of life and an absolutely unmolested opportunity of autonomous development'.

In his address to congress of 11 February 1918, Wilson had declared that the war had its roots 'in the disregard of the rights of small nations and of nationalities which lacked the union and force to make good their claim to determine their own allegiance and their own form of political life'. He then listed four further principles for the peacemaking process. The second of these stated that peoples and provinces were not to be bartered about from sovereignty to sovereignty as if they were mere chattels and pawns in a game. The third demanded that every territorial settlement must be made in the interest and for the benefit of the population concerned, and not as a part of mere adjustments or compromise of claims among rival states.[5] There was nothing in these principles to indicate that the newly drawn borders should coincide precisely with ethnic frontiers. On the contrary, the fourth and final demand of the 'Four Principles' emphasised 'that all well-defined national aspirations shall be accorded the utmost satisfaction that can be accorded them without introducing new or perpetuating old elements of discord and antagonism that would be likely to break the peace of Europe, and consequently of the world'.[6]

Wilson showed little enthusiasm during the peacemaking process for endorsing the multitude of petitions from disgruntled ethnic groups from the Habsburg, Romanov, and Ottoman empires who sought self-determination based on ethnicity. He had hoped that the political system of his own country—where many (white) ethnic groups lived in relative harmony, and which was based on government through the consent of the governed without reference to ethnicity—might be implemented elsewhere.

His secretary of state, Robert Lansing, was sceptical. National self-determination, he said, 'is bound to be the basis of impossible demands on the Peace Conference and create trouble in many lands. What effect will it have on the Irish, the Indians, the Egyptians, and the nationalities among the Boers? Will it not breed discontent, disorder, and rebellion?' He made the grim prediction that 'the phrase is loaded with dynamite. It will raise hopes which can never be realised. It will, I fear, cost thousands of lives ... What a calamity the phrase was ever uttered. What misery it will cause!'[7]

But the genie would not go back into the bottle.[8] As an American authority on the peace treaty sums it up:

> [T]he very idea of popular sovereignty, when applied
> to the crazy quilt of heterogeneous population in

post-war Europe, inevitably acquired an ethnic dimension in spite of Wilson's original interest. His ambiguously defined principle of self-determination became the miraculous means of salvation in the eyes of discontented folk all across the continent who were struggling against those whom they regarded as their oppressors (and who not coincidentally spoke a different language and practiced different customs).[9]

The importance placed on the term 'national self-determination' during the peacemaking process obscures other issues on the peacemaking agenda. Weighty factors had to be taken into consideration in the task of creating new states from the ruins of disintegrated empires. Economics were important: longstanding trade connections, communication networks, and complex matters of ownership existing in the old empires could not be simply erased. Legal and judicial traditions came into play, as did historical alliances. Geopolitical considerations were also important, particularly in the settlement with the German empire.

Some continue to hold the view that the peace conference constituted a conflict between two opposing approaches, personified by Clemenceau on the one hand and Wilson on the other: that Clemenceau's insistence on a vengeful and vindictive peace stood against Wilson's fair and just 'peace without victory'. This is pure myth.

The president was not in a particularly German-friendly mood as he headed to Paris. Had he contemplated a peace without indemnities, he was in no position to put it into effect. The U.S. contribution to the war effort had been vital.

The Allies had to rely upon American financial assistance and on American imports of food and vital war supplies. Around 600,000 U.S. soldiers had arrived in France by the summer of 1918, though they did not play a major part in the Allied breakthrough of August–September or in the subsequent defeat of the German army. The British, with the support of their empire, had fought hard and had sustained large losses. The same was true of the French, who, in addition, had seen their country devastated. Wilson could not have ignored their legitimate concerns.

Moreover, a peace seen as pro-German would not have been accepted back at home. The president had just lost the mid-term Congressional elections, which had returned a Republican majority in both houses. This had been largely brought about by domestic issues unrelated to the war, but the warning was on the wall, and his opponents, in particular ex-president Theodore Roosevelt, and Wilson's lifelong opponent Henry Cabot Lodge, Republican chairman of the Senate committee on foreign relations, were thundering no end against his Points, Principles, and Particulars. According to Roosevelt, these had 'ceased to have any shadow of right to be accepted as expressive of the will of the American people'.[10]

His critics need not have worried. Notwithstanding his numerous attempts to bring about an end to the war, by 1918 Wilson had clearly sided with the Allies. He had taken no great interest in Europe before the outbreak of the war. In his scholarly career as a political scientist, he had been greatly impressed by the democratic traditions of the United Kingdom, and he remained a lifelong Anglophile. He had also praised the administrative efficiencies brought about by Prussian reformers such as Stein, Hardenberg, and Gneist, although he was critical of what he regarded as the strongly authoritarian system of government under Kaiser Wilhelm II. When war broke out, he was bitter about German conduct, and in particular the destruction of Louvain, but he saw strict neutrality as the only course open to the United States.

His attitude did not change until spring 1917, when he stopped advancing the idea of a 'peace without victory'. He had become convinced that the war had been started by the 'military masters of Germany', who had planned and executed the conquest of Europe and Asia 'from Berlin to Baghdad ... from Hamburg to the Persian Gulf'. He regarded Germany's leading establishment and its political system as the embodiment of evil 'without conscience or honor or capacity for covenanted peace'.[11] A compromise peace with Germany's military rulers was out of the question. Nevertheless, he did not hold the German people responsible for the aggression of their government, seeing them as victims rather than as participants in the German empire's drive for world domination. Once the military autocracy had been replaced by orderly democratic government, Germany would become a constructive member of the community of nations.[12]

This positive assessment of the German people changed when the rapacious terms of the Treaty of Brest-Litovsk showed what a German peace would look like. When even the Social Democrats, whom Wilson up to that time had regarded with respect, failed to vote against Brest-Litovsk, he was once more disillusioned:

Brest-Litovsk not only caused Wilson to drastically step up America's military contribution to the war, it also had an effect that, in the long run, was far more fateful for Germany. The failure of the Majority Socialists to fight the annexationist peace terms seems to have convinced him that even the civilian population, if not most of the German people, had been inculcated with the spirit of militarism ... he no longer exempted the German people from blame for the deeds of their rulers. On the contrary he had come to believe that in the final analysis, the German people themselves were behind German militarism.[13]

Wilson still maintained that, while Germany had to remain a viable nation state and should not be saddled with an unbearable burden, nevertheless the Germans could not escape punishment for their crimes.

Settling peace with Germany on the principle of national self-determination would have meant that Germany's national territory would have been far greater than Bismarck's Reich. Its population would have increased by around ten million, and it would have gained prosperous industrial regions. As William Keylor aptly comments, 'with a postwar redistribution of territory based purely on considerations of nationality or ethnicity, Germany's penalty for its military defeat [and the destruction the nation had caused] would have been the acquisition of *Lebensraum* more extensive than the vast terrain acquired by Hitler through diplomatic intimidation by the beginning of 1939'.[14] Such a redistribution would have been absurd.

Equally absurd are the claims that Austria and the German-speaking population of Bohemia should have merged with Germany—claims still found today, even in scholarly works. This view was first peddled by Germany's chief negotiator, Ulrich von Brockdorff-Rantzau, in his reply to the peace terms at Versailles on 7 May. This claim was made chiefly for domestic purposes, but it was also a first step in a long and skilfully conducted public-relations exercise by the German empire to discredit the Versailles Treaty.

Wilson may have been idealistic, but he was neither ignorant nor incompetent. 'Wilsonianism' is a concept that overemphasises the nationality principle and refers ad nauseam to his 'peace without victory' speech. The arguments that only a Germanophile settlement would have blessed the country with a stable democracy—and that any punitive aspects would only cause damage—were not Wilson's. These were the criticisms later made by disgruntled members of the British Treasury and Foreign Office and, above all, by John Maynard Keynes. Such arguments overlook the fact that after the 'peace without victory' speech came the introduction of unlimited submarine warfare, the American entry into the war and heavy U.S. casualties, the repugnant peace treaties of Bucharest, Brest-Litovsk, and Moscow, and a further eighteen months of war. Wilson himself was not a 'Wilsonian'.

Start of proceedings

The *George Washington* reached Brest on 13 December. There, the American president was given a rapturous welcome. Thousands of people, many in traditional Breton costumes, had lined up for the jubilant and colourful reception. The music of Breton bagpipes filled the air. Wilson's arrival in Paris was even more magnificent. Guns were fired as the train pulled into Luxembourg station, where he was greeted by French president Raymond Poincaré and the prime minister with his government. As the car ferried the president and his wife to their residence, soldiers struggled to hold back the huge, wildly cheering crowds that gathered along the streets. Most of the French media gave the impression that the League of Nations which Wilson had promised to create would be a victors' club, an alliance to curb future German ambitions, and that the United States would play a vital part in restricting renewed Prussian militarism. After spending a few days in Paris, Wilson crossed to London, where there was a repetition of the scenes of euphoric citizens welcoming a man they considered a saviour. The same happened in Rome, where he finished his whirlwind December tour.

David Lloyd George arrived in Paris on 11 January 1919. He was in a buoyant mood, having won a landslide victory in the 14 December election. The chief reason for the convincing win was his determined leadership during the war. Two catchy slogans concerning the imminent peacemaking process were thrown in to rally the electorate. The first was the demand to 'hang the Kaiser'—that is, to bring the German war leaders to account for the crimes they had committed during the war. The second was to make Germany pay fully for the costs of the war. Making promises that are difficult to fulfil is nothing new in electioneering. Since the dawn of democratically elected government there has always been a discrepancy between the great promises of candidates and the modesty of the goods they are able to deliver. Most of the time, gullible electorates acquiesce, and are content with partial fulfilment. In this case, loud declamations to 'hang the Kaiser' were impractical simply because Wilhelm II had acquired political asylum in the Netherlands, and the Dutch government had no intention of handing him over to the Allies.

The excitement over bringing Germany's war conduct to account soon faded. President Wilson showed little enthusiasm. He agreed to the setting up of a commission to investigate who was responsible for the war and how to punish war crimes. The German government, however, refused to hand anyone over to the special military tribunal, and the Allies eventually sent a list of a few hundred names to be tried in Germany. The list included Hindenburg and Ludendorff, as well as most members of the OHL. Twelve were eventually brought to trial, and most were immediately acquitted. A couple of submarine commanders who had sunk lifeboats of wounded survivors were sentenced to four years' imprisonment, but, allegedly, escaped after a few weeks and were never found.[15]

Lloyd George's other campaign trump card, to 'make Germany pay', caused him constant difficulties during the peace negotiation process. He was aware that compensation had to remain within reason, and he had emphasised 'that members of the government should not be responsible during the election for arousing any false hopes in the minds of the electorates'.[16] However, he did little to restrain the media's demand to 'bleed the Hun dry'. Nor did he rebuff the demand of First Lord of the Admiralty, Sir

Eric Campbell Geddes, that the German government be 'squeezed as a lemon is squeezed—until the pips squeak'. On the contrary, the prime minister himself announced in a speech at Bristol two days before election day that 'we have an absolute right to demand the whole cost of the war … those who started it must pay to the uttermost farthing, and we shall search their pockets for it'.[17]

This statement was one big problem that Lloyd George faced over the next five months. The composition of the British delegation to Paris was another. The four hundred delegates comprised not only members of the British military, diplomatic, and civil service, but also delegates from the white Dominions (Canada, South Africa, Australia, and New Zealand), as well as India. Because the Dominions had played a substantial role in the defeat of the Central Powers, they were not to be pushed aside when it came to collecting the spoils. And they could be very difficult and vociferous—none more so than the Australian prime minister, William 'Billy' Hughes.

On 18 January 1919, the Peace Conference opened officially in the presence of plenipotentiaries from 28 countries. Among them were delegates from China, which had made a valuable contribution to the Allies' war effort. After declaring war on Germany in the summer of 1917, about 100,000 Chinese labourers had helped in the construction and maintenance of trenches, freeing Allied soldiers for combat. The Chinese had suffered severe casualties at the front, and over 500 had died when a French ship was sunk by a German submarine. China held high hopes of regaining full possession of the Shandung peninsula. Portugal had contributed 60,000 soldiers to the Western Front, but was angered that it was allowed only one official delegate, whereas Brazil, which had sent only medical aid, was allowed three.[18] Even this exceeded the contributions of Chile, Haiti, Honduras, Guatemala, Nicaragua, or Panama, and a century later it is hard to discern why these countries should have even attended the peace process in Paris.

The day after the long-winded palaver of the pretentious plenary session, Lloyd George, Wilson, Clemenceau, Italian prime minister, Orlando, their foreign secretaries, and two Japanese representatives formed of a 'Council of Ten'. Commonly referred to as the Supreme Council, this was the chief decision-making body for the first ten weeks of the conference. The spadework of formulating the peace conditions was delegated to 58 specialised committees, many of which were divided into sub-committees.

Laying the foundation of the League of Nations was the first item on the agenda, an act of courtesy granted the U.S. president. Although the idea of a transnational body to conduct global affairs in the post-war era was upheld unanimously, none of the other chief decision-makers shared Wilson's enthusiasm or his unbound optimism for such an organisation. Clemenceau, in particular, was sceptical. France had lost 1,500,000 men—half its male population under thirty—and with no counter-weight in the east, it faced a large military imbalance with Germany. Clemenceau preferred an international league able to provide military protection. He wanted 'teeth' put into the league, but he found no backers.

A committee to create the League of Nations, set up on 25 January, met for the first time on 3 February, and produced a comprehensive draft by 14 February. All league members were pledged to each others' independence and territories, but the league was not to have its own military. Its primary aim, as stated in its covenant, was to prevent war through collective security and disarmament. International disputes were to be settled through negotiation and arbitration, but neither disarmament nor arbitration was compulsory. Other issues dealt with in the twenty-six paragraphs included global health and labour conditions, human and drug trafficking, the arms trade, treatment of prisoners of war, and protection of minorities in Europe. The organisation was to have a general assembly of all members, a secretariat, and an executive council made up of a member from each of the 'big five'—the U.S., the U.K., France, Italy, and Japan—and four smaller nations, which would ensure a small majority for the major powers.

The reality differed. The United States failed to enter the league, which encouraged deadlocks in the executive council, and this was later blamed for its ineffectiveness. Germany, at the insistence of the French, was not admitted, and would not join until 1926. But, pleased with the speedy creation and the overall structure of his pet project, Wilson left for Washington on 14 February to attend to domestic matters. When he returned on 4 March, it was decided to replace the Council of Ten, which had proven too awkward and laborious to deal with the myriad of problems it faced, with a Council of Four—Wilson, Lloyd George, Clemenceau, and Orlando. The Japanese, who had contributed little to the work of the Supreme Council, were excluded, and as Orlando generally participated only when Italian matters came up, the peacemaking at Paris became essentially the work of the first three.

The question of what to do with the German navy was not easily dealt with. As far as its submarines were concerned, all but ten—which had been given to France—were destroyed. However, there was disagreement between the admiralties of the United States and Britain about the fate of the surface fleet. In line with armistice conditions, the German ships had left their base in November 1918, and were now anchored at Scapa Flow in the Orkneys. Lloyd George suggested that they be sunk unceremoniously in the mid Atlantic, but Wilson thought it foolish to destroy perfectly good ships. However, dividing the spoils on the basis of the contribution to the war effort or of losses incurred would have favoured the British. There were acrimonious quarrels between admirals on both sides[19] until the politicians declared a truce.

The distribution of German colonies also proved a burdensome enterprise. By 1914, the German empire had embraced a large area of Africa divided into four colonial districts: German East Africa (today's Tanzania); Togoland; Cameroon; and German South-West Africa (today's Namibia). Germany also ruled parts of Melanesia and Micronesia, forming the 'Imperial Colony of German New Guinea', covering about 6,400 square kilometres of the Pacific Ocean.

It was unanimously agreed that Germany, because of its maladministration and ill-treatment of the indigenous people, should lose its overseas possessions, but there was one major point of disagreement. The European Allies envisaged a swap-around in colonial administration, while president Wilson opposed a continuation of traditional colonialism. Instead, and in line with the fifth of his Fourteen Points, he stood for 'a free, open-minded, and absolutely impartial adjustment of all colonial claims, based upon a strict observance of the principle that in determining all such questions of sovereignty the interests of the populations concerned must have equal weight with the equitable claims of the government whose title is to be determined'. To achieve this, he suggested the establishment of mandates, a kind of trusteeship run either directly by the league or by powers mandated by the league. The length of such mandates would depend on the progress made by local populations.

Wilson's ideas did not find favour with the French. Given Germany's greater population, they wanted to be assured that in case of renewed aggression from her they could rely on soldiers drafted in from their colonies. A compromise in France's favour was reached, but strong opposition also came from the British Dominions, in particular from South Africa, Australia, and New Zealand. They had been counting on outright annexation, and were critical of the mandate system—none more so than the Australian prime minister. After frantic dealing behind the scenes, a three-tier mandate system was agreed upon. Class A constituted those relatively advanced communities previously part of the Turkish empire, which were expected soon to run their own affairs. Class B included the three central African colonies. They were to be administered 'under conditions securing freedom of conscience and religion, the prohibition of such abuses as the slave trade and the liquor trafficking'. The military training of natives other than for police purposes and the defence of territory was outlawed.

All league members were to be given equal opportunity for trade and commerce in these regions. Class C covered German South-West Africa and all former German colonies in the South Pacific. They, 'owing to the sparseness of their population, or their small sizes, or their remoteness from the centres of civilisation, or their geographical proximity to the mandatory' would be administered by the mandate as part of its territory. However, there were the same safeguards in regard to the indigenous populations as in the African colonies.[20]

Discussion of the mandate system in the Supreme Council led to heated exchanges at times—none more vicious than the encounters between Hughes and the American president. Wilson loathed Hughes, seeing him as a 'a pestiferous varmint'.[21] The feeling was reciprocated: the Australian held Wilson, his principles, and the league in contempt. At one point in the discussion about Australia's claim for the New Guinea mandate, Wilson asked whether the Australian government would allow the sale of alcohol to natives. Having received an affirmative answer, he asked whether there would be unlimited access to missionaries. Of course, Hughes replied. 'There are many days when the poor devils do not get half-enough missionaries to eat'.[22]

Two days later, after the Australian prime minister had taken a particularly stubborn stand on the Solomon Islands, Wilson angrily asked whether he was 'to understand that if the whole civilised world asks Australia to agree to a mandate in respect of these islands, Australia is prepared still to defy the appeal of the whole civilised world?' Hughes, who was deaf both literally and figuratively to arguments he did not want to hear, fiddled with his cumbersome hearing aids, claiming he had not heard the question. After Wilson had repeated himself, he answered, 'That's about the size of it, Mr. President'. Although this did not raise Hughes' standing in Wilson eyes, it did increase his already substantial popularity among the French.

By the end of January, arrangements were agreed. France acquired possession of Togo and most of the Cameroons; Britain, a small strip of Cameroon and virtually all of German East Africa. After Belgium bitterly complained that it had been left out of the African settlement, Britain reluctantly agreed to hand over the East African provinces of Rwanda and Burundi to a Belgian mandate. In the Pacific, Japan received the former German islands north of the equator, and Australia received German New Guinea. In addition, the two Pacific Dominions divided up the remaining islands south of the equator between themselves.

Nation states and minority rights

By the time the conference officially opened, the peacemakers faced a *fait accompli* in large parts of eastern and south-eastern Europe. The Czechs had set up the state of Czechoslovakia, made up of the Bohemian parts of Cisleithania (the Austrian half of the Habsburg empire) and the northern parts of Transleithania (the Hungarian half of the Danube Monarchy). Also referred to as Upper Hungary, the population here was chiefly Slovak. The Serbs were in the process of creating a southern Slavonic state, and Poland had become a nation again, having been wiped off the political map by its three neighbours,

Prussia, Russia, and Austria in 1795. Around the Baltic, Finland, Estonia, Lithuania, and Latvia had declared their independence, leaving the small most easterly inlet of the Baltic Sea around Petrograd (renamed Leningrad in 1924 and St. Petersburg in 1991) as the last remnant of Russian possession.

There were two guiding principles behind the creation of the new states that would fill the power vacuum left by the collapse of the Habsburg, Romanov, and Ottoman empires. First, for geopolitical, military, and economic reasons, they had to be of a sustainable size geographically and in population. Second, there was a widespread belief, particularly among the political and intellectual elites, that the era of the multinational state was over: that it was not capable of adapting to democratic principles. This belief was strengthened by the concept of national self-determination that had started to dominate the peace conference. It was now widely upheld that the modern state could only be realised in the form of the nation state. Central to this was the notion of the 'actual' nationality of the state, best rendered by the German term *Staatsvolk*. However, given the heterogeneity of these parts of Europe, the creation of a nation based on ethnicity was an impossibility. Outside observers noted again and again when asking about their nationality that peoples identified themselves as Catholic or Orthodox, as subjects of the government in Vienna, or a local ruler, or a member of a clan in the former Ottoman parts. This hurdle, it was hoped, would be overcome by the 'minority principle'.

The minorities treaty aimed to guarantee ethnic minorities equal rights with the majority of the *Staatsvolk*.

It was initially designed by the Allies to provide protection for the Jewish population of Poland (which had been viciously attacked by Polish forces immediately after the proclamation of Poland's independence).[23] Under this principle, citizens were not to be discriminated against on the grounds of their mother tongue. The state was obliged to provide schooling for minorities, which had the right to use their first languages in business and administration, in the courts, the media, and in religious observance. These rights, however, were granted to individual citizens within minority groups, not to whole communities as collective bodies. The reason for this was to safeguard the state against attempts by minority groups to secede or to join the countries of their mother tongues. As with many other decisions made in Paris, the good intentions of the peacemakers were to face grave difficulties in the turbulent post-war political life of central and eastern Europe.

Czechoslovakia, alone among the new nations, was genuine in its pursuit of the guidelines laid down in the peacemaking process. There were five minorities in Czechoslovakia: Germans, Hungarians, Ruthenes, Ukrainians, and Poles. Edvard Beneš, who ranked as the most prominent and influential political figure in Czechoslovakia until his death in 1948, recognised the need for all the nationalities to live together harmoniously. The new system, he advocated early in 1919, would have to be similar to the Swiss. He did not mean that the new state should adopt the Swiss political model, but was referring to the spirit of Switzerland, where several nationalities co-existed peacefully. The Czechoslovak Republic granted all of its citizens full civil rights: political and legal equality;

liberty of expression; freedom of association, press, and religion; access to education and basic health care; and a modest degree of social security. Policies pursued in the early years illustrate the Czechoslovak Republic's liberal, democratic character. This positive trend could have been built on, had stability persisted.[24]

The term 'minority' was scarcely applicable to the German-speaking population of Czechoslovakia. Numbering over three million, it wielded immense economic, political, and cultural power. The more farsighted of the Czechoslovak leaders recognised the need to 'win the Germans over'.[25] The second prime minister of the republic, Vlastimil Tusar, stressed that it was essential to 'have other bonds than the peace of St Germain and Versailles to tie the Germans to the state'.[26] But the attitude of Bohemian and Moravian Germans towards the new state was ambiguous. Parties that took up a negative or irredentist position garnered small followings during the 1920s, while their opposites, referred to as 'activists', entered governments in the mid-1920s and held three ministerial positions. The impact of September 1929 and 30 January 1933 drove most 'Sudeten-Germans' to rally behind Konrad Henlein's *Sudetendeutsche Partei*, which led them straight into the arms of Adolf Hitler and—eventually—into the abyss.

The Germans were expelled at the end of World War II, and joined another eight million ethnic Germans forced to leave their homes in central, eastern, and south-eastern Europe. The Republic of Czechoslovakia became the 'Socialist Republic of Czechoslovakia' and, when the end of the Soviet empire heralded the demise of socialism, the Czechs and Slovaks went their own ways peacefully. A set of friendly special clauses regulating old economic and cultural ties recall a time when they formed a single nation. Today, both the Czech and the Slovak Republics have become part of the European Union.

If one were to rate the newly emerged nations on their compliance with the benevolent principles to which they had committed themselves, the Kingdom of Serbs, Croats, and Slovenes would stand in stark contrast with Czechoslovakia. The kingdom, established by Serbia, embraced Orthodox Serbians, Catholic Croatians, and Slovenes, and the Muslims of Bosnia-Herzegovina. Given the importance of religion and dynastic traditions played for the bulk of the population, basing a political unit on the sole principle of southern Slavonic ethnicity was ill-conceived, as soon became apparent. And if the concept was flawed, its execution was worse.

The new nation, which in October 1929 would be renamed the Kingdom of Yugoslavia, was proclaimed on 1 December 1918 by Prince Alexander of Serbia. With the collapse of Austria-Hungary, Serbian forces quickly ensured that non-Serbian military units were disbanded. All vital positions in government and administration went to Serbs, and Belgrade was declared the capital. The Serbs' dream of re-establishing the mediaeval empire of Stepan Dušan, held since they had liberated themselves from Ottoman rule in 1867, had come a step closer. This empire covered most of Serbia, Albania, Macedonia, and all of northern and central Greece. The newly founded state included Croatia (Serb statesmen and thinkers regarded the Croatians as Serbs) and parts of the eastern Adriatic, including Trieste, as well as large parts of Hungary.[27]

King Alexander took the oath of allegiance on 28 June, the anniversary of the battle of Kosovo, the most important day in Serb history. On this day in 1389, legend has it, the Christian Serbs, led by Prince Lazar, were through treachery defeated by the Ottoman Turks. The prince, who the night before had experienced a vision that he could have either a kingdom in heaven or one on earth, chose the former. The Serbian people, true to their faith, would one day rise again to restore the Serbian empire. Historians today have great difficulty substantiating much of this. There is little evidence of Lazar's empire; he is seen rather as one of a number of princes struggling for dominance in the region. There is also considerable doubt that Lazar lost the battle: some records maintain that he won; others, that it was a draw. But, as the saying goes, never let the facts get in the way of a good story. Lazar the martyr, and Kosovo, the supposed site of the battle, were symbols kept alive in monasteries for centuries until, in the wake of nineteenth-century nationalism, they were revived to provide the ideological backing for Serbian expansionism.[28]

The Kingdom of Serbs, Croats, and Slovenes was three times the size of the old Serbia. Once the Serbs had charted their new boundaries, the peacemakers at Paris could only rubber-stamp them. France, greatly worried about the power vacuum left by the war in eastern Europe, wanted strong successor states there, able to assist should it come to future conflict with Germany. Support for the new kingdom among its non-Serb nationalities—who comprised about half the population—was limited. Orthodoxy having been declared the state's official religion, the attitude of other religions to the new arrangements was ambivalent. Catholic Croats and Slovenes objected—not unjustifiably—to being swept up in a Greater Serbia; they had been content as part of the Catholic Habsburg empire. Irredentist movements, confined to a few intellectuals and nationalist zealots, had no popular base. Nor did Muslim Bosnians welcome the fact that they were now run by Belgrade. The domestic political violence of the pre-war kingdom continued, reaching a climax in 1928 when the leader of the Croatian Peasant Party, Stjepan Radić, was assassinated in the Belgrade parliament. A year later, the king declared a royal dictatorship.

Thanks to their shameless territory-grabbing, the numbers of enemies the Serbs faced from within was matched by the numbers without—as became clear in the Second World War. The Croatian fascist *Ustasha*, in particular, excelled in murdering Serbs. After the War, Josip Broz (Tito) pieced Yugoslavia together again, managing to keep the nation united, not only by force and coercion, until his death in 1980. Little more than a decade later, the Serbs resorted again to violence and genocide. In July 1995, 'ethnic cleansing' by the Serbian army resulted in the slaughter of 8,000 Bosnian Muslims. In 2015, a number of high-ranking Serbian officers were sentenced at the International Court of Justice in The Hague to life imprisonment or to lengthy jail sentences for participating in the massacre at Srebrenica. Of the chief culprits, Radovan Karadžić, former president of the Serbian Republic of Bosnia-Herzegovina, was given 40 years' imprisonment in March 1916, and Bosnian Serb army leader Ratko Mladi is still facing trial at the time of writing.

The Polish state that emerged after World War I was not a creation of the peacemakers, although defining the borders of the new Poland had seen more commission meetings than any other aspect of the conference. The Polish National Committee that had been formed during the war advocated a return to the boundaries of 1772, which would have meant the inclusion of millions of Lithuanians, Belorussians, and Ukrainians. The French, ever in search of a counterweight in the east against potential German aggression, favoured a strong Poland. The Lithuanians, Belorussians, and Ukrainians did not; nor did the British and Americans. They favoured a smaller Poland, along what became known as the Curzon line. Poland's new western borders included a small strip of Pomeranian territory around the River Vistula in order to allow the Poles access to the sea, as stipulated in Wilson's Fourteen Points.[29] Its eastern boundaries were decided in a war with Russia, which lasted from February 1919 to September 1920. The Poles were victorious, and the expanded territory added a further two million Jews, four million Ukrainians, and one million Belorussians to their minority population.

Initially, this large state was governed by the *Sejm*, a democratically elected parliament based on the French model. However, the 92 political parties, the introduction of proportional representation, and the exuberant individualism of the Polish intelligentsia made parliamentary government difficult. In 1927, Marshal Józef Piłsudski, who had played a major part in the formation of the new Poland, decided to end the 'chaos', and established a military dictatorship. His government lasted for twelve years before it was terminated by Hitler and Stalin. After the Second World War, the country was stripped of its eastern 'minorities', and the German-speaking population was expelled. Poland became the homogenous nation it is today.

Romania, although it had played only a minor part in the defeat of the Central Powers, did well in Paris, where it received Bukovina from Austria, and the Banat and Transylvania from Hungary, doubling its population and territory. In 1920, it also wrested Bessarabia from Russia. Like their Polish and Yugoslav counterparts, the Romanian leaders had been loud in their support for ethnic self-determination when it came to their neighbours, but did little to follow such principles at home. Impressive lists of minority rights had been enacted, but they were scarcely adhered to, leaving large populations dissatisfied and unwilling to be mobilised when the need arose.

The new states—characteristically referred to by the Germans as 'season states'—looked impressive on paper, but they failed to provide domestic stability. To this was added their failure to ensure harmonious relations between themselves. Consider, for example, the fate of the small duchy of Teschen, located in the west of the former Austrian province of Galicia, which bordered the Upper-Silesian coalfield. The population of half a million people was around two to one Polish. The Czechs claimed Teschen because its coal was vital to Czechoslovakia and because the railway junction there connected the Bohemian and Slovak parts of the new state. Although little stood in the way of a cordial settlement, Teschen led to acrimonious quarrels between the Czechs and Poles during the peace conference and after, until a compromise pleasing neither side was reached.[30] A close political and military alliance between the two countries would have benefited both, but as a result of the Teschen conflict, relations remained tense in the inter-war period. This was symptomatic of the entire region, and French hopes that Yugoslavia, Romania, Poland, and Czechoslovakia would provide a reliable counter-balance to Germany in the east did not eventuate.

Of the defeated powers, Bulgaria escaped relatively unscathed. The Treaty of Neuilly stipulated that it had to return some of the lands it had gained in the peace of Bucharest, and the Bulgarians lost access to the Aegean Sea, about 10 per cent of their territory. They also had to pay reparations of £90 million and reduce their army to 20,000 men, neither of which they ever did.

Austria and Hungary, the two pillars of the Habsburg Monarchy, did not fare well. Both were reduced to rump states. Hungary received harsher treatment because at the time of the peacemaking its government was in the hands of a Soviet council.[31] Austria was politically isolated and economically cut off from its traditional trade links, and found it hard to make ends meet in the inter-war years. This helps to explain why the Austrians accorded their fellow countryman Adolf Hitler such a tumultuous welcome in Vienna on 12 March 1938. The aspect of the St. Germain peace treaty the Austrians most resented was the loss of South Tyrol, a German-speaking region south of the Brenner Pass. This was awarded to Italy.

The Italians had originally been part of the Triple Alliance with the Austro-Hungarian and German empires, but did not join the war in 1914. For nine months they watched to see which way the wind blew. They joined the Allies in May 1915, enticed by the promise of rich rewards, among them South Tyrol. Thus the Allies were saved from having to fight on another front, and one potential enemy had joined their own ranks. In practice, Italy's military contribution to the defeat of the Central Powers was modest. All attempts to invade Austria-Hungary from the south were rebuffed, the attackers suffering huge losses. The Allies, however, kept their promise, offering up a sizeable stretch of territory around the northern Adriatic coast and South Tyrol. President Wilson had qualms about allocating this German-speaking community to Italy, because Point Nine of the Fourteen Points held that the frontiers of Italy should be effected along clearly recognisable lines of nationality. The Italians, however, reasoned that without possession of the lands south of the Brenner Pass, their country would be left open to future aggression from the north, and to this Wilson assented. Nevertheless, the original list of Italian expectations had been much longer,[32] and they were angered in particular by not being awarded the city of Fiume. Dissatisfaction with the peace treaties, coupled with never-ending political and economic instability—the post-war Italian governments stumbled from one crisis to the next—led to Mussolini's 'March on Rome' on 28 October 1922. Italy would become the first country to fall to fascism.

The ink on the treaties had not dried before loud claims were being made that the Allied peacemakers had dealt arrogantly with the fate of millions—assigning national minorities here, taking whole folks-groups away there, and all by the stroke of a pen. Such claims are too generalised, and in many instances false. To have imposed every condition of the Fourteen Points would have involved major military intervention, something that was out of the question in 1919 or early 1920. Given the ethnic pluralism of the region, no border was immune from the cry of foul play from those who claimed to have lost out. As stated above, the peacemakers faced a *fait accompli* in central and eastern Europe, and they agreed to borders that had been established by the states themselves. The development of fair, co-operative, and productive policies that might have led to a better outcome for the post-war world was in the hands of the rulers of the new 'nation states'. Their failure to develop such policies contributed to the catastrophic course history was to take in the 1930s and 1940s.

Key issues

In making peace with the German empire, which was the chief item on the Paris agenda, the Allies were confronted by two key issues: how to set compensation for the costs of war, and how to provide France with security against an eastern neighbour whose superiority in size and industrial potential could not be altered even after its defeat in war. In his various announcements during the war, president Wilson had stated that the settling of war costs should not include indemnities, payments for expenditure incurred in military operations, and the staging of the war. These, to him, were relics of a bygone age. Restitution was only to be made for unlawful acts of war.

This vague concept met opposition from the Europeans. They were not willing to abandon the traditional principle ruling European peacemaking for the past hundred years: loser pays, winner takes all. In the November 1815 Treaty of Paris, which ended the Napoleonic chapter in French history, France was made to pay 700 billion francs and the cost of an occupation army of 150,000 men for three years. The Kingdom of Prussia, together with Austria, collected handsomely from Denmark after winning the first of Bismarck's 'unification wars', the Kingdom of Denmark losing one-third of its territory and almost half of its population. Prussia did even better from the 'Second Unification War' fought chiefly against Austria. The Kingdom of Hanover was annexed outright, and Bismarck also confiscated the assets of the royal dynasty, the Guelphs, amounting to about five million goldmarks. The electorate of Hesse and the Free City of Frankfurt were also annexed, the citizens of Frankfurt having to pay an indemnity of over 30 million guilders. The Kingdoms of Bavaria and Württemberg and the Grand Duchy of Baden, too, paid heavily for siding with the Austrians. Bavaria, for example, was obliged to pay an indemnity of 51 million goldmarks, making the 32 million Ludwig II needed for the construction of his fanciful castles, which so enraged the Bavarian political establishment of his time, look relatively modest. The thrifty Bavarians could not know that the *Neuschwanstein* Castle would, a century later, rank as the state's main tourist attraction, and, courtesy of Walt Disney, would become the fairly-tale castle par excellence, giving joy to millions of children around the world.

For strategic reasons, Austria was let off the hook, although the Austrian emperor had to give assurances that the empire would never again meddle in German affairs. In the peace of Frankfurt that ended the Franco-Prussian War of 1870–1, France had to pay to the newly founded

Second German empire 20 billion goldmarks, in addition to occupation costs. The plundering of defeated enemies peaked in the Treaties of Bucharest with Romania—which had to cede large territories to the Habsburg Monarchy and Bulgaria and its oilfields to Germany—and the Treaties of Brest-Litovsk and Moscow with Russia.

For the European Allies, it was now Germany's turn to pay. They had no intention of plundering Germany but, not unreasonably, they wanted to be reimbursed for the damage done by German occupation and to recover at least part of their outlays.

The Pre-Armistice Agreement of November 1918 had stipulated that Germany had to make compensation for all the damage done to the civilian population of the Allies and their property by its aggression on land, sea, and air. This suited France, where most of the fighting on the Western Front had taken place. In the ten French departments that had seen the heaviest fighting, around 600,000 houses, 20,000 factories, and 6,500 schools had been destroyed, 4,000 villages levelled, and three million people driven from their homes. This region also contained the centres of the French iron, coal, wool, and cotton industries. Under a strict interpretation of the Pre-Armistice Agreement, France (and Belgium) could expect to receive the largest reparation payments.

The British did not share this point of view. Limiting reparations to damage done to civilians would mean that they could claim reimbursement only for the loss of merchant shipping. Yet Britain's war expenditure had been greater than that of France's, huge loans having to be raised to meet the costs. Britain owed the U.S. government loans amounting to $4.7 billion, and a further $2 billion to U.S. banks. The British had also lent large sums to Russia, which had defaulted on its debts, and to other European nations such as Italy and Romania, which were in no position to repay. France itself owed Britain $4 billion. In the emotion-charged aftermath of the war, it would have been difficult to explain to the people why their taxes had to pay for the costs of the war. The British Dominions, in particular, raised strong objections to a peace without compensation. The Australian prime minister, Billy Hughes, became their spokesman.

Hughes was convinced that he had a strong case. Australia had suffered a high casualty rate, and its soldiers had made valuable contributions to the defeat of Germany. Australian General John Monash had led the Australian and Canadian Corps in their breakthrough of the German trenches on the Somme on 8 August 1918,[33] and had contributed to the collapse of the Hindenburg Line a month later. Australian troops had also distinguished themselves by halting some of the most advanced units of the German March offensive at Villers-Bretonneux, the beginning of the collapse of Operation Michael. Hughes had already bitterly attacked the Pre-Armistice Agreement, being among the first to recognise its implications. In a series of passionate speeches and letters to the press, he maintained that, by accepting the agreement, Britain had forfeited her rights to war indemnities and that this would have dire consequences for the Dominions.[34] If Wilson's views were to be sustained, Belgium, which had contributed little to the outcome of war, would be compensated, while countries like Australia would go empty-handed. To Hughes, there was no valid distinction between restoration and compensation:

> Australia lost nearly 60,000 men killed and many
> more maimed for life. She has incurred a war debt
> of some £300,000,000—a crushing burden for
> 5,000,000 people. And what is true of Australia, is
> true *mutatis mutandis* of the other Dominions and
> peoples of the British Empire. In the way of the
> destruction of civilian life and property, they may
> have suffered little. Yet the sacrifice they have made
> and damage they have suffered, have not been less.
> There must be for them, as for all the Allies full
> compensation.[35]

He dismissed the American rejection of high reparations
as unprincipled and self-serving.[36]

Hughes' criticism was not unfounded. For all Wilson's
talk of the 'moral advantage' in not claiming reparations,
the United States did well out of the war. Its civilian war
damage was small, as was the size of the its war debt. The
United States had seized twice as many German merchant
ships as it had lost, and had confiscated German property
in North America to the value of $425 billion.[37] The United
States also reaped enormous war profits from Europe.
The French and British governments had hoped that the
U.S. would provide financial assistance in the settling of
their obligations. Indeed, there were even suggestions
of cancelling outright all intra-allied debts. But neither
president Wilson nor his government was interested in this.

On 10 February, Hughes was made chair of the
Commission on Reparation. Most members of the

commission were hardliners on reparations. Lord Cunliffe, a retired governor of the Bank of England, was a member, as was Lord Sumner, a Law Lord. They were supported by the Northcliffe Press, and took up a catch-cry on bleeding the Hun dry. The pair was called the 'heavenly twins' because of the astronomical estimates they advanced—initially $120 billion. This figure was reduced to $47 billion, but was still in striking contrast to sums suggested by the Treasury, whose representative, John Maynard Keynes, argued that Germany could pay $10 billion at the most. This sum, however, would have been unpalatable to an Allied public that had been promised rich rewards for its efforts in the defeat of the enemy. Eventually, to the relief of Lloyd George and Clemenceau, who had both made vast promises to their people, it was decided to leave settling the final sum to the work of a further commission.

The establishment of this commission helped to solve the impasse between Wilson and the European leaders. The South African minister for defence, General Jan Smuts, maintained that the Pre-Armistice Agreement allowed the Allies to include separation allowances for soldiers' families, as well as pensions for widows and orphans. This was seen by opponents of the treaty as a further example of the piling up surrealistic reparation claims. In reality, the inclusion of allowances and pensions did not add to the final bill owed by Germany, but it did affect the amount each ally was to receive.[38] The share gained by Britain, which had suffered relatively little physical damage requiring repair, but had huge unfunded pension liabilities, was increased by reducing the shares of other allies.[39]

It had also been agreed by then that there was to be

an unlimited *theoretical* responsibility, but a much smaller *actual* German liability. Lloyd George and Clemenceau had explicitly insisted that Germany should acknowledge an obligation for all the war costs. The Americans feared that this would be a violation of the Pre-Armistice Agreement, and offered a compromise that would assign unlimited theoretical and moral responsibility for all the damage caused by the war to Germany and its allies, but confine the actual German liability to specific damages. This would greatly reduce the amount Germany was expected to pay. The British and French agreed to the compromise, which was placed in the reparation chapter of the Versailles Treaty (in paragraphs 231 and 232).

Solving the problem of France's future position towards her powerful eastern neighbour proved equally difficult, threatening at times to break up the conference. It was important for the French to be compensated adequately for the devastation caused by war and occupation. Although the minister for finance, Louis-Lucien Klotz—according to Clemenceau, the only Jew who knew nothing about finance—joined for a time the ranks of those demanding surrealistic figures, French reparation expectations were on the modest side. As with so much regarding the reparation issue, the discrepancy of the sums given to the public and the amount realistically expected was vast. The future of French security, however, was of paramount importance. Twice within fifty years, the country had been invaded by Germany, the second invasion amounting to near apocalypse. In addition to the physical destruction of the countryside, towns, and cities, and the damage done to French industry, France had lost 1.5 million men. Double that number had been injured. Although two million young Germans had also died, Germany would still have a post-war population of around 65 million, compared to France's 40 million. No foreign soldier had set foot on German soil, no village been razed, no industrial compound dismantled or blown to pieces. The Rhenish-Westphalian industrial region—Europe's largest coal-mining and steel-producing area—was still able to work at full capacity.

France's hopes rested on two pillars: to confine Germany to the east of the River Rhine, and to continue the wartime alliance with the United Kingdom and the United States. French president Raymond Poincaré demanded that the peace treaty should push the French border with Germany to the Rhine, a position shared by the bulk of the media and a large part of the population. This would mean that the Saarland, the Rhenish Palatinate, and the Rhineland would become part of France. The Rhine had been the German border in the past, and the Rhenish, it was claimed, were in character and lifestyle much closer to the French than to the Prussians. Like the French, they were Catholic, enjoyed good food and wine, and (by reputation) took a more joyful approach to life than their eastern compatriots.[40] Such a view found no support with Lloyd George or the American president, who reasoned that downright incorporation of the left bank would create a new Alsace-Lorraine, a certain recipe for future disaster. As they could expect no assistance from the Allies, Clemenceau pointed out to those of his countrymen demanding this frontier the sacrifices that French occupation of the region would entail. Two hundred and fifty thousand men would have to be withdrawn from the workforce to guard the Rhine, stifling economic growth, and there would have to be wholesale reform of the region's administration and governing structures.

French army chief Foch also wanted to restrict Germany to the east of the Rhine, but his suggestion was for the creation of an independent buffer state militarily and economically linked to France, Belgium, Luxembourg, and Britain. This, too, was rejected outright by Lloyd George and Wilson.

There is another reason Foch's scheme would have been impractical. Konrad Adenauer, the mayor of Cologne and the later the first chancellor of the Federal Republic, seemed willing to participate in the secession of the Rhineland from the Reich. Early in 1919, he joined a group of Centre Party members who had become concerned about the Workers' and Soldiers' Councils that had formed during the November Revolution. They feared the spread of socialism, and they were apprehensive about the Berlin government's school policy, which they saw as an assault on the Catholic religion and on local autonomy.

However, Adenauer soon found out that the Rhenish had no desire to be separated. This was in no way surprising. The Rhineland, assigned to Prussia in the Peace of Vienna, had (along with Westphalia) become Germany's industrial leader during the industrial revolution of the nineteenth century. This had brought rich benefits to its inhabitants. Many of their sons and daughters had died in what they saw as the defence of their fatherland. To now be forced to join a new state under the tutelage of the enemy was deeply resented. Adenauer carefully tested the possibility of an autonomous Rhineland state within the Reich to escape what was feared to be Prussian-Socialist domination, but his scheme found no significant support among the population.

Clemenceau could claim some success for his efforts. The French were given temporary ownership of the Saar coalmines for fifteen years. The League of Nations was to administer the region, and in 1935 the inhabitants were to decide in a plebiscite whether to remain independent, or become part of France, or re-unite with Germany. The Rhineland was to be demilitarised, and the French Rhenish occupation zones around the three bridgeheads would continue. The northern zone around the bridgehead of Cologne was to be evacuated in five years, the second zone around the bridgehead of Koblenz in ten years, and the third zone in the south around the bridgehead of Mainz in fifteen years—subject to Germany's having met its reparation commitments. The Anglo-American Alliance was to continue under a separate Treaty of Guarantee with Britain and the United States.

The terms were attacked by Clemenceau's opponents. President Poincaré described him as morally blind, a pawn in the pocket of the Anglo-Saxons, a swollen-head and sleepwalker, a scatterbrain and blunderer who, having signed the Armistice prematurely, was now bound to lead the nation into the abyss.[41] Foch wanted to indict Clemenceau for high treason before the High Court. But in the end their rage withered away. On 25 April, the French Council of Ministers unanimously backed the prime minister.

It soon turned out that Clemenceau had little reason to celebrate his success. The United States' Senate failed to ratify the Treaty of Versailles, which also meant the end of the Special Treaty with France. Senators had asked for amendments to the Versailles Treaty, but Wilson insisted on all or nothing. Not a single alteration was to be to his handiwork. Even his lifelong Republican opponent Henry Cabot Lodge regretted that the president made no effort to save his life's great ambition, the creation of a global organisation to secure the peace and harmony of a democratic world. For France, the Special Treaty with the U.S. was not worth the proverbial crumpet. And the same can be said about the Treaty of Guarantee with Britain: it was dependent upon American acceptance of the Versailles Treaty.[42]

Germany arrives

Germany's unexpected and rapid transition from monarchy to republic initially took place under peaceful conditions. Workers' and Soldiers' Councils that had formed all over Germany governed the country for ten weeks until the first democratic elections on 19 January 1919. The Majority Social Democrats had rediscovered their revolutionary spirit, and joined the Independent Socialists in the Council of Peoples' Deputies that had taken over government in Berlin. The moderate Social Democrats wanted to ensure that there would be an orderly beginning to the life of the Republic, and that things would not drift towards chaos as in Russia a year earlier. There was widespread fear among the Germans, and also among the Allies, that Germany might follow the path of the Bolsheviks. This fear was unfounded because left-wing extremism was confined to a small minority on the fringe of the workers' movements. Speedy agreements between the Majority Social Democrats and the army and industry leadership calmed anxiety. The election of 19 January 1919 ended the period of revolutionary government, and led to the formation of coalition government made up of Majority Social Democrats and members of the Centre Party and Liberal Parties.

Demobilisation of the armed forces was the first task to be completed. In some places there were scuffles between army officers and local Workers' and Soldiers' Councils, but by and large the returning soldiers were given a hero's welcome. In Berlin, they were greeted by the leader of the Majority Social Democrats, Friedrich Ebert, soon to become the Republic's first president, who praised them for their bravery and claimed that 'no enemy has conquered you'. Similar scenes were repeated in many cities and towns. The fact that Germany had actually lost the war seems to have been ignored.

The country's desperate food shortage was given prime importance. The cessation of hostilities led to a slight increase in the weekly food rations. Whereas previously the army was given priority, the end of the war enabled a more equitable division. In particular, the release from army service of a large numbers of draught horses led to a temporary abundance of horse-meat, putting to an end the meatless weeks that had caused much hardship among the civilian population. Food imports were vitally important, and the Allies had agreed as an Armistice condition that Germany be allowed to bring in food, provided it used its own merchant shipping. But German ship-owners refused, because they feared that their ships, having left their harbours, would be confiscated.

A further difficulty arose over the method of payment.

The German government suggested it could pay for its food purchases with a loan from the United States. When the Allies objected that such a loan would never pass Congress, the Germans offered to pay with their gold reserves. This caused anxiety among the French, who wanted the German gold for reparations. After several weeks, however, the French caved in, and by late March American food was arriving.

The Germans initially had great faith in Wilson's Fourteen Points, despite the fact that they spelt out clearly that post-war Germany would be different and that the differences would not be in Germany's favour. As German theologist and liberal politician Ernst Tröltsch saw it, people were living in a 'dreamland', 'where everyone, without grasping the conditions and consequences, could portray the future in fantastic, pessimistic or heroic terms'.[43] Perhaps, as one historian suggests, the terrible sacrifices and efforts of the war had destroyed people's ability to realistically judge their place in history.[44] In any case, most Germans viewed the post-war situation with optimism. Some sort of indemnity would have to be paid, but this would stay within reason and would not involve the costs of war. They expected, too, that the Republic would become a member of the League of Nations, that there was to be no significant territorial amputation, that Germany would keep its colonies, and that the principal of self-determination would decide whether the Austrians and Bohemians would become part of the nation.

Wishful thinking also extended to Germany's political leaders. They would have had sufficient information about the Allies' attitudes, but continued to believe that they were receiving full parity in Paris. They did not expect that the harsh treatment they had meted out to others would be reciprocated. When the Allies rejected complaints about their proposals by referring to the treaties imposed on France at Frankfurt and on Russia at Brest-Litovsk, the Germans insisted that negotiations should only be on the basis of the Fourteen Points and the Armistice. The German political leadership interpreted, or wilfully misinterpreted, the Fourteen Points and the Armistice conditions as and when it suited them—something they continued to do throughout the course of the reparations.[45] The position Germany would take at Paris was to ignore the military verdict of the war and the fact that 'peace without victory' had long been overtaken by events, while trying to resume as much of its negotiating strength as was possible. Sally Marks' assessment of the German stance on the reparation issue can be applied to the whole treaty:

> As to tactics, [the German cabinet] agreed on loud and constant repetition of its views, numerous countercharges, and maximum propaganda to rouse world opinion, especially socialists, and to split the Entente, which it hoped was crumbling. Further, Germany would insist on absolute equality and an equal voice, demand neutral arbiters, and make an inflated offer, proposing to pay it in paper marks at the 1914 exchange rate or roughly triple their current value on neutral exchanges. In addition every means was to be used to lure the Allies into negotiation.[46]

The Allies would not have a bar of any of this. They agreed that Germany should not be consulted formally before the peacemakers in Paris had formulated a common draft. The Allies' statesmen, facing a myriad of domestic problems in the aftermath of the war, were neither willing nor able to be bogged down in lengthy negotiations with the former enemy. They knew the Germans would attempt to follow the example set by the French a century earlier during the Congress of Vienna — to draw out proceedings, attempt to split the alliance of their victorious opponents (which the French did successfully), and then use division in their ranks to achieve favourable terms for the loser. But almost a hundred years had passed. International communications and the media had advanced, illiteracy had almost been wiped out, and there were now democratic governments. The public was better informed, and was able to challenge policies that greatly disadvantaged or exploited them. Under the dynastic system, rulers could ride roughshod over their subjects. In 1919, after all the damage and blood-letting, the public would not have accepted that their leaders sit down with the enemy and leisurely put the war to rest.

There is still a view, and not only in Germany, that German participation in the Paris peacemaking process would have led to a more successful post-war arrangement. There is no evidence to support this view. The position of the German delegation that made its way to Paris at the end of April was that of the government: to retain the status quo of 1916 and to resist any attempt to reduce Germany's pre-war territory or industrial capacity. The chief of the delegation, Count Ulrich von Brockdorff-Rantzau, the physical epitome of the stereotypical Prussian aristocrat, was just as arrogant. He had been selected because of his criticism of some of the extreme war policies of the OHL.

The economic experts in the German delegation had all been members of the old industrial and commercial elite, and included Otto Wiedtfeld, a Krupp director; Wilhelm Cuno and Philipp Heineken, directors of the HAPAG and Norddeutscher Lloyd shipping lines; and Ewald Hilger, an Upper Silesian mining magnate. These men could be expected to object to a treaty that, apart from ceding Alsace-Lorraine, temporarily mortgaged a proportion of Germany's future coal production, surrendered most of her merchant fleet, and threatened to sever Upper Silesia from the Reich.

The French government had ordered that the trains bringing the delegation to Paris should loiter so that their passengers might see first-hand the results of their invasion. The sight of miles upon miles of a devastated landscape and razed towns and villages affected some of the delegates. After seeing this, how could they not be daunted by the prospect of what they faced in the negotiations? Arriving at the station, they were carted away in heavily guarded buses to the Hôtel des Réservoir, where their luggage had been dumped in the courtyard. They had to carry it themselves to their rooms. The Hôtel des Réservoir was where the French leaders had stayed during the negotiations with Bismarck in 1871. It was now surrounded by a stockade, the French claiming—with some truth—that this was for the delegation's own security. The writing was clearly on the wall.

CHAPTER FOUR

Versailles

The day of facing the facts for the Germans came on 7 May 1919, a week after their arrival at Versailles. Representatives of 27 nations had assembled in the dining-room of the Trianon Palace Hotel, where the final chapter of the war opened at three in the afternoon. Clemenceau wasted no time in coming to the point:

> This is neither the time nor the place for superfluous words. You see before you the accredited representatives of the Allied and Associated Powers, both great and small, which have waged war without respite for more than four years, the pitiless war that was imposed on them. The time has come for a heavy reckoning of accounts. You have asked for peace. We are ready to grant it to you.[1]

As the large white folio volume containing the peace

conditions was handed to Brockdorff-Rantzau, the prime minister reminded the Germans that there was to be no discussion, that all observations had to be in writing, and that they had fifteen days to submit their comments. On completion, Clemenceau asked whether anyone else wanted to speak. The head of the German delegation did.

Acknowledging defeat and accusing the Allies of making Germany pay as the vanquished party and submit to punishment as the guilty one, Brockdorff-Rantzau immediately turned to the question of war guilt, which he called a lie. He claimed that Germany had been waging a defensive war, and insisted that it should not be burdened with sole responsibility. He maintained that the war had been the product of European imperialism, and blamed the Allies for cold-bloodedly causing the deaths of hundreds of thousands of non-combatants by the continuation of their blockade. He also asked for a neutral commission to investigate objectively who was responsible for the outbreak of war, and he reiterated that peace was to be on the basis of the Fourteen Points and the Pre-Armistice Agreement. Germany accepted liability for civilian damage in Belgium and in occupied France, and would agree to contribute to their reconstruction with 'the technical and financial participation of the victors'. He added that 'experts on both sides will have to study how the German people can best meet their obligation of financial reparation without breaking down under the heavy load'.[2]

Neither what he said nor the way he said it was well received. Brockdorff-Rantzau, 'a most sinister looking person, an incarnation of the whole Junker system', according to chief secretary of the war cabinet, Maurice

Hankey, spoke in German, 'in a harsh rasping voice' and, contrary to international diplomatic protocol, remained seated. Billy Hughes, as the text was being translated, approached Lloyd George, asking him whether Clemenceau 'would allow this fellow to go on like this'. Clemenceau had turned red with anger. Wilson was exasperated. 'The Germans are really a stupid people', he commented on the way out. 'They always did the wrong thing during the war, and that is why I am here. They don't understand human nature. This is the most tactless speech I ever heard'. Lloyd George agreed: 'it was deplorable to let him talk'. His private secretary, Phillip Henry Kerr, summed up the feeling in the room: 'At the start everybody felt a little sympathy with the Hun, but by the time Brockdorff-Rantzau had finished, most people were almost anxious to recommence the war'.[3]

It had not been the aim of Brockdorff-Rantzau's speech to soothe the Allies. Aside from the fact that it was chiefly addressed to the German domestic audience, it gave a clear indication that Germany would fight the Peace Treaty tooth and nail. The Trianon Palace address was the beginning of a long propaganda exercise to discredit the victors. The Germans would refer continuously over the next weeks to the 'hunger blockade' (which did not exist), and would wage an unrelenting campaign against the assumption of 'unilateral war guilt'—something that no country other than Germany detected in the treaty. Throughout its time in Paris, the German delegation, in the manner of Leon Trotsky at Brest-Litovsk, flooded the Allies with notes, constantly delayed procedures, and involved itself in as much public diplomacy as possible to engage the world's sympathies.[4]

At the same time, the German cabinet in Berlin pursued numerous attempts to erode the treaty conditions. Like the delegation in Paris, it put the responsibility for the outbreak of war on Russia. It conceded only that the invasion of France through Belgium had violated international law, and hence would pay only for the damage done in those countries, not for the destruction in Poland, Russia, Serbia, Montenegro, Romania, and Italy, nor for damage done to shipping. When this made no impression on the Allies, the German government made a counter-proposal that it claimed was in line with the Fourteen Points. Territorially, Germany would agree to a cessation of part of Poznan to Poland, but there had to be plebiscites in Alsace-Lorraine and northern Schleswig. Germany would provide Polish access to the sea. The Germans of Austria and Bohemia would be allowed to join the Reich, and there was to be no occupation of the Rhineland. Further points of the counter-proposal were immediate German entry into the League of Nations, and a German mandate over its colonies. Germany would keep its merchant fleet and, like the delegates, the government demanded a neutral enquiry into responsibility for the outbreak of war. In return, Germany offered to pay 100 billion goldmarks, the first payment to be made in 1926 and the rest in interest-free annual instalments amounting to no more than one billion per annum over the first ten years. Germany would also participate in the reconstruction of France and Belgium, provided it could join the Reparation Commission, the power of which was to be greatly reduced.[5]

This proposal was also rejected by the Allies. Nevertheless, the strategy of the German peace delegation to spread disunity in the Allied camp does seem to have borne fruit as the signing of the treaty drew closer. In Britain, some politicians and a section of the public at large began to feel uncomfortable about the Peace Treaty, which they regarded as too harsh. The most outspoken criticism came from the South African delegate, Jan Christian Smuts. He attacked the reparation demands, which he judged as too high, conveniently overlooking his key role in deciding reparation payments. He also argued that some of the territorial clauses were a menace to Europe's future. Lloyd George took the wind out of Smuts' sails by raising the issue of German South-West Africa, about to become a South African mandate, which Smuts was in no way willing to give up.

Even so, on 1 June, Lloyd George called a meeting of the British empire delegation at which he agreed to go back to the Council of Four to ask for modification of some terms, including the reparation issue. When he told Wilson and Clemenceau the next day that his colleagues would not authorise him to sign the treaty as it stood, they were incredulous. Horrified at the prospect of redoing months of work, they concluded that the British prime minister had lost his nerve. Wilson, who had had enough of the wily Welshman, accusing him privately of having no principles whatever of his own and that expediency was his sole guiding star,[6] refused to budge this time except on two points. Lloyd George managed a concession on Upper Silesia (where there would be a plebiscite) and an agreement that Germany could enter the league once Europe had settled down. On 16 June, the German delegation was told that they had three days to sign.

The growing concern with which German people had been watching developments in Paris soon turned to despair and hatred. Woodrow Wilson, originally hailed as a saviour, became the object of unlimited scorn. Novelist Thomas Mann spewed his anger upon Clemenceau, in whom he saw a 'poisonous old man … with oval eyes', a sign that the French prime minister might possess the blood-stock which would 'carry Western civilisation to its grave and create Khirgizian conditions'.[7] Reference to the barbaric east was also to be found in Max Weber's comments. Weber, who had joined the German delegation as an expert adviser, claimed that there was no way that in August 1914 the German empire could avoid conflict with Russia. He claimed that 'Tsarism [was] the most horrible system of subjugation of human beings and nations ever devised'—matched only by the peace treaty the Allies were about to impose.[8] Leading Centre-Party deputy Konstantin Fehrenbach described the treaty as 'the immortalisation [*Verewigung*] of the war', predicting that 'German women will give birth to children, and [that] these children will break the slave-chains and wash away the shame, which has been done to the German countenance'.[9] Historian Antony Lentin has hit the nail on the head:

> [T]here is no denying the historical importance of the profound psychological unwillingness to look facts in the face and the 'apocalyptic' despair that gripped many German thinkers by no means conservative in outlook. Victims not merely of imperial tradition and wartime propaganda, but of a heady succession of undeniable victories and massive annexation in the east, at the same time convinced that Germany had

fought a war of self-defence, they gave little thought
to the consequences of defeat and of Allied fears of
Germany. This explains perhaps part of the depth of
their shock and disillusion. One has the impression
that Germany was as blinkered intellectually and
imaginatively as it was blockaded physically: a
'dreamland' indeed.[10]

The German government now faced the reality of
the treaty. 'The hand that signed the treaty must wither',
commented chancellor Phillip Scheidemann on receiving
the terms. He and his entire cabinet resigned, but not
before adding the term *Schandparagraph* [disgrace-
paragraph] to the illustrious list of derogatory German
terms about the Allies' peacemaking. Scheidemann's
resignation was a fitting end to a political life in which no
objective biographer would find major merit. Hidden away
in his drawers was documentary evidence that the German
high command bore a major share of responsibility for
August 1914.[11]

In the end, it was all to no avail. Following intelligence
reports from Germany that the government was not willing
to sign, the Allies on 20 June ordered the preparation of an
assault into central Germany by over forty divisions. The
British also took steps to renew the naval blockade. On 21
June, the German navy scuttled itself at Scapa Flow. By
the time the British awoke to the operation, all but a few
ships had been sunk. All told, 400,000 tons of shipping—a
fortune in scrap metal—was gone.

The Germans were divided as the deadline drew closer
by the hour. Brockdorff-Rantzau demanded that Germany

should stand firm and not sign; the Allies were bluffing, and there would be no occupation. Field Marshal Hindenburg also wanted to hold out: better an honourable defeat than a disgraceful peace. On 22 June, the German National Assembly voted in favour of signing, provided that Germany would not have to accept Article 231. The Allies did not budge: sign or we move. There was one final dramatic parliamentary session the next day. Catholic Deputy Matthias Erzberger, who had signed the Armistice and who held the most realistic view of the situation, urged that the treaty be signed. (He would be murdered by nationalist thugs two years later.) Army chief Wilhelm Groener informed the house that Germany was in no position to renew military action. At three that afternoon, by a margin of 237 to 138, the National Assembly voted to accept. The note reached the peacemakers one hour and twenty minutes before the deadline ran out.

The signing ceremony took place on 28 June, the fifth anniversary of the assassination of the crown prince and his wife at Sarajevo. At 3.45 p.m., the German signatories, foreign minister Hermann Müller and minister of transport Johannes Bell, signed the treaty in the Hall of Mirrors. The audience included all of the plenipotentiaries who had witnessed the opening five months earlier. Only the Chinese were missing; they had left the conference in protest against the handing over to Japan of the former German base of Tsingtao on the Shantung peninsula.

The Treaty of Versailles—Parts I to VII

It is necessary to analyse the content of the Versailles

Peace Treaty to establish whether it contributed politically, economically, militarily, geographically, or in any other way to the failure of democracy in the Weimar Republic and the 'seizure of power' by the National Socialist German Workers Party (NSDAP). Part I of the treaty contained the 26 paragraphs establishing the League of Nations. The German delegation had objected to not having been invited to become a foundation member, which, it claimed, violated promises president Wilson had made in his speeches to congress on 8 January and 27 September 1918. This was repudiated. Wilson maintained that he had made it clear from the outset that Germany would not be included because it had proven untrustworthy, but that after redeeming its character, 'not by what happens at the peace table but by what follows', it should be allowed to join. Although it is reasonable to question why Germany should agree to the establishment of an organisation to which it was barred entry, membership of the League can hardly be said to have been a major political issue before it did join in September 1926.

Part II (Articles 27–30) defined Germany's new borders. Part III dealt with 'Political Clauses for Europe' (Articles 31–117). Many of these articles were uncontroversial. As far as Luxembourg was concerned (Articles 42–43), for example, the Germans declared that the Grand Duchy would no longer enjoy the benefits of membership in the German Customs Union, to which the Allies responded that, because of the violation of its neutrality during the war, Luxembourg itself had already decided to quit the union. A plebiscite in Schleswig (Articles 109–114) was not questioned by either side. When it was held in

February 1920, the vote went along ethnic lines: the northern parts voted to return to Denmark, the southern to remain with Germany. There was no objection from Germany to the dismantling of all military equipment on the island of Heligoland (Article 114). Germany reaffirmed Article 15 of the Armistice Agreement, renouncing the treaty of Brest-Litovsk and all subsequent treaties with Russia (Article 115–116), and also declared that it had no intention of shifting the Austrian-German frontier by force (Article 80). No reference was made to Articles 81 to 86, which concerned the Czechoslovak state. In line with Armistice conditions, Articles 40 to 42 stipulated that the demilitarised zone on the left bank of the River Rhine was to extend 50 kilometres to the east. This provoked an angry German reaction, but the failure of the United States to ratify the military-assistance agreement with France, and Britain's steady withdrawal from continental European affairs, meant that there was no military value in the left bank clauses, as Hitler's reoccupation of the Rhineland in March 1936 was to illustrate.

With the exception of northern Schleswig, Germany objected to the loss of its pre-war territory. Belgium, which had severely suffered from four years of German occupation, was rewarded with the district of Prussian Moresnet near Liège, as well as the territory between the small towns of Eupen and Malmedy, all told about 400 square miles with a population of 50,000 (Articles 31–39). This region was heavily forested, and so Belgium recovered some of the timber it had lost during the war. Germany objected on the ground that the population was German—incorrect, as far as Malmedy was concerned, as it belonged to the

Walloon (that is, French-speaking) part of Belgium. The Allies responded that Eupen and Malmedy had been separated from the neighbouring Belgian lands of Limburg, Liège, and Luxembourg in 1814–15 when these had been assigned to Prussia and when, they alleged, 'no account was taken of the desires of the people, nor of geographical or linguistic frontiers'. Moreover, the region 'continued in close economic and social relations with the adjacent portion of Belgium ...' and, at the same time, 'had been made a basis for German militarism'.[12] However one may view the correctness of the decision to award Eupen and Malmedy to Belgium, the loss to Germany was negligible. The same goes for Germany's handover to Lithuania of the Baltic port of Memel with its hinterland (Article 99), thus providing the newly founded state with a harbour. Memel's population was about equally divided between Lithuanians and Germans.

The return of Alsace-Lorraine to France (Articles 51–79), however, was no small matter. Germany had acquiesced in Article Eight of Wilson's Fourteen Points, 'that the wrong done by Prussia to France in 1871, as regards Alsace and Lorraine, which has disturbed the peace of the world for nearly fifty years, must be righted in order that peace again may be assured in the interest of all'. Nevertheless, Germany now maintained that Alsace-Lorraine was old German territory, having become part of the German empire more than a thousand years before. Claiming that 'racial and political characteristics of the inhabitants have been so little influenced that even to-day four-fifths of the country's population is still German in its language and customs',[13] it argued that a plebiscite should be held here. This was refused outright. The Allies claimed that the inhabitants had been annexed against their will, and were only too ready to throw themselves back into the arms of France, 'as into those of a long-lost mother'.

Articles 45 to 50 dealt with the Saar Basin, the population of which was 90 per cent German. The French initially wanted to annex outright the Saar district, with its rich coalfields, to compensate for the destruction of mines in northern France and as part of the overall payment due from Germany for war damage. After heated debate in the Council of Four, Clemenceau had to settle for a compromise that gave the French fifteen years' possession of the coalmines. As the Saar did in fact vote to return to Germany in 1935, production figures for the Saar coal industry, or indeed for *Saarland* generally, after that date cannot be included in the calculation of German economic losses caused by the Peace Treaty.

By far the most territory Germany had to cede went to its new eastern neighbour. As part of the Polish-Lithuanian Commonwealth, the Kingdom of Poland had in early modern times been a formidable power in eastern Europe, but by the eighteenth century political life in Poland had reached a stage of near anarchy. Its kings were the puppets of powers abroad and rival noble families within. With no effective government, the land-owning class, the *szlachta*, exploited the Polish peasantry to such a degree that their living conditions were the worst in rural Europe. Their status has been compared with that of West Indian slaves.[14] An ultra-conservative Catholic clergy, with its emphasis on otherworldly fulfilment, added to the burdens on Poland's villages. In a rare act of political cannibalism beginning in 1772, even by eighteenth-century European standards, the Russian empress, Catharine the Second, the Prussian king, Frederick the Second, and Empress Maria-Theresa of Austria carved the kingdom up among themselves. For those Poles who became part of Prussia, living conditions greatly improved. Most Polish patriots who clamoured for the restitution of their homeland came from those parts that had fallen under Habsburg and tsarist rule.

After six unsuccessful uprisings through the course of the nineteenth century, World War I provided the chance for rebirth. Point Thirteen of the Fourteen Points had stipulated that there was to be an independent Polish state, 'which should include the territories inhabited by indisputable Polish populations, which should be assured a free and secure access to the sea'. Given the geography of the region, this access could only be provided by the River Vistula, which runs into the Baltic just east of Danzig, on its way passing through the territory of the Prussian provinces of Pomerania, West Prussia, and Poznan. Originally purely Polish in population, 150 years of Prussian rule, with its vigorous Germanisation policy, had created a mixed population of Poles and Germans, with most of the land owned by Prussian Junkers. The part ceded to Poland by the treaty (Articles 87–98), after lengthy and often inimical deliberations in the Council of Four, was inhabited mainly by Poles. Attempts to enlarge this area, commonly referred to as the 'corridor', in Poland's favour by incorporating into it parts of East Prussia were stopped by plebiscites. The corridor also surrounded the city of Danzig (the Polish Gdansk), where there was a major German population. Danzig became a Free City (Article 100–108) under the auspices of the League of Nations, but maintained its strong economic and cultural ties with the Reich.

The fate of Upper Silesia, because of its large industrial area, was strongly contested by both sides. The population was 65 per cent Polish-speaking. A quarter of German coal came from here, four-fifths of it zinc, and almost a third of its lead. Both countries claimed that their economies could not function without Upper Silesian coal. A plebiscite held two years later brought no clear result—the north and west choosing to stay with Germany, and the south preferring to become part of Poland. The centre, where the industrial area was located, although largely Polish-speaking, returned a fifty-fifty vote.

Many Poles may have decided to vote for Germany from fear of recrimination by their employers, as Germans owned most of the mines and steel mills, or in the belief that living conditions even in a defeated Germany were better than those in Poland. An independent commission set up by the League of Nations finally awarded 70 per cent of the total area to Germany, but handed two-thirds of the industrial part to Poland. However, Article 90 of the treaty, which had stipulated that for a period of fifteen years Germany could purchase all products of the mines at the same price as the Poles, was re-affirmed. Neither the German mine and steel-mill owners nor the rural landowners were dispossessed. Nevertheless, the Upper Silesian settlement accounts for the bulk of Germany's industrial losses.

What does this amount to? Almost all of the figures circulating about Germany's territorial and population losses state that the Reich lost almost 70,000 square kilometres of its territory, amounting to 13 per cent, and 6.5 million inhabitants or 10.2 per cent of its population. Robert Boyce has recently queried these statistics. He points out that much of the land in question had been acquired in the previous half-century by military conquest, and was neither historically nor ethnically German. He stresses that even the Nazis made little protest over the loss of Alsace-Lorraine and northern Schleswig, but—with the exception of Eupen-Malmedy—focused all their anger upon German losses in the east. If one accepts this reasonable argument, the loss of territory is reduced to 9.4 per cent and of population to 7 per cent. Moreover, Boyce contends that German losses are overstated for three further reasons. First, a large number of people in pre-war German or Prussian territory were ethnically non-Germans. Second, when territory was transferred, some ethnic Germans refused to be transferred with it, but moved to other parts of Germany. Third, the German statistics that almost all historians use most likely overestimate the German losses. On this point, Boyce refers to a 1919 British study, which noted:

> The figures of the 1910 census are demonstrably falsified, and even if they were accurate they would describe a state of things artificially created by the police of ruthlessly suppressing the Polish language and of substituting German for Polish peasants on the land by the expenditure of public money to which the Poles as taxpayers are compelled to contribute, and this on top ... of the presence of large numbers of German officials (railway porters and post office clerks, &c) and their families.

However, even if the German population moving out of the transferred region is left to one side, the non-Germans are counted in the territorial changes, and the official German statistics are accepted, Boyce concludes that the population loss amounts to 1.8 per cent, a fraction of the 10 per cent invariably claimed.[15]

Similarly, just as the Upper Silesian mines and plants constitute the only industrial loss that can be substantiated, claims that Germany lost a third of its pre-war coal production and three-quarters of its iron capacity are dubious. The output of Germany's coal and heavy industry had surpassed pre-war figures by the mid-1920s, much earlier than that of the United Kingdom,[16] and the same goes for the chemical and electrical sectors of Germany industry.

There can be no genuine talk of a 'Carthaginian Peace'. Had Germany won the war, it would have incorporated large parts of eastern Europe and European Russia, much of northern France, and the whole of Belgium and Luxembourg. Compared to this, and taking into account the terms imposed by Prussia on defeated states in the second half of the nineteenth century, German losses at Versailles were moderate.

Part IV of the treaty, 'German Rights and Interests outside Germany', began with the German colonies (Articles 119–127). In its response to the Versailles Peace Treaty, Germany claimed to have been an exemplary colonial power, having abolished 'devastating and incessant predatory warfare between the tribes' and the 'high-handedness of the chiefs and witch-doctors and the kidnapping of slaves and the slave trade'. All told, Germany had always looked to the welfare of the natives. In particular, it had brought peace and order to its colonies, and a well-organised system of native education provided vocational and agricultural schooling. The Allies dismissed these claims. They referred to pre-war studies, private and official, conducted in Germany into the Reich's colonial administration, which pointed to cruel and methodical repression, arbitrary requisition of territory, and various forms of forced labour.[17] The first administration of Heinrich Ernst Göring (the father of the notorious Nazi) in German South-West Africa stood out for its brutality. The year 1904 saw the twentieth century's first genocide, when General Lothar von Trotha drove the Herero people into the Namibian desert, where up to 100,000 perished from thirst and starvation.[18]

The Allies' accusation of German colonial maladministration was an example of the pot calling the kettle black, and with hindsight the loss of the colonies was a blessing. None of the other colonisers had objected to the German empire's belated acquisition of territory overseas, as the richest pickings had long been made. In terms of nineteenth-century colonialism, the German possessions in Africa and the Pacific yielded few returns and had to be subsidised, and they did not provide an outlet for Germany's rapidly expanding population. By 1913 the number of Germans in the African colonies totalled 18,362, many of whom were military and administrative staff and temporary residents engaged in railway construction. The actual number of German settlers would have been around ten thousand, most of them in German South-West Africa.

Economically, the colonies provided Germany with only

2 per cent of its so-called 'colonial wares': cotton, rubber, tobacco, and copra palm kernels. Less than a third of one per cent of Germany's total foreign commerce came from the African colonies, and trade with the Pacific Islands was even less. By the time the twentieth-century mining boom had reached Africa and the Pacific (and in particular New Guinea), national liberation movements had brought the mandate system to an end. The seeds of anti-colonialism were being planted at Paris even while the peacemaking process was in progress. Ho Chi Minh, a young Vietnamese working as a kitchen hand at the Ritz Hotel, presented a petition seeking Vietnam's independence from France.[19] As the French and Americans were to find out decades later, it would have been wise to have listened to him.

The loss of its colonies meant that Germany was spared humiliation and cost when, after World War II, liberation movements in 'Third World' countries pushed out their European overlords. The German population of what had been German South-West Africa supported the Union of South Africa, with its apartheid system. When the African National Congress put an end to apartheid, Nelson Mandela returned the government of the former mandate to its original inhabitants. Like other white minorities of southern Africa, the German settlers acquiesced peacefully, and in Namibia, as the ex-colony is now called, black and white now live in harmony.

Treaty Articles 128 to 158 specified that treaties made by Germany with a number of states in North Africa and Asia[20] previous to and during the war were to be invalidated. The most important of these concerned the Chinese Shantung peninsula (Articles 156–158) where, since 1898, Germany had held a 99-year lease for 100 square miles at Kiachow Bay in the south. Here, at Tsingtao, they constructed a harbour where the German Cruiser Squadron was stationed. Tsingtao was overrun by the Japanese in the early months of the war, and they expanded their base far beyond the territory leased to Germany. The Allies, keen to secure continued Japanese assistance in East Asia and the Pacific, had assured Japan in 1917 that it could take over from Germany in Shantung after the war, but U.S. delegates at the peace conference objected to the acquisition. Under pressure to finalise the treaty in the last days of April, Wilson agreed to a compromise: Japan could take over Germany's economic rights in Shantung—the port, the railways, and the mines—but had to pull out its occupation forces. When the Chinese delegates were handed these terms, they left the conference. Japan withdrew from Shantung in 1922, but invaded the Chinese mainland, including Shantung, fifteen years later. It was the beginning of a war and an occupation that was to take the life of twenty million Chinese.

Part V of the treaty—Military, Naval and Airforces (Articles 159–221)—was severe. Germany had to reduce its army to 100,000 men, of whom only 4,000 could be officers. The latter were allowed to serve for 25 years; the other ranks, for twelve. Germany was also banned from possessing tanks or armoured cars, heavy guns, poison gas, or other chemical weapons. Only a limited amount of smaller armaments was exempt. Likewise, the navy was to be reduced to 36 smaller ships and 15,000 personnel, and Germany was allowed no submarines or military aircraft. Arms and ammunition could only be produced in a number of designated plants. In addition to the Articles on the

Rhineland referred to above, all existing stocks of weapon and fortifications in the region had to be destroyed. There were to be restrictions on the manpower and training of organisations such as the police, customs, and coastguards. Private societies such as veteran's associations were not to pursue military goals. The system of cadet students in high schools and universities was to be discontinued. These restrictions were aimed at reducing the likelihood of renewed German aggression.

It was characteristic of the Peace Treaty and the peacemaking process that what was demanded on paper and what happened in reality did not match. 'Military men', comments Versailles expert Stephen Schuker, 'no more believed in the permanent disarmament of a major industrial nation than they gave credence to the tooth-fairy'.[21] Implementation of the 62 disarmament articles was to be carried out by the Germans themselves, supervised by an Inter-Allied Military Control Commission (IAMCC) in an arrangement characterised by one historian as 'like the ropes of the Lilliputians over Gulliver'.[22]

The Allies felt satisfied by the middle of 1921 that naval and aerial disarmament had by and large been achieved. But while ships and aeroplanes could not easily be hidden, other armaments could. The IAMCC had a staff of only 1,200 soldiers, and could not extend its control over the whole of Germany. Obstruction was common. Allied inspectors were given a hostile reception in most plants and barracks, and were hindered in carrying out their task.

There were widespread violations of the military articles of the Peace Treaty. Large caches of war material were frequently discovered,[23] and German arms producers soon found ways to circumvent Allied control. Rheinmetall, for example, produced artillery under the guise of railway equipment. Factories that had previously manufactured tanks now fabricated inordinately huge tractors. The joke was told in Berlin's cabarets of the worker who smuggled parts out of his pram factory for his newborn, only to find when he put them together that he had assembled a machine gun.[24] The bulk of post-war armament production was moved outside the country, with manufacturers transporting their plants to neutral countries such as Switzerland, Holland, and Sweden. Leading arms producer Krupp, for example, set up a giant firm in the Netherlands, and was able to gain control of Swedish armament producer Bofors.[25]

German avoidance of the disarmament demands reached its peak after the Treaty of Rapallo, signed with the Soviet Union on 16 April 1922. Rapallo was a spin-off from the Genoa conference held in April and May 1922, in which representatives of 34 countries, including Germany and Russia, discussed ways to tackle the economic problems left by the war. With the conference making little headway, the German and Soviet foreign ministers, Walther Rathenau and Georgi Chicherin, slipped away with a team of delegates to nearby Rapallo to settle the differences between their countries.

Officially, the treaty was to normalise diplomatic and economic relations and to renounce all territorial and financial claims resulting from the war. Unofficially, the result was clandestine military co-operation, which enabled the Reichswehr to test on Soviet soil weapons and equipment forbidden by the Versailles Treaty and to train military personnel in their use. In return, German know-how was to improve the Soviets' deficient and backward military.

A number of German firms (among them Junkers, Krupp, Rheinmetall, and Stolzenberg) participated in the reconstruction of the Soviet armaments industry, and in 1924 a German-Soviet company was set up to manufacture poison gas, ammunition, and aircraft. The enterprise failed because of economic, technical, and personnel problems, but not before a shipment of 300,000 rounds of ammunition was discovered heading for Germany—causing a storm of indignation in the Western media.[26]

The treaty with the Soviet Union also assisted in circumventing the demands made in the Versailles military clauses to reduce the size of the German army. During the peacemaking processs, the British delegate on the commission dealing with disarmament, Henry Wilson, had argued for a volunteer army where members would serve for a number of years. French commander Foch, however, warned that the creation of such an army led by long-serving officers would form the nucleus of a much larger force and, to avoid this, demanded a system in which conscripts would serve no longer than a year. The French lost out, at Lloyd George's insistence, and the concept of a conscript German army was abandoned. By the end of 1920, the British members of the IAMCC believed that Germany had reduced the size of its army to the required 100,000 men. The French were more sceptical, and they were supported by Brigadier-General J. H. Morgan, a dissenting voice among the British in the IAMCC. Morgan was active in uncovering German attempts to circumvent the clauses of the treaty. In two articles published in *The*

Times in September 1921, he pointed out that Germany had enough personnel, clothing, and armaments for 800,000 men.[27]

Foch's fear that the volunteer army would grow around a large nucleus of well-trained officers proved well founded. Because the peacemakers failed to place restrictions on the number of non-commissioned officers in the *Reichswehr*, the number of sergeants and corporals amounted to 40,000.[28] This contravention assisted Nazi Germany with its re-armament policy of the mid-1930s.

Part VI (Articles 214–226) of the treaty specified that there should be a speedy, orderly, and humane repatriation of prisoners of war and interned civilians, and that the fallen on both sides should be buried in their respective territories as far as this was possible. Part VII on penalties dealt in part with Kaiser Wilhelm. He was to be extradited from the Netherlands and put on trial for 'supreme offence against international morality and the sanctity of treaties' (Article 227). The next Article recognised the right of the Allies 'to bring before military tribunals persons accused of having committed acts in violation of the laws and customs of war'. The committee in charge of drawing up penalties had also been charged with establishing responsibility for the outbreak of war, a task that could not be carried out because members did not have at their disposal material to investigate. The conclusion to Part VIII stated the optimistic demand that the German government provide all documents and information necessary to deal with the criminal acts and the perpetrators (Article 230).

Reparations and Article 231: 'Paragraph of disgrace', or 'Paragraph of good fortune'?

By the time the details of the Versailles Peace Treaty had been made public, interest in the prosecution of war crimes had all but vanished, at least in Britain and the U.S. The question of 'war guilt' was another matter. Article 231, introducing Part VIII on 'Reparations', stated 'That the Allied and Associated Governments affirm and Germany accepts the responsibility of Germany and her allies for causing all the loss and damage to which the Allied and Associated Governments and their nationals have been subjected as a consequence of the war imposed upon them by the aggression of Germany and her allies'. There was no reference suggesting that Germany was responsible for the outbreak of war. The term 'aggression', as it did in the Pre-Armistice Agreement, referred to German violation of international conduct as spelt out in The Hague Convention of 1907, and in particular to Imperial Germany's unprovoked attack upon neutral Belgium. Article 231 was merely an introductory clause stating the ethical and jurisdictional justification for the reparation liability. Insisting that Article 231 assigned 'war guilt' (*Kriegsschuld*) to Germany, the German response was strident. No other part, sentence, or paragraph of the Versailles Treaty was attacked with such ferocity.

The insistence on Article 231 as the source of all evil that was to befall Germany has surprised treaty specialists outside Germany for some time. Given the importance of the issue for this book, I have taken the liberty of quoting one of these specialists at length:

The issue of German responsibility—as specified in the notorious article 231 of the peace treaty—has given rise to the most egregious popular misconceptions about the reparation settlement that have persisted down through the decades. The truth of the matter is that this provision had been inserted at the behest not of some French or British hardliner (such as the devious 'Klotzkie', the bombastic 'Billy' Hughes, or the obdurate 'heavenly twins'), but rather of the American representatives of the Reparation Commission, Norman Davis and John Foster Dulles. The courtly southern gentleman and the stolid Wall Street lawyer had been conscientiously seeking diplomatic language that would mollify the British and the French while reducing the amount of Germany's financial obligation were it held liable for the totality of war costs, as Clemenceau and Lloyd George had been frantically demanding in order to satisfy their publics' insistence on integral repayment. By affirming [in article 231] Germany's *moral responsibility* for the war and its *legal liability* for the damage to persons and property, while implicitly acknowledging [in article 232] her financial incapacity to pay the enormous bills that was certain to result from an objective inspection of the devastated regions of France and an actuarial projection of pension costs, Davis and Dulles thought that they had devised a brilliant solution to the reparation dilemma: Here was a means of furnishing what Arthur Walworth has aptly called a 'psychological sop' to Allied public opinion

as compensation for the loss of the huge German
payments that Allied leaders knew could and would
never be made.[29]

There is one obvious reason for Germany's sensitivity
about Article 231. To concede that the German empire
bore responsibility for the events of July–August 1914
and the calamity that followed them was unthinkable. To
admit that the sacrifices—the two million of their people
dead, the four million crippled, blinded, or otherwise
incapacitated, the sufferings demanded of the bulk of the
population—may have been of Germany's own making, no
upright German could contemplate.

There was another reason why Article 231 was vilified.
The German government was aware of its true meaning.
Before negotiations commenced, it was reluctant to
bring the question of war guilt to the table, and it was
not altogether in agreement with Brockdorff-Rantzau's
decision to jump the gun and base the attack in his reply
of 7 May on the issue of German war guilt.[30] The German
note of 29 May referred to Article 231, but did not mention
that it implied war guilt.[31] When the Allies became aware
of the furore created by the clause, they pointed out that
the German delegation had 'misinterpreted the reparation
proposals of the treaty'.[32]

The Austrian and Hungarian governments, which had
faced provisions similar to Article 231, had not questioned
their inclusion, but accepted them as what amounted to
petty legal points to back up the Allies' reparation claims
as specified in the Pre-Armistice Agreement. Had the
German government acted likewise, there would have

been little justification for dissent. On the contrary, if German politicians and opinion-makers had disputed or challenged the Allies on this point, attention would have been drawn again to the collapse of the German war effort in September–October 1918, to the acceptance of the Fourteen Points with the Pre-Armistice Agreement, and to Germany's signing of the full Armistice terms—in short, to the fact that the nation had in all but name made an unconditional surrender. Had such a discussion occurred, it would have countered the ever-increasing feeling of the German public that the empire had not lost the war.

Weeks before the collapse, the public believed that the fatherland was set for victory. Because no foreign soldier had set foot on German soil, SPD leader Ebert, soon to become president of the German Reich, could welcome the troops with the proud assurance 'that no enemy has conquered you'. With the political right recovering from the sudden shock of defeat, and with war hero Ludendorff (who had fled in November to Sweden in false whiskers and tinted glasses) and his companions from the former OHL proclaiming the story of the brave German soldier, undefeated in the field but stabbed in the back by shoddy left-wing politicians and Jews (long before anyone had heard the name Adolf Hitler), renewed discussion about the true nature of the ending of the war could be avoided.

With Article 231 discounted as an Allied attempt to blame Germany for the outbreak of war and make it pay on that basis, myriad possibilities emerged for the Germans to mount a crusade against the Versailles Peace Treaty. 'Expert' historians could be (and were) used to provide volumes—forty in all—of counter-evidence as to the reasons for the war. A government department could be (and was) set up to spread the message that the war had not been Germany's fault, and endless propaganda countering such a false assumption could be (and was) circulated around the world. And if it could be shown that the German empire did not cause the war, then not just the reparation clauses, but the Versailles Peace Treaty as a whole, was based on a falsehood, was an attack by the Allies, and was null and void. Article 231 could be (and was) blamed for the entire malaise that befell the Republic—economic difficulties such as inflation, high prices, low wages, and unemployment, and the country's permanent political instability—and, above all, for the Republic's inglorious end in January 1933. Viewed in such terms, Article 231 for Weimar Germany was not a paragraph of disgrace but of good fortune.

Article 232 of the treaty assured Germany that, Article 231 notwithstanding, the amount to be paid would be within the limits of the country's capacity to pay. The amount was to be estimated by an Inter-Allied Reparation Commission (Article 233). This commission would determine the extent of Germany's obligation on 1 May 1921, after taking into account all the evidence and allowing the German government 'a just opportunity to be heard'. An initial payment of 20 billion goldmarks was to be made (Article 235) before this deadline. The remaining clauses (Articles 236–244) and their annexes spelt out the details for this initial payment.

Like the territorial settlement, the reparation terms of the first payment were modest. Payment could be made either in cash or, as happened for the most part, in kind.

Reparation credit was given for coal, timber chemicals and dyes, industrial and agricultural machinery and locomotives, rolling stock, and shipping. Germany was credited for confiscated military equipment, and for its colonies and transferred territories, including the Saarland but excluding Alsace-Lorraine. As far as the transfer of industrial equipment and plants from occupied territory was concerned, no levy was imposed. Included in the first payment were the Rhineland occupation costs and the Allies' expected outlays in providing Germany with food and raw materials — an amount of eight billion goldmarks.

Germany was to surrender all ships over 1,600 tons gross, half of those between 1,000 and 1,600 tons gross, a quarter of its steam trawlers and fishing boats, and a small part of its river fleet. This was to compensate for the losses caused by German submarine warfare, Britain alone having lost eight million tons of shipping. Over 2.6 million tons were handed over during the next two years. The loss of shipping, however, did not have an undue impact on the German economy. Ships were handed over only gradually, and by the end of 1919 leading German shipping companies such as HAPAG and Norddeutscher Lloyd were beginning to use agencies to run their former fleets.[33] Ship-building replaced the losses and helped to revive Germany's post-war economy, and by 1921 the German merchant fleet was greater than its pre-war size.[34]

All of these requirements were within Germany's capacity to pay, and did not effectively cripple the immediate post-war economy.[35]

The subsequent part 'Special Provisions', which dealt with the return of items of historical importance, has sometimes given critics of the treaty grounds for ridicule. Article 245, which covered the restoration to the French government of trophies, archives, historical souvenirs, and works of art carried away in the two previous wars, was reasonable, although one does wonder why, of all the confiscated documents, 'the political papers taken by the German authorities on October 10, 1870, at the Chateau of Cercay, near Brunoy, belonging to Mr. Rouhier, formerly Minister of State' should have been singled out for special mention. The subsequent clauses could perhaps have been settled privately.

Article 246 specified that the original Koran of the Caliph Othman, which had been taken from Medina by the Turks and handed to Wilhelm II, should be returned to the King of Hedjaz (the western part of today's Saudi Arabia), and that the skull of Sultan Mkawa, which had been removed from the Protectorate of German East Africa, should be handed over to the British government in good condition.

Article 247 required the replacement of all items of value (manuscripts, incunabula, printed books, maps, and other objects of collection) destroyed by the burning of the Library of Louvain, for which Germany would be given reparation credit. No such credit was allowed for returning the leaves of the Triptych of the Mystic Lamb, painted by the Van Eyck brothers, from the Berlin Museum to the Church of St. Bavon at Ghent; nor for the return of the Dierick Bouts' triptych of the Last Supper to the Church of St. Peter at Louvain.

The remaining seven parts of the treaty were concerned mainly with post-war arrangements for international financial and economic matters, customs and international traffic regulations, maritime and river navigation, aerial navigation, postal and telecommunications systems, and ports, waterways, and railways. Clauses here did not arouse the acrimony that accompanied the earlier parts, especially those on reparation. In its reply, Germany objected again to its exclusion, short-term, from the League of Nations and its affiliated organisations, and even more so to not being immediately admitted to all of the post-war trade arrangements. The Allies responded by pointing to the economic reality that had resulted from the war:

> The illegal acts of the enemy have placed many of the Allied States in a position of economic inferiority to Germany, whose territory has not been ravaged, whose plant is in a condition enabling manufactures and trade to be at once resumed after the war. For such countries, a certain freedom of action during the transition period is vitally necessary ... hence during the transitory period formal reciprocity with Germany is not practicable.[36]

Reciprocity would be forthcoming once economic balance was restored.

The Reparation Commission

After two years of deliberations, the Reparation Commission announced a total reparation debt of 132 billion goldmarks enshrined in the London Schedule of Payments presented to Germany on 5 May 1921. The amount was regarded as the lowest figure that would not cause a major public backlash in the Allied countries, but in reality it was for public consumption only; the commission consigned all but 50 billion goldmarks to never-never land.

The commission, in a highly complicated payment schedule, divided the reparation debt into A, B, and C Bonds. A and B Bonds, which amounted to a nominal value of 50 billion goldmarks, covered genuine German war debts such as occupation costs, coal deliveries, reparations, and food purchases as specified in Articles 233 to 244 of the treaty and their annexes. A and B Bonds would bear a modest interest rate of 5 per cent, and were to be delivered to the Reparation Commission by 21 July and 1 November 1921 respectively.[37] Repayments were to be made at the rate of two billion goldmarks per annum, in addition to a variable annuity of 26 per cent of the value of Germany's exports. The annual payment would thus be linked to the county's economic performance—an obvious invitation for the German government to cook the books.

C Bonds were also to be delivered to the Reparation Commission by 1 November, but authorisation and repayment was not to occur until the obligations under the A and B Bonds had been met. To meet this target, Germany would need to export to the value of approximately 21 billion goldmarks per annum. Because this was a near impossibility, it was estimated that the A and B Bonds would not be settled for 36 years, and only then would C Bond repayments begin. The likelihood that a recovered Germany would then meet any such obligations was nil. In fact, as the whole C Bond business 'would depend upon complete German good faith, favourable political conditions, and extraordinary German prosperity, and even then, would remain improbable',[38] the 83 billion goldmarks worth of C Bonds was phony money and was never meant to be anything else. Gaston Furth, assistant secretary of the Belgian delegation to the Reparation Commission, put it bluntly:

> [T]he Authors of the Schedule of Payments knew themselves that the C Bonds were only a fiction and that, if they had not wished or dared to touch the total of the debt, they had deliberately arranged to reduce in fact to 50 billion the nominal amount of 132 billion. In this there was an undeniable deception but an undoubtedly useful and even necessary deception. The men who had been studying the reparations question for several years knew then that one could not reasonably require of Germany more than 3 billion per year and that, consequently, there was no hope that she could pay off a debt of more than 50 billion gold marks. But the statesmen believed that public opinion in the allied nations was not sufficiently enlightened not to rebel at the brutal announcement of a total so short of its expectations. In brief, the Schedule of Payments elegantly resolved the difficulty on which all previous negotiations had foundered: the German debt was reduced in fact to a reasonable amount but this reduction was sufficiently cleverly disguised to keep public opinion from perceiving it and becoming aroused.[39]

To reiterate, the total sum Germany was obliged to pay in reparations was effectively 50 billion goldmarks. Yet even this was only a nominal figure. Experts recognised that the bonds could not be marketed at nominal value at the interest rate of only 5 per cent. Estimates of the 1921 *present* value ranged between 25 billion goldmarks (Keynes) and 35 billion (Furth), but whatever the exact figure, it is clear that the extent of the obligation Germany was to meet in 1921 was considerably less than 50 billion goldmarks in value. By coincidence, Germany had made a previous offer to the U.S. government to pay reparations to a *present* value of 50 billion marks.[40] This was refused, because the sum was not considered large enough to allow for public acceptance in the receiver countries.

Germany made its first cash payment in the summer of 1921, but paid only a fraction of the subsequent annuities. It also fell short on payments in kind, in particular on the delivery of coal. The destruction of coalmines by retreating German troops prior to the Armistice had deprived France of 50 per cent of its coal production. As coal was the chief source of energy at that time, France was dependant on German deliveries. Saar coal, which totalled eight million tons per annum, brought some relief, but the key to French supplies was the delivery of the 27 million tons Germany was obliged to provide under the terms of the Peace Treaty. Germany's chief coal region, the Ruhr, was so rich that Weimar should have been able to deliver. Yet Germany consistently defaulted, even though the Allies offered five dollars per ton as a goodwill gesture, and the quotas were constantly revised downward until they met barely half of the required amount. By the end of 1922, the London

Schedule had run into great difficulties.[41]

In January 1923, the Germans defaulted in their coal deliveries for the thirty-fourth time in 36 months. As a consequence, French, Belgian, and Italian engineers, accompanied by a small contingent of troops, entered the Ruhr. Britain, the fourth member of the Reparation Commission, was highly critical of this action, but for France more was at stake than collecting coal. With a few exceptions, the whole peacemaking process had failed to work in France's favour. It had lost on the issue of war criminals, and Germany was failing to comply with provisions on disarmament and assistance with the costly reconstruction of France's provinces. Were it to lose out on reparations as well, the French prime minister at the time, Raymond Poincaré, knew that the post-war balance would tilt against his nation. The fundamental issue of the Ruhr occupation was not the delivery of coal or timber: it was a last-ditch effort to force Germany to acknowledge defeat in World War I and the validity of the Versailles Peace Treaty.[42]

Occupation of the Ruhr coalfields netted the Allies 900 million goldmarks, but Germany did well, too. The mark had been rapidly depreciating since the war, partly because the Weimar government wanted to avoid budgetary and currency reform, but mainly because that way it could escape reparations. As the German government financed the resistance to the Ruhr occupation from an entirely empty treasury, hyper-inflation resulted. The hyper-inflation of 1923, a nightmare for the bulk of the German population, was brought about not by reparation costs or the Ruhr occupation, as the government claimed, but by Germany's deliberate decision to undermine the reparation demands and to dismantle the mountain of debts caused by the war. Hyper-inflation netted Germany 15 billion goldmarks held by foreign investors in German bank accounts. Against this, Germany had paid less than 1.5 billion goldmarks in cash reparations up to 1923. Furthermore, the inflation took care of war bond obligations totalling around 60 billion goldmarks, and reduced other state debts to zero. Sections of big business also profited from the collapse of the German mark, and so did people who owed money.[43]

The Ruhr occupation also spelt the end of the London Schedule of Payments. In 1924, the United States placed itself in charge of reparations and other aspects of post-war Europe with the introduction of the Dawes Plan. Washington's renewed interest in Europe was caused by a growing concern over the loss to America of overseas markets. American producers of wheat, pork, cotton, tobacco, and other commodities were suffering severely from the economic instability of the old world.[44] An international committee chaired by American banker and U.S. vice-president Charles Dawes reduced the overall reparation amount and scaled down the annual payments to one billion goldmarks for 1924–25.[45] This amount was to increase each year to 2.5 billion by 1928–29. In return for Germany's introducing a program of currency stabilisation and austerity, a consortium of American lenders arranged substantial loans to Germany (totalling, in the end, 12 billion goldmarks) to meet initial reparation payments and to provide a stimulus for the economy.

Germany paid the first Dawes Plan instalment mainly from the American loan, but asked for renegotiation before the 2.5 billion reparations threshold was reached. The resulting Young Plan, which further reduced Germany's commitment, was cut short by the world Depression that began in September 1929. Three more years of futile international wrangling followed before reparations met their de facto death at the Lausanne Convention of July 1932.

Altogether, Germany had paid between 20 and 21 billion goldmarks in reparations. Of the approximately 7 billion goldmarks paid in cash, 2 billion were paid by Germany itself. The remainder was paid out of loans from the Dawes and Young Plans. Cash reparation payments for the 13 years of the Weimar Republic amounted to 0.91 per cent. The gross burden on the German economy for the same period was 2.72 per cent.[46] This was scarcely an insurmountable economic strain on the Weimar economy.

Even these loans were later repudiated by Hitler. But the Nazis did not have the final word. When the 'Thousand Year Empire' met its end after twelve years, the United States, in the post-World War II settlement, insisted that $100 million still be paid for the Dawes loan bonds. This was a fraction of the approximately $3.5 billion U.S. losses incurred during the Weimar years. The story of the reparations part of the Treaty of Versailles ended on 3 October 2011, when Germany made its last payment.

In the end, the burden of paying for the damage done by the war had to be met by the victors. They had to pay for the reconstruction of devastated regions, the pensions of disabled veterans and war widows, and their own debts. I can find no better summary of this sad aspect of twentieth-century history than the conclusion of the American reparation expert Sally Marks:

In addition to reinforcing German economic superiority, the history of reparations generated a vast bureaucracy, a mountain of arcane documents, much bitterness, endless propaganda [and] more than its share of historical myths, ... It is evident that Germany could have paid a good deal more if she had chosen to do so, particularly since she paid little out of her own considerable resources. But Germany saw no reason to pay and from start to finish deemed reparations a gratuitous insult. Whether it was wise to seek reparations from Germany is arguable, although the consequences of not seeking them would have been far-reaching, as the failure to obtain them proved in time to be. Certainly it was unwise to inflict the insult without rigorous enforcement. In the last analysis, however, despite the fact that reparations claims were intended to transfer real economic wealth from Germany to the battered victors and despite the financial complexity of the problem, the reparations question was at heart a political issue, a struggle for dominance of the European continent and to maintain or reverse the military verdict of 1918.[47]

Winners and losers

The United States did well out of both the war and the peace. It seized twice as many merchant ships as it had lost, and sequestrated $425 million worth of German property.

American business benefited from fortunes made during the war by the Allies' demand for foodstuffs, raw materials, and ammunition, and banks profited from big loan operations to facilitate business.[48] In the Paris negotiations, the United States claimed six billion goldmarks, of which it eventually received 400 million.[49] Its war debt, by contrast, was relatively low. The war left the United States in a class of its own, as the leading world power economically and politically.

The United Kingdom's position was different. To its advantage, the German naval threat had been eliminated, and some overseas possessions had been added to its empire. There is a popular textbook claim, sometimes making its way into academic literature, that Britain also benefited from ridding itself of a major trade competitor. This was not the case. The German economy recovered faster and more strongly in the inter-war period.[50] Before the war, Britain had been a firm supporter of the global system of free trade, which, it hoped, would be restored as soon as possible. This support, as will be shown below, greatly guided her policies in the 1920s, to the detriment of France and the benefit of Germany. No one in British politics or industry contemplated taking out continental Europe's largest industrial nation.

Britain's post-war economic performance was dismal. Its share of global industrial production sank by a third (from 14.1 to 9.4 per cent), while that of the United States rose from 35.8 to 42.2 per cent. Key British industries such as textiles, coal, and steel suffered a substantial decline after the war, as did shipbuilding. Formerly the pride of British industry, shipbuilding employment figures declined 4.6 per cent, and the tonnage produced fell by 2.7 per cent per annum.[51]

On paper, Britain was a creditor state, but the bulk of this debt was owed by tsarist Russia (which had ceased to exist) or by countries on the verge of bankruptcy. The British government had also made commitments to support its war victims (veterans unable to work and dependents of fallen soldiers) and its unemployed, without foreseeing the persistence of long-term unemployment in the years after the war. With no reparations coming in, it soon became clear that British economic life faced grave difficulties post-war. As Trevor Wilson correctly remarks, the victory, far from enhancing Britain's position in the world, constituted a burden that its economy could not sustain.

The outlook for another alleged winner, Belgium, was even grimmer. The German invasion had been accompanied by a wave of violence directed at the Belgian civilian population. All told, 4,700 Belgian civilians lost their lives. Following the example of the persecution of alleged *francs-tireurs* during the war of 1870–71, German soldiers from the first day embarked on a rampage of pillage, arson, and murder, culminating in the burning of the mediaeval town of Louvain in the last week of August 1914. The brutality of this act shocked the world. The German Foreign Office blamed the Belgians for the disaster, but as observers from neutral countries had witnessed what was happening, their claim found little acceptance. A manifesto addressed by 93 German professors and intellectuals to the 'Civilised World', which stressed the civilising aspects of German culture and denied any German wrongdoing, also made no impact, in view of so much evidence to the contrary.[52]

During its occupation of Belgium, Germany picked the country clean, dismantling factories, tearing up railway tracks, and transferring livestock to Germany. Industries that might have competed with their German counterparts, such as the spinning industry, were wiped out. The coke, iron, and steel industries were also hit. Of the 60 blast furnaces Belgium had before the war, only nine survived intact. Coke production fell to one-seventh of pre-war levels, steel to less than one-tenth, lead to a fifth, and zinc production to one-twentieth. The situation for the chemical industry, cement production, and glassworks was almost as dire. In addition to machinery and tools, the Germans removed stocks of industrial goods, semi-finished products, and spare parts 'down to the smallest screw'.[53] In total, 85 per cent of Belgium's industrial production was paralysed after the Armistice, and three-quarters of its workforce (900,000 out of 1,200,000 people) were still unemployed six months after the war's end. A third of the main railway tracks and half of the local lines were either carried off to Germany for steel, or destroyed, or heavily damaged. Destroyed, too, were 350 railway bridges, and of 3,500 locomotives, only 81 survived. The small quantity of rolling stock left was in poor condition after four years of no maintenance.

Farming was equally affected. The Germans had moved livestock out of Belgium even during and after the Armistice, in contravention of its terms. It had lost two-thirds of its horses, over half its cattle and pigs, 35,000 sheep and goats, and two million chickens. The Belgian population during the period of the peace conference was kept alive only through large-scale American aid.

Only coalmines escaped destruction. The authorities

had planned to flood them as they had in France, but held back probably because of Woodrow Wilson's request late in the Armistice negotiations. Though the mines were spared, they were still in poor shape. There was a substantial lack of tools and a severe shortage of pit ponies.[54] From 1916, Belgian men and women had been forced to work in German mines and plants, and the few miners left for Belgian pits were suffering from malnutrition. As a result, Belgian coal production fell to 40 per cent of pre-war levels.

After the war, Belgium's hopes of receiving generous compensation for the damage done were soon dashed. Lloyd George and Clemenceau were not impressed by the Belgians' claims at the peace conference, although the Americans were more sympathetic.[55] Wilson agreed to Belgium's being the only country allowed to add its war costs to the reparation bill, and consequently it was awarded a priority payment of $500 million—although some of this was used to pay for settlement of its pre-Armistice debt to the U.S. Belgium also received a stretch of forest between Eupen and Malmedy, to make up for the deforestation carried out by the Germans, along with a small slice of the former German East African colony.

Arguably, the French contributed most to the German defeat in the battlefields. For this, Alsace-Lorraine was returned to France. It also gained Togo and the Cameroons in Africa, as well as some former Turkish territories. It was entitled to receive Saar coal for fifteen years (with the prospect—albeit slight—that the people of the Saar might choose to stay with *la Grande Nation*), and was entitled to German coal deliveries for an unspecified amount of time (of which not much actually arrived). On paper, there was also the promise of German physical assistance in the repair of war-caused damage (which never arrived). The gains were modest compared with French expectations. France, like Britain, emerged from the war disadvantaged.

Trevor Wilson's summary of the reality of post-war Europe is concise:

> The crucial fact about Germany's situation after 1919 was that the internal upheaval at the end of the war and the territorial settlement which followed it had brought neither the social dislocation which had befallen Russia nor the dismemberment which had taken the Habsburg and Ottoman regimes. Germany remained the greatest power on the Continent. It overshadowed France, as before, in terms of population and economic development. So potentially, it overshadowed France in war-making capacity.
>
> In truth, not only had the war failed to alter the fundamental imbalance between France and Germany in the former's favour, in important aspects it had moved the balance yet further to Germany's advantage. The apparent restoration of France's status in Europe which had developed after 1890 was fatally undermined by events beginning 1917. After all, the Franco-Russian alliance had from 1894 confronted Germany with a potent deterrent to war-making—the menace of a war on two fronts. If despite its potency, that deterrent had failed in effect in 1914, how much more threatening was the situation for France after 1919,

with no major power on Germany's eastern frontier on whom France could rely for assistance. That is, the withdrawal of Russia from a clear-cut, regular place in the European power alignment following the Bolshevik seizure of power had introduced a fatal element of instability into European affairs such as had not existed prior to 1914—itself not an era of surpassing stability. Should a regime arise in Germany tempted to seek a replay of the endeavours of 1914–1918, the circumstances of the post-war years were altogether more menacing for supposedly victorious France.[56]

French strategists repeatedly pointed to the threat to peace posed by the undiminished strength of nationalist and imperialist sentiments within the German political, economic, and military elites. Their view found no acceptance, and instead the French were (and in most of the literature still are) criticised for being unreasonable, obstinate, aggressive, and unforgiving. London, in particular, took the high moral ground: 'The British wrapped their policy in rectitude, complete with elevated oratory about the only route to permanent peace, and soon convinced themselves and much of the Western world that they had a monopoly on international morality'.[57] The French saw the dividends of the Versailles Peace dissipate one by one. The Dawes Plan ended France's leading influence in the Reparation Commission with its right of sanction in case of German default, and forced the French to lift the economic and military occupation of the Ruhr.[58] Having won the war, France lost the peace.

All of the European belligerents suffered heavy losses, but Germany, as Stephen Schuker commented long ago, 'emerged from World War I despite military defeat less damaged in terms of human and economic resources than the other European combatants'.[59] With its economy intact, the Reich had not endured invasion. It had suffered no transfer of entire industrial plants to enemy territory, no devastation of agricultural land, no complete denuding of forests. Despite the loss of Lorraine's iron ore and its temporary loss of Saar coal, Germany remained Europe's industrial powerhouse. When the five-year constraints written into the Peace Treaty lapsed in 1925, Germany was heading for industrial hegemony in Europe. If to this we add the weaknesses of the successor states in eastern Europe following the collapse of the Habsburg and tsarist empires, and the weak state of France, Germany's position in geo-political and military terms was arguably stronger than it had been in August 1914. In the converse of what befell France, though it may have lost the war, it won the peace.

CHAPTER FIVE

Weimar

After the wounds left by the bitter division over Germany's role in the war, chances that a united workers' movement would give strength to the newborn republic were slight, as was evident almost immediately. The speed with which the monarchical system was wiped away within less than a week—having been regarded as invincible little more than four years previously—stunned Germany's political establishment. On 10 November 1918, the two socialist parties formed a revolutionary government that consisted of three Majority Socialist and three Independent Socialist members, under the impressive title of 'The Council of the People's Deputies'. Far-reaching social and constitutional reforms were decreed.

Behind the scenes, though, a less united picture was emerging. Frightened, like most Germans, that the revolution would lead to Bolshevik chaos, Friedrich Ebert, the SPD leader and member of the council—a man known for his saying that 'he hated revolution like sin'—made an agreement with General Groener (who had succeeded Ludendorff as commander-in-chief) to secure the survival of the Reichswehr. Less than a week later, Karl Legien, the leader of the German trade union movement, made a pact with industrialist Hugo Stinnes not to tamper with the existing economic structure. This was the logical continuation of the reformist approach most party and union leaders had followed before the outbreak of war. The SPD leaders' objective was clear: the establishment of democracy, already decreed in the final stages of the war, as quickly as possible. Social changes were to come gradually through the ballot box and through the trade unions, taking onto account prevailing economic conditions. The SPD saw their role as a caretaker government, to thwart radicalism until a National Assembly had been elected.

The Independent Socialist Party favoured a parliamentary system with majority rule as a long-term aim, but they wanted to use the council system to clear the path for more genuine social democracy. In their opinion, the nation's institutions had to be reformed and the power of the old establishment had to be curbed. They doubted that those who ran the public service, the army, judiciary, and police, the universities, the education system in general, and other vital institutions would accept major political and social changes. There was substance to this view. Conservative ideology in pre-war Germany had little respect for Western parliamentarianism, which was considered to have an aura of corruption, if not decadence. The ruling establishment thought that the Prussian bureaucracy was more efficient than the Western system, as Germany's rapid developments in all fields had shown. Subsequently, the Reichstag was often referred to as a *Schwatzbude* (the chatter box). Moreover, the people who had acquired power in the revolution, the workers, were detested by the class-conscious German upper and middle classes. Even when the party supported the empire by voting for the war credits in August 1914, the reaction of the conservatives was 'ice-cold', as chancellor Bethmann-Hollweg noted, not without concern. Conservatives feared that, one day, concessions would have to be made. The warnings sounded by the Independent Socialists, as the subsequent history of the Weimar Republic was to reveal, were justified.

Calls for Marxist revolutionary action were confined to the Spartacists, a small but vociferous group of radicals. The Spartacists had no significant following at the end of 1918, and were in no position to stage anything resembling a proletarian revolution. This did not stop some fanatical editors from vicious and aggressive polemics in their media, heightening fear of the Bolshevik threat. Indiscriminate shots by members of the old army into a peaceful demonstration in Berlin on 6 December, which killed several workers, marked the beginning of the bloody end of the Revolution. Confrontation between supporters and opponents of the SPD's policies continued throughout December. In the Workers and Soldiers Council, the uncompromising attitude of the Majority Socialists leaders towards workers' dissent led to the withdrawal of the three Independent Socialists by the end of the month. Three SPD members took their place.

Bloodshed reached its first peak in the so-called 'Spartacist Putsch' of early January in Berlin. The name is misleading because, although Spartacists participated, it was revolutionary shop stewards who organised this ill-fated attempt to take control of the capital. In practice, they got no further than occupying several newspaper offices. Rosa Luxemburg, one of the leading theoreticians of the Spartacists, had spoken against the coup plan, foreseeing that such action would not only be ineffective but would also lead to unnecessary bloodshed. To Luxemburg, the revolution had already failed. She believed that only a properly educated working class in the Marxian sense could achieve a successful revolution—a working class that had understood its historical mission. However, when fighting broke out, she expressed solidarity with the rebellious workers. Troops loyal to the government soon gained the upper hand, particularly as Gustav Noske, one of the new SPD members on the Council of Peoples Delegates, had called in the 'Freecorps', newly formed military units made up of officers and soldiers of the old army establishment. Noske, having been placed in charge of this 'cleaning-up' operation against militant workers, became known for his saying that someone had to take on the role of the 'bloodhound' of the revolution—illustrating the neo-Machiavellian attitude prevailing in sections of the SPD. The Freikorps, aptly described as the 'vanguard of fascism', staged a massive bloodbath. Among the many victims were Rosa Luxemburg and fellow Spartacist leader Karl Liebknecht. Both were murdered and their bodies thrown into the Berlin Canal.

The election of the National Assembly on 19 January resulted in a three-party centre-left coalition of Majority Socialists, left-liberals, and Catholics, which had gained more than three-quarters of the total vote. The Independent Socialists received only 7.6 per cent of the vote, compared to the SPD's 38 per cent. This is easy to explain. The Majority Socialists were in a much stronger position to fight the election, controlling most of the workers' media and enjoying the support of the imperial establishment. Its calls for a return to law and order, and slow, peaceful progress, were more attractive to the bulk of the workforce weary of instability after more than four years of war. In particular, the SPD leaders made effective use of the 'Bolshevik threat'. Nevertheless, the two workers parties together had gained an impressive 45.5 per cent of the vote, an increase of almost 10 per cent over the last peacetime election. Had they managed to overcome their differences and agree on a common program, with such a large following they would have held a strong position in the new political system.

Dissatisfaction with the SPD's decision to form a coalition with middle-class parties soon emerged, however, and spread rapidly through much of the workforce. Over the next fifteen months there were uprisings in Berlin, the Ruhr region, parts of central Germany, Munich, and other industrial centres. They served as a reminder of how much revolutionary potential had been accumulated. Unrest in Berlin after the suppression of the 'Spartacist Putsch', for example, was so strong that members of the National Assembly preferred to leave the capital and hold their constituent sessions in the Thuringian town of Weimar, a centre of German cultural tradition. The Weimar Republic took its name from this town. In the end, the workers' uprisings proved to be too disorganised, lacking in sufficient support, military equipment, and central leadership. They were eventually put down by the Freecorps in bloody fashion. In the Ruhr uprising of March 1920, for example, over a thousand workers lost their lives.[1]

On 6 June 1920, a new Reichstag election was held. The result was a bitter blow for the SPD and its policies. Its share of the vote almost halved from 38 per cent to just over 21 per cent. Its opponents in the labour movement, the Independent Socialists (at 17.9 per cent) and the newly founded Communist Party, which had emerged from the Spartacists (2.1 per cent), together almost matched the SDP vote.

The Independent Socialists enjoyed their election success only briefly. The party split four months after the 6 June election over the issue of admission to the Third International, which Lenin had established in Moscow in 1919. The main conditions of entry required the adoption of the name 'Communist Party', and a firm commitment towards working for a proletarian revolution. Of the 900,000 party members, only a third supported common cause with the communists. Subsequent elections showed that the Independent Socialists had no electoral appeal, and they disappeared from the political scene. The Communist Party became the third largest in the Reichstag, gaining between 12 and 14 per cent of the vote in all subsequent Reichstag elections. This following was not enough to challenge, let alone topple, the political, economic, or military establishment of the Republic, but it was enough to ensure that fear of communism remained a key issue until the Nazi 'seizure of power'. The Bolshevik threat joined the Treaty of Versailles as the chief spectre haunting Weimar Germany's political life and, in the opinion of many Germans, was the chief reason for the Republic's inglorious end.

The SPD recovered from the setback of the June 1920 election. It continued working constructively for the success of democracy, occasionally joining multi-party coalitions, even forming government itself for a brief period. But it was to no avail in the end. When an Austrian lance-corporal managed to established himself at the helm, communists and social democrats alike ended up in concentration camps, where few survived.

Although labour movements worldwide were affected by the success of the Bolsheviks in the Russian Revolution and their subsequent attempt to take over workers' movements everywhere, nowhere was the resulting split so harmful as in post-war Germany.

Weimar politics and the Versailles Peace Treaty

The Weimar constitution was among the most advanced in the world. There was universal suffrage, with all men and women above the age of 21 having the right to vote. Provision was made for small parties to have a voice in the Reichstag: under a system of proportional representation, each political party was entitled to one member for every 60,000 votes received. There was no censorship of the press, and freedom of speech, as well as political, religious, and artistic expression, was guaranteed. The union movement was legalised—a longstanding goal of the German labour movement—and the eight-hour day, minimum wages, collective bargaining, and unemployment payments were decreed. Above all, an impressive free and comprehensive health and welfare system for all citizens was introduced (as it turned out, a fair share of these generous schemes were paid for with American money).[2] Organised labour in small to medium enterprises fared well. Industrial barons in the huge iron, steel, and mining industries, however, were as reluctant as ever to abandon their 'Herr im Haus' (master in the house) stance, and firmly opposed these welfare policies and the system of collective bargaining. Not surprisingly, many of the workers in their plants turned to communism.

Proportional representation did not necessarily assist with the formation of stable coalition cabinets, but the claim that Weimar's electoral system undermined government does not bear scrutiny.[3] More serious shortcomings of the Weimar constitution were articles providing the president with emergency powers: article 53 allowed for the dismissal of cabinets at will; article 25 enabled the president to dismiss the Reichstag at any time and to call new elections; and, in particular, article 48 provided sweeping emergency powers enacting rule by decree and e of the army in times of trouble. Although article 48 was intended to be used only in exceptional circumstances, Weimar's first president, Ebert, applied it 136 times. During the Ruhr conflict of 1920, he frequently enforced the article to give post-facto legal sanction to summary executions of members of the workers' Red Army.[4] In the final years of the Republic, president Hindenburg's continuous reliance on article 48 contributed to the rise of the Nazis.

The June Reichstag election saw the vote of the three democratic parties—the SPD, the Catholic Centre Party, and the German Democratic Party or DVD, the successor of the pre-war left-liberal Progressive People's Party, reduced from 76.2 per cent to 43.6 per cent. They were not able to form a government in their own right in subsequent elections, and government could only be formed in co-operation with opponents of Weimar's political system. Coalition with the communists—detested by the other parties as much as the communists detested them—was out of the question. There were two right-wing parties. The German National People's Party or Nationalists (the DNVP, the conservatives of the Kaiser's time) were opposed to the Republic and wanted the return of the Bismarckian Reich and the Kaiser. They gained, on average, 20 per cent of the vote, but participated—reluctantly—in only two of Weimar's 21 cabinets. More inclined to compromise was the German People's Party (DVP), the successor of the pro-Bismarckian National-Liberals. Although they would have preferred a return to the pre-war order, they were willing to regularly participate in coalition governments.

Governing Weimar was a difficult and tedious process. In the fourteen years of the Republic, there were 20 different coalitions. Reichstag coalitions normally had to settle for the lowest common denominator, and added little to the overall quality of the Republic's political life.

A compounding difficulty was the political attitude of the dominant sections of German society. The old guard of the Kaiser's time still held key positions in the upper levels of the civil service, the judiciary, the army, and the education system, and they held little sympathy for the new order. Many senior civil servants were opposed to the Republic, but they carried on their administrative duties, and by and large refrained from undermining the Weimar system. More damaging was the stand taken by the German judiciary.

Whereas in the British legal system, judges were appointed to their position after a long period at the bar, the German judiciary was trained for this task from the beginning of their university education. The majority of Weimar's judges had served during the Kaiser's time, and still adhered to the principles and values of Imperial Germany.

Imperial law-making in pre-war Germany has been branded as 'Klassenjustiz'—justice meted out according to social standing. As a result, the German working class suffered from legal injustices, a process that continued into the Weimar Republic. Crimes committed by the political left received severe sentences; criminals of nationalist right-wing persuasion were more lightly dealt with. A contemporary critique pointed out that the twenty political murders committed by the left between 1919 and 1922 resulted in ten executions and prison sentences averaging 15 years. In contrast, of the 354 murders which were said to have been committed by right-wing activists, only 24 led to convictions, there were no executions, and prison sentences amounted to a mere four months on average. Twenty-three right-wing murderers who had confessed to their crimes were in fact acquitted by the courts.[5]

Right-wing terrorists targeted leading politicians. Reichstag Centre Party deputy Matthias Erzberger was assassinated in August 1921. The assassins escaped to Czechoslovakia, were given hero status in Nazi Germany, and received short prison sentences after the Second World War in the Federal Republic.

Walther Rathenau, at the time of his murder the Republic's foreign minister, fell victim in July 1922. Of the thirteen people charged, one was sentenced to fifteen years jail for having been an accomplice to murder, three were acquitted, and the rest were given prison sentences ranging from one year to five.

Independent Socialist leader Hugo Haase was shot on 8 October by Johann Voss, a leather worker. Haase died a month later. His assassin was judged mentally ill, and no charges were laid.

In March 1920, when it seemed that Freecorps units were about to be disbanded, its mercenaries marched on Berlin, where they installed a government lead by Wolfgang Kapp, a former public servant with extreme right-wing views. The Reichswehr refused to support the legitimate government, which again sought refuge in Weimar. Rebuffed, it was forced to move to Stuttgart, the capital of Württemberg, in the south-west of Germany. The ineptitude of the *Putschists*, together with a general strike, brought about the collapse of the Kapp Putsch. Five hundred people were involved, but charges of high treason were laid against only one hundred, of whom a handful were eventually put on trial. All that resulted was a single sentence. General Lüttwitz, one of the leaders of the putsch, was forced into retirement on his general's pension.

By and large, it was individuals who suffered from legal improprieties during the Weimar Republic, but the wholesale maladministration of justice in the November 1923 uprising in Munich had more far-reaching consequences. Commonly referred to as the 'Beer Hall Putsch', its chief instigator was Adolf Hitler, the leader of the Munich based National Socialist German Workers' Party (NSDAP). He was charged with and found of guilty of high treason. Four policemen had been shot dead in the attempt, offences which should have carried the death penalty. Instead, Hitler was sentenced to a mere five years' confinement in the prison fortress of Landsberg. The jury felt that even this was too severe, but the presiding judge assured them that the prisoner would be eligible for parole after six months. In the end, Hitler spent nine comfortable months at the castle, working on an account of his life that was published a year later under the title *Mein Kampf* ('My Struggle'). Had proper justice been meted out, Hitler's career would have been over.

Historians have long warned against overrating the importance of the individual in history. In his monograph *In Defence of History*, Cambridge don Richard J. Evans raises the question of whether history would have taken a different course had Hitler, for example, died in 1928. The chances of Weimar's democracy surviving the 1929 Depression, he argues, were small. A right-wing dictatorship or the return of the monarchy, 'would almost certainly have led to a similar sequence of events to that which took place anyway: rearmament, revision of the Treaty of Versailles, *Anschluss* in Austria, and the resumption, with more energy and determination than ever before, of the drive for conquest which had been so evident in Germany's war aims between 1914 and 1918'.[6] Even anti-Semitism was by no means confined to the Nazis. Nevertheless, it is doubtful whether without Hitler's tireless dedication and, eventually, his large popular appeal, the NSDAP would have gained office and the subsequent course of history would have plunged to such a unique level of evil.

The German army was even more opposed to the Republic than the judiciary was. At its head stood General

Hans von Seeckt, an authoritarian reactionary who, wearing a monocle over his left eye, epitomised the old Prussian officer class. He refused to assist the government during the Kapp Putsch, and worked consistently towards undermining Weimar democracy. Evans' claim that as far as foreign policies were concerned, there was little difference in the ambitions of the German military and the policies pursued later by the National Socialists, can readily be demonstrated. Consider, for example, a memorandum prepared in 1926 by Colonel Joachim von Stülpnagel, a leading army official, on behalf of the Reichswehr for the German Foreign Office:

> The immediate aim of German policy must be the regaining of full sovereignty over the area retained by Germany, the firm acquisition of those areas at present separated from her and the reacquisition of those areas essential to the German economy. That is to say: (1) liberation of the Rhineland and the Saar area; (2) the abolition of the Corridor and the regaining of Polish upper Silesia; (3) the *Anschluss* of German Austria; (4) the regaining of her world position will be the task for the distant future ... It is certainly to be assumed that a reborn Germany will eventually come into conflict with the American-English powers in the struggle for raw materials and markets, and that she will then need adequate maritime forces. But this conflict will be fought on the basis of a firm European position, after a new solution of the Franco-German problem has been achieved through either peace or war.[7]

Establishment of a 'firm European position' implied armed conflict and territorial annexation.

The one unifying element in Weimar Germany's political system was hatred of the Versailles Peace Treaty, coupled with a determination to repudiate most of it. Article 231 was the chief target. To combat the allegation that Germany had been responsible for the outbreak of war in 1914, the German Foreign Office arranged for the publication of a large number of documents aimed at illustrating that Germany was no more guilty than any other of the great powers. The scholars chosen to carry out this project were Johannes Lepsius, a Protestant missionary and orientalist; Albrecht Mendelssohn-Bartholdy, professor of law at Hamburg University; and the librarian Friedrich Thimme. Published between 1922 and 1927, *Die Grosse Politik der Europäischen Kabinette* amounted to a collection of forty volumes, in 54 parts, of German Foreign Office documents on various aspects of international relations between 1871 and 1914. The enterprise was financed by the Foreign Office itself, though this was hidden from the public. The editors' claim that their selection was guided solely by scholarly considerations and made in complete objectivity is unconvincing.

Until this time, foreign-policy matters had not been published in a major way. The documents provide some insight into the conduct of Europe's diplomatic history in the decades preceding the war. The material presented in *Grosse Politik* illustrates that there was rivalry and a steady deterioration in European relations, and that the foreign policies pursued by all the powers were influenced by vested national and/or imperial interests, security matters, and defence arrangements.

There was nothing new or of major importance in the documents published, and they do not provide an answer to the question of how war had come about in 1914. Documents were selected only from files of the pre-war Foreign Office, and there was no material from other offices involved in war preparations, such as the War Ministry, the General Staff, the Navy Office, or the bureau responsible for the economic preparation for war. The documents selected were often shortened and, indeed, falsified. In particular, the 1914 July crisis is inadequately dealt with:

> [T]he editors failed to include (perhaps destroyed) a number of utterly critical documents: the discussion on 5 and 6 July at Potsdam not only among German leaders but also with Austro-Hungarian representatives, the detailed analysis of the Viennese ultimatum to Serbia, missing in *Die Grosse Politik* but handed to the Baden plenipotentiary on July 20, any and all contacts between Wilhelm II and his political as well as military leaders after the monarch's return from his northern cruise on 27 July, and, last but not least, any and all notes pertaining to important telephone calls, telegraphs or other verbal communications.[8]

The only three documents listed for July 1914 concern a planned British-Russian Naval agreement.

The Foreign Office also established a 'war guilt department' (*Kriegsschuldreferat*) to distribute material. It published an historical journal, *Die Kriegsschuldfrage*, which influenced scholars in Britain and the USA to adopt a more pro-German attitude in regard to the outbreak of war and the Versailles Peace Treaty.

All historical accounts and history textbooks from primary to tertiary levels continued to glorify Germany's Prussian past and to allege that the Allies had encircled the German empire and wanted to destroy the German nation—and, to top it off, they now blamed Germany for the outbreak of war and were attempting to ruin the country economically.

On the other hand, anything implying German responsibility for the events of July–August 1914 was suppressed, and authors were persecuted. Some of the documents that should have been included in *Grosse Politik* were presented in a further study, conducted by Hermann Kantorowicz, relating to the origins of the war. *Gutachten zur Kriegsschuldfrage 1914* ('Report on the question of war guilt 1914') was never published during the Weimar Republic. It was brought out decades later in the wake of a revisionist debate about the causes of the war that was set off by Fritz Fischer.

Kantorowicz was born in Posen in 1877, the son of a Jewish spirit merchant who had moved his business to Berlin around the turn of the century. He studied law in Berlin, and was appointed lecturer in 1907 at the University of Freiburg, where he became professor in 1913. Frequent contact with British officer POWs during the war resulted in his admiration of England and contributed to his embracing the new parliamentary democracy with enthusiasm. He attracted negative headlines in late 1921 when he wrote a newspaper article criticising the glorification of Bismarck and his policies, which he saw still permeating

German thinking. The article provoked a backlash from the university's establishment and the political right. But surprisingly, it was he — 'a Jew, an Anglophile, a pacifist, a republican, and a democrat'[9] — who was asked to write a report on the events of July 1914.

Kantorowicz had gained the support of Eugen Fischer-Baling, general secretary of the Reichstag's commission investigating the causes of the war, who was impressed by Kantorowicz's democratic fervour and his lucid thoughts. Kantorowicz worked on the project between 1921 and 1927, and, on its completion, was confronted by strong opposition from the Foreign Office, which wanted the publication stopped at all costs. He also saw his academic future impeded. The Foreign Office did everything to prevent his appointment to the chair of the Law Faculty at the University of Kiel. Foreign Minister Gustav Stresemann, in particular, warned that the publication of Kantorowicz's findings and his appointment to the Kiel Chair would greatly damage Germany's international reputation:

> The report, if published, will definitely damage our reputation abroad because by laying the chief blame for the outbreak of the World War upon Austria and Germany he plays into the hands of the Entente propaganda. Professor Kantorowicz's meagre and quibbling method to judge and evaluate events according to legal principles strips his presentation of all credibility. Moreover his arguments are based on such poor scientific foundations that there should be no difficulty to prove him wrong. But what I object to most is the spiteful way the report is presented.

> As there is no scientific objectivity to his argument, and as we have succeeded thanks to untiring efforts over the last years to persuade practically the entire world of a more realistic assessment of the events leading up to the war, his work will be viewed with embarrassment even in countries not favourably inclined to us. All told we are dealing with a sorry effort, which because of its low quality, is not likely to cause the damage that I originally feared.[10]

Kantorowicz was eventually appointed to Kiel, but the Nazi takeover of power in Germany forced him to flee to England. Cambridge University offered him the position of assistant director of research in law, an office he held until his death in 1940.

Gutachten zur Kriegsschuldfrage was shelved by the Foreign Office, but was rediscovered in microfilm form by American scholars twenty years after World War II. The Foreign Office's fury at Kantorowicz's survey is easy to understand, because his findings undermined the official version of German innocence peddled by the *Kriegsschuldreferat*. Documents referred to in Kantorowicz's study include Wilhelm II's 'Blanco-Vollmacht' (blank cheque) for Austria-Hungary to take any action considered necessary against the Kingdom of Serbia, and the Kaiser's subsequent confirmation that the German empire would honour its alliance obligation to Habsburg should tsarist Russia declare war.[11] He also pointed out that under article three of the Triple-Alliance agreement, Germany had not been obliged to come to Austria-Hungary's assistance in July 1914. Article 3 stipulated that the *casus foederis*

(*Bündnispflicht*) in the Triple Alliance would come into existence only if one of the partners were the victim of an unprovoked attack by two major powers. This was not the case in July 1914. Russia had not attacked the Danube Monarchy; instead, the Austrian government declared war on Russia on 6 August on German insistence. In the absence of an unprovoked attack, Kantorowicz lamented that the German people 'had been led to the slaughter' via a treaty obligation that did not exist.[12]

Subsequent documents illustrated Austria-Hungary's determination to cripple Serbia, which was supported in Berlin, and showed that warnings from the British government failed to stop Vienna's declaration of war on 28 July. Kantorowicz did not see the mobilisation of the Russian army as a necessarily aggressive act. The tsar's claim that this step was a precautionary measure may well have been valid; the Netherlands and Switzerland had also ordered full mobilisation on that day. Kantorowicz felt that Berlin was responsible for the subsequent escalation of the war: although the government regarded the Russian mobilisation as a defensive measure, it nevertheless embarked upon preventive warfare as outlined in the Schlieffen Plan.[13] The German declaration of war on Russia on 1 August and on France on 3 August, together with the German invasion of Belgium in the morning of 4 August, turned a regional war into a global war.[14]

The Foreign Office was further outraged by Kantorowicz's account of the extent to which the principle of preventive warfare had gripped Germany's political and military elites. His references to statements made by Bethmann-Hollweg in the final days of peace, that the impression had to be be given 'that Germany was forced into the war', that under no circumstances should the German people get the impression that this was otherwise, and that it was 'most important that Russia must be seen as the guilty party' for the widening of the conflict, brought the office's anger to boiling point.[15] With the *Gutachten* unpublished, Kantorowicz saw six years of intense work wasted.

Worse was the fate of the left-wing journalist Felix Fechenbach, who was charged after having published in 1919 Bavarian files suggesting Germany's responsibility for the First World War. He was accused of having damaged Germany's position at the Versailles Peace Conference, and was sentenced to eleven years imprisonment by a 'People's Court'. These courts had been set up during the Bavarian Revolution of 1918 to dispense summary justice to looters and murderers. Their function, however, was soon widened to deal with 'treason' cases. They were outlawed by the Weimar constitution, but 'People's Courts' continued to function in Bavaria for a further five years. Those charged had no right of appeal against their verdicts.[16]

The leading Social-Democratic revisionist Eduard Bernstein urged the party at its first post-war congress, held in Weimar in June 1919, to tell the truth about the war, but he was firmly opposed. Refusal to face reality was bound to have grave consequences:

> The incessant din about the injustices heaped upon
> a defeated Germany, allegedly undefeated in the
> field and stabbed in the back at home, in effect serve
> to reinforce an idea that things would be normal
> if only the external burdens, imposed by the allies,

could be lifted. That is to say, the constant—indeed ritual—complaints about Versailles in effect served to disguise the extent to which the War really had impoverished Germany … These illusions were dangerous … [because] … as long as the truth about the War, its causes and consequences remained excluded from mainstream public political discussion, it was impossible to face harsh economic and political realities … Responsible politics remained a hostage to myths about the First World War, and Weimar democracy eventually had to pay the price.[17]

John Maynard Keynes and other appeasers

Enlargement of the German navy had led Britain to abandon its policy of 'splendid isolation' and to enter into an *entente cordial* with France in 1904 and with Russia in 1907. The subsequent years saw a general deterioration in British-German relations. This policy of moving away from their 'racial cousins' on the continent by siding with the Latin French and the Slavonic Russians caused apprehension among sections of Britain's social and intellectual elite and middle classes. Throughout the nineteenth century, Oxbridge historians had emphasised Britain's Germanic past, and German achievements in the arts and sciences were widely admired. An image of two Germanys began to emerge: the traditional Germany of cultural achievements, of Goethe, Schiller, Hegel, and Wagner, and the Prussian

Germany—expansionist, militarist, aggressive, and arrogant.[18]

Apart from a small group of pacifists, Britain's war effort enjoyed the full support of the country, but this consensus started breaking down during the peacemaking process. Parliamentarians, leading churchmen, journalists, and members of the British delegation at Paris claimed that the terms imposed on Germany were far too harsh. Perhaps spending the war in the safety of the workplace or home had inclined some to call for a generous peace. Younger civil servants in the Treasury and Foreign Office may also have seen their hopes for a new and better world dashed. Among these was John Maynard Keynes.

First Baron Keynes of Tilton was born at Cambridge in 1883, son of John Neville Keynes, a lecturer in moral sciences at Cambridge University, and his wife, Florence Ada Keynes, a local social reformer. John Maynard showed from his early youth great talent in all subjects, and above all in mathematics. He won a scholarship to Eton College in 1897, entered King's College at Cambridge in 1902, and graduated with a first class B.A. in mathematics in 1904. His career as public servant began in October 1906 as a clerk in the India Office. The quality of his publications on various economic aspects over the next years saw him appointed to a position at the Treasury shortly after the outbreak of war. This appointment was soon to lead him into moral conflict.

In his Cambridge days, Keynes had befriended a group of young intellectuals with pacifist leanings known as the Bloomsbury Circle. Most of his friends had applied for exemption from military service as conscientious objectors—and were facing severe consequences. Keynes himself toyed with the idea of becoming a conscientious objector, which would have meant resigning from the Treasury, but eventually decided against it. A bitter confrontation with his Bloomsbury friends followed.[19]

Sent to Paris as chief Treasury representative of the British delegation at Versailles, he established himself as the leading advocate for moderate peace terms. His estimate that Germany would not be able to pay more than £3 billion brought upon his head the wrath of the chair of the Reparation Commission, Billy Hughes, and of the 'heavenly twins', Lords Cunliffe and Sumner. The German counter-proposal of £5 billion in gold undermined his reputation.[20] Although the final amount Germany would pay was yet to be specified, Keynes felt that the treaty was repugnant, resigned from the Treasury, and immediately began to work on what would become *The Economic Consequences of the Peace*.

According to his biographer, it was not only the Peace Conference that led to his furious attacks upon Wilson, Lloyd George, Clemenceau, and other participants in the peacemaking process. He felt guilt for his part in the war. Other historians saw the reasons for the jeremiad that flowed from his pen in his resentment 'at seeing his authority usurped by the deaf little Australian Prime Minister and the detestable "heavenly twins".'[21] An American observer claimed that 'Keynes got sore because they wouldn't take his advice, his nerve broke and he quit.'[22]

The Germanophile sentiments of his social class and peer group influenced his *Economic Consequences*. The fact that he fell in love with a German financial delegate to the conference, the banker Dr. Melchior, was another influence,[23] as was his dislike of the French. Keynes did not want to be objective. Passions were to guide him. The book, he admitted, 'is the child of much emotions'.[24]

'Paris', he wrote, 'was a morass, a nightmare, and everyone there was morbid', the atmosphere 'hot and poisoned', the halls 'treacherous', the conference rooms 'a thieves' kitchen'. The statesmen at the conference were 'dangerous spellbinders ... most hypocritical draftsmen', inspired by 'debauchery of thought and speech'. Their labours were 'empty and arid intrigue'. President Wilson was a 'blind and deaf Don Quixote ... playing a blind man's bluff'. He was 'bamboozled' by the French Chauvinist and the Welsh Siren. The treaty was clothed with a 'web of Jesuit exegesis', its provisions were 'dishonourable', 'abhorrent and detestable', revealing 'imbecile greed' reducing 'Germany to servitude', perpetrating its economic ruin, starving and crippling its children. All told, Versailles was a 'Carthaginian Peace', a huge repository of vindictiveness, masquerading as justice — 'one of the most outrageous acts of a cruel victor in civilised history'.[25]

Overpowering emotions have led to outstanding literature. They do not provide a good basis, however, for the writing of a monograph on the economic consequences of the Versailles Peace Treaty, and Keynes' book is flawed.

Keynes reiterated the false claim made by Count Brockdorff-Rantzau in his speech replying to the presentation of the Fourteen Points that the treaty 'would sign the death-sentence of many millions of Germans, men, women, and children'. The malnutrition that observers noticed was caused by a distribution system which favoured the military and kept rations for the civilian population scarcely above subsistence levels. The ending of the war brought internal improvements in distribution, and food entered Germany from neutral countries.

It was ambitious of Keynes to attempt a major analysis of Germany's ability to meet reparation claims in view of the huge overall dislocation of industry and commerce in all countries brought about by the war, the uncertainty of international trade conditions post-war, and the absence of reliable data about Germany's economic potential. Other factors affecting the viability of his study were questions not yet settled at the time of writing, to do with collecting the booty and the liability amount. None of Keynes' Cassandra calls eventuated.

Nevertheless, his arguments were accepted more or less without question by an increasingly guilt-ridden English-speaking world. Those who finally analysed his claims in detail found them wanting. French economist Étienne Mantoux wrote *The Carthaginian Peace, or the Economic Consequences of Mr. Keynes* during the Second World War. He was killed in action one week before Germany capitulated. His monograph, which debunked Keynes's book as a self-fulfilling prophesy, was published posthumously by his son Paul Mantoux, but went virtually unnoticed,[26] perhaps because the author was a Frenchman. It is worthwhile presenting his conclusions, which left the emperor with few clothes, verbatim:

> In *The Economic Consequences of the Peace*, Mr. Keynes predicted that the Treaty, if it was carried into effect, 'must impair yet further, when it might have

restored, the delicate, complicated organisation, already shaken and broken by war, through which alone the European peoples can employ themselves and live'. Europe would be threatened with 'a long, silent process of semi-starvation, and of a gradual, steady lowering of the standards of life and comfort'. Ten years after the Treaty, European production was well above its pre-war level, and European standards of living had never been higher.

He predicted that the iron output of Europe would decline as a consequence of the Treaty. In the ten years that followed the Treaty, the iron output of Europe, which had fallen considerably during the War, increased almost continuously. In 1929, Europe produced 10 per cent more iron than in the record year 1913, and would no doubt have produced still more had not the producers combined to restrict output for fear of injuring prices by overproduction.

He predicted that the iron and steel output of Germany would diminish. By 1927, Germany produced nearly 30 per cent more iron and 38 per cent more steel than in the record year 1913, within the same territorial limits.

He predicted that the efficiency of the German coal-mining industry lowered by the War, would remain low as a consequence of the Peace. By 1925, the efficiency of labour, which had dropped seriously in the meantime, was already higher, in the Ruhr coal industries, than in 1913; in 1927 it was higher by nearly 20 per cent; and in 1929 by more than 30 per cent.

He predicted that a pre-war level of output could not be expected in the German coal industry. In 1920, 1921, and 1922, coal output was well above the average level of the five years preceding the war, within the same territorial limits. It fell sharply in 1923, and was slightly below pre-war average in 1924. It was above that average in 1925; and in 1926, it was already higher than in the record year 1913.

He predicted that Germany 'cannot export coal in the near future … if she is to continue as an industrial nation. In the first year following the Treaty, Germany exported (net) 15 million tons of coal; and in 1926 she exported (net) 35 million tons, or *twice* [Mantoux's italics] the amount of the average (1909–13) pre-war exports of *all* [Mantoux's italics] her pre-war territories.

He predicted that the German mercantile marine 'cannot be restored for many years to come on a scale adequate to meet the requirements of her own commerce'. The total German tonnage was a little above 5 millions in 1913. It was reduced in 1920 to 673,000; but in 1924 it already approached 3 million tons; in 1930 it was well above 4 million, and German liners were the wonder of the transatlantic world.

He predicted that 'after what she has suffered in the war and by the Peace', Germany's annual savings would 'fall far short of what they were before'. The monthly increase in German savings bank deposits was 84 million in 1913; in 1925 it had become 103 million; and in 1928 it was nearly 210 million.

He predicted that Germany's annual surplus would be reduced to less than 2 milliard marks. In 1925, the net accumulation of domestic capital was estimated at 6.4 milliards, and in 1927 at 7.6 milliards.

He predicted that in the next thirty years, Germany could not possibly be expected to pay more than 2 milliard marks a year in Reparation. In the six years preceding September 1939, Germany, by Hitler's showing, had spent each year on re-armament alone about seven times as much.[27]

With new sources becoming available in the second half of the twentieth century, Mantoux's *Economic Consequences of Mr. Keynes* has been vindicated by scholars in the field. Their studies have shown that a relatively moderate increase in taxation, coupled with an equally moderate reduction in consumption, would have enabled the Weimar Republic to meet the reparation debt.[28] In fact, Stephen Shuker has shown that the net capital inflow ran towards Germany in the period 1919 to 1933 at a minimum of at least 2 per cent.[29]

The reparation terms obliged Germany to pay 50 billion gold marks. Keynes—expecting that the C Bonds would eventually be cancelled—advised the German government to accept.[30] Despite his undisputed command of economics, he did not pick up that most of the London schedule was phony money. When, by the second half of the 1930s, it had become clear that Germany had not been ruined by the Treaty of Versailles but was recommencing its attempt to take possession of most of continental Europe, he saw that he had erred, and regretted having written *The Economic Consequences of the Peace.*[31]

It was too late. There is little to challenge Antony Lentin's summary of the Keynesian tragedy:

> Despite his personal aversion towards the President, Keynes's vision of regeneration was in its way as humane and inspiring as Wilson's. His book was conceived as an instrument of correction and enlightenment, a vehicle 'for the assertion of truth, the unveiling of illusions, and the dissipation of hate' … If, as Colonel House had warned, 'we are so stupid as to let Germany train and arm a large army and again become a menace to the world, we would deserve the fate which such folly would bring upon us'. But the accepted wisdom of centuries was overturned, the sagacity of ripe practitioners set at naught, the deep policy and nice calculations of Clemenceau or Foch dismissed at a stroke of the pen by a Cambridge don 35 years old. '*Nous avons changé tout cela*' he wrote in effect; and such was the national mood which he expressed, that his paradoxes passed for home-truths. But Clio is not lightly defied: and to those who flout her admonitions, she brings if not nemesis, then certainly consequences. In this case, they came with disconcerting, with devastating speed. Keynes had assured the world of Germany's utter prostration, her condemnation by the Treaty to decades of hopeless servitude and impoverishment—and now German, not French sentries, stood on the Rhine, armed to the hilt and not noticeably undernourished. Keynes

> awoke, dumbfounded at the spectacle, and, noted
> [Harold] Nicolson, 'very defeatist', as well he might
> be. It would be a melancholy pastime to speculate,
> of acreage of territory, of bridgehead secured, of
> tactical advances, of bloodless victories, on the value
> to the Wehrmacht of *The Economic Consequences of
> the Peace*.[32]

Harold Nicolson, another of the young public servants, should also have had second thoughts. He was a member of the Foreign Office delegation at Versailles, which had little influence on the peacemaking process. 'Seldom in history', he wrote, 'has such vindictiveness cloaked itself in such unctuous sophistry'.[33] Published in 1933, his *Peacemaking 1919* presented the treaty as a product of confusion, turmoil, stress, overwork, and time pressure. To him, Paris was the 'scurrying cacophony', a 'riot in a parrot house' which created an atmosphere that made it impossible to devise a peace of moderation and fairness[34]—only a 'bloody bullying peace'.[35]

Many liberals soon joined the German attack on the *Kriegsschuld* article and other aspects of the treaty, and the need to redress the wrongs of Versailles became a basic part of the *Weltanschaung* of the chattering classes.[36] Oxbridge soon joined the club. In October 1920, 57 eminent Oxford academics signed a letter expressing regret about the disruption of relations with their German and Austrian counterparts during the war, and appealed for the restoration of 'a wider sympathy and better understanding between our kindred nations'. A few months later, students of the Cambridge and Oxford Union defeated motions to continue the Anglo-French Entente as the guiding principle of British foreign policy. Subsequent motions passed by unions at both universities regretted the crushing defeat of Germany, attacked the Treaty of Versailles, and—illustrating the ever-present racism of the English educated classes—claimed that 'the selfishness of French policy since 1918 has condemned humanity to another World War'.[37]

Historians followed. George Peabody Gooch, the president of the Historical Association, took the lead by blaming the outbreak of war on all the major European powers, on the division of the continent, and on the 'international anarchy' that had caused a breakdown in international relations.[38] Historians Goldsworthy Lowes Dickinson and W.H. Dawson also declared that the alliance system and the conduct of secret diplomacy was the fundamental cause.[39] Raymond Beayley, vice-president of the Royal Historical Society, went furthest in his desire to clear Germany of major war guilt. He argued that 'she had not plotted the Great War, had not desired a war, and had made genuine, though belated and ill-organised efforts to avert it'.[40] These historians, when Hitler proceeded to dismantle the Versailles system in the 1930s, 'urged acceptance of his aggression on the grounds that Germany's grievances were valid'.[41]

From the start, British leaders had sought to undo anti-German aspects of the treaty. Lloyd George, to whom Versailles was merely 'a temporary measure of a nature to satisfy public opinion',[42] was the first to undermine such critical aspects of the treaty as French security and reparation demands. They did this not necessarily through guilt or shame, but because Britain wanted to restore the international trade and payment system that had run the world's pre-war economy. This needed Germany to be reintegrated again into the global system, which in turn meant dismantling the framework of European security created in Paris. Lloyd George's unfortunate comment that 'we all slid into the war' was aimed at wooing German economic co-operation.

British governments over the next ten years worked towards reducing German reparation payments, ended military inspections, accelerated the withdrawal of troops from the Rhineland, and hastened the return of the Saar to the Reich. At the same time, they pressured France to disarm and to abandon its alliances with eastern European countries, and expressed sympathies for German revisionist ambitions in this region.[43] The French, understandably, were increasingly concerned about their security. They pointed out that those who sought to restore authoritarianism, militarism, and aggression still held key positions in the civil service, the judiciary, the military, and the boards of heavy industry. Were Germany to gain control of central and east-central Europe, it would be too powerful for the Western powers to restrain. Marshal Foch warned repeatedly:

> [Germany] would burst asunder all the provisions of the Treaty of Versailles, one after the other. First the Polish Corridor would disappear, and then Czechoslovakia and Austria would rapidly follow, and instead of an already sufficiently powerful Germany of some 65 million inhabitants, we should be faced

with a Germany of well over 100 millions, and then
it would be too late for us to endeavour to check
their ever-growing land hunger of power.[44]

J.H. Morgan, a member of the Inter-Allied Control
Commission, drew attention to Germany's extensive flouting
of the disarmament clauses in 1925 and 1926. He reiterated
that the High Command had not been suppressed, but
reconstituted in a new guise; there had been a large intake
and training of short-term recruits; few munitions factories
had been converted to civilian production; and vast stock
of arms had been found. Morgan warned that Germany,
'the least idealistic nation in the world and the most realist,
watches, waits, plans and despite her dynastic catastrophes,
remains after the war more identical with what she was
before than any other nation in Europe'.[45]

It was in vain. British leaders — convinced, or pretending
to be convinced, that Germany was in the safe hands
of democracy and fair government — would not listen.
On 30 January 1933, the reactionary German political
establishment brought Hitler into power. This was not the
fault of the Versailles Peace Treaty.

The Nazi takeover of power

The Reichstag election on 19 January 1919 seemed a
victory for forces working towards democracy in post-war
Germany. The three parties that gained a majority, having
between them secured three-quarters of all votes cast — the
Social Democrats, the left-liberal German Democratic

Party (DDP), and the Centre Party—had sponsored the Reichstag's 'Peace Resolution' of July 1917. This resolution blamed the Allies for having caused the war and for wanting to destroy Germany; and its mover, Matthias Erzberger, proclaimed that Germany was entitled to keep the conquered territories in east and west. Because of their support for the 'move to peace', these three parties were seen as providing evidence that the German empire was starting to embrace parliamentary democracy. This interpretation is wrong. The political uncertainty and disorder that followed the collapse of the Kaiser's Germany, and above all the fear that the nation would be submerged in Bolshevism, encouraged people to vote for parties they hoped would prevent the worst. How far did these parties, referred to as the 'Weimar Coalition', stand behind the Republic?

The SPD leaders had embarked upon reformist policies and continued to stick with them. The party program, however, was still Marxist, expecting capitalism to end, with the workers replacing the bourgeoisie as the ruling class. Formal disassociation from Marxism in the form of a new party program, as happened after World War II, would have alienated a large part of the rank and file. Nevertheless, the SPD was a pillar of the Weimar Republic.

With qualifications, this was also true of the Centrists, who participated in most coalition governments. The Centre Party was above all Catholic, looking after the interests of a large Catholic minority in a Prussian-dominated Protestant Germany. In particular, the *Zentrum* defended Catholic interests in the education system, and fought against such evils of modern society as pornography and contraception. Catholic political conduct, however, was determined in

Rome, and throughout the 1920s the Papacy was concerned about the spread of leftism that accompanied the process of democratisation.

The DDP was the only committed member of the Weimar Republic to participate in all governments. The democratic liberals, however, were victims of a huge swing in the 1920 Reichstag elections towards the conservative former national liberals. They lost thirty-six of their 75 seats, whereas the National Liberals increased theirs from nineteen to 65. The DDP continued to lose voters—only fourteen seats were won in the 1930 election, and by then they had ceased to play a significant part in the Republic's political life.

Following the June 1920 election, as stated above, the Weimar Coalition parties never gained a majority, which meant that from thence government had to be formed with parties opposed to the Republic. The 1920 election also showed that if there was support for Weimar democracy among the middle classes, it was neither deep-seated nor long-lasting. Their disillusionment reached a peak with the hyper-inflation of 1923.

A steady decline in the mark had commenced during the war, when the German government resorted to the printing press to meet the ever-rising costs of war without having the economic resources to back it up. After the war, successive governments continued to print money rather than tackle the problem with more responsible economic policies, such as raising taxes (as most other national participants in the war had done). The mark declined from eight to the dollar in December 1918 to 7,000 to the dollar in December 1922. The subsequent occupation of the Ruhr was disastrous: by

November 1923, the mark had fallen to 4,200 trillion to the dollar.

This was good luck for those who owed money, but for most other citizens the hyper-inflation was a frightful experience. Savings were wiped out. Employees had to carry home the mass of banknotes that made up their pay packets in baskets and wheel-barrows. People rushed to buy basic essentials before their salaries became worthless. Food was worst affected. It is reported, for example, that the cost of a cup of coffee, listed at 5,000 marks at the time of ordering, had risen to 8,000 by the time the customer asked for the bill. The price of a loaf of bread, 163 marks at the beginning of 1923, had risen to 229 billion by November. Families had to sell possessions to meet rising costs. Crowds rioted, shops were looted, and there were gunfights between miners invading rural areas to strip the fields bare and farmers who did not want to see their goods stolen or sold for worthless money.[46]

The nightmare was ended by DVP leader Gustav Stresemann, who was appointed chancellor and foreign minister in August 1923. He remained foreign minister until his death in October 1929. His chancellorship lasted only months, but that was enough time for him to succeed in negotiating the withdrawal of French troops from the Ruhr in return for a guarantee to meet reparations. By the end of the year, economic stability was restored.

The years of relative social peace that followed the turmoil of hyper-inflation saw a flourishing of cultural life. A large number of the twentieth century's most outstanding artists were part of Weimar culture. They included painters Max Ernst, Paul Klee, and Max Beckmann, and novelists

Alfred Döblin, Erich Maria Remarque, and the brothers Thomas and Heinrich Mann. The novel of the last mentioned, *The Blue Angel*, a biting satire on bourgeois society, was made into a film starring Emil Jannings and Marlene Dietrich. Fritz Lang's expressionist films *Metropolis* and the *Cabinet of Dr. Caligari* became world famous. *The Three-Penny Opera*, an all-out attack on the decadence of capitalist society, ran for months in Berlin to capacity audiences every night. The text was written by Bertolt Brecht, and Kurt Weill composed the music. To Brecht, however, the box-office success of the play was a disappointment. Most of the crowd came to enjoy the catchy tunes and the witty lyrics, but were not interested in Brecht's social message.

The *Bauhaus* was created by architects Walter Gropius and Mies van der Rohe in March 1919 in Weimar. Designed primarily as an educational centre, it accommodated artist from all fields. Gropius saw no difference between a craftsperson and an artist. 'Architects, sculptors, painters, we must all turn back to craft'. Art and architecture should be functional, contributing to a new future. Teachers at the Bauhaus included painters Wassily Kandinsky, Oscar Schlemmer, Paul Klee, and Laszlo Moholy-Nagy. The modernity of the paintings and architectural designs was not appreciated by Weimar's general population, nor the liberal lifestyle of the school's male and female students. Funding was withdrawn in 1924. The Bauhaus then moved to Dessau in the small central German state of Anhalt, where it continued a troubled existence for a few more years before being closed down by the newly elected Nazi town council in 1931. The Bauhaus movement, nevertheless, continued to influence international modern architecture.

Because of the left-leaning tendencies of writers such as Bertolt Brecht and Alfred Döblin, the journalists Kurt Tucholsky and Carl von Ossietzky, and Bauhaus director Hannes Mayer and other intellectuals, the broader public coined the term 'Cultural Bolshevism'.

Most people did not like the new forms of entertainment from across the Atlantic either. American-style variety shows and new dances such as the Charleston and the foxtrot offended social conservatism. Jazz, in particular, angered traditional music lovers. Alfred Einstein, Germany's leading music critic, wrote that jazz 'was the most disgusting treason against all occidental civilised music'.[47] That most jazz musicians performing in German nightclubs were black made things worse.

Promiscuity encouraged by the comparatively mild censorship laws in many German states also caused outrage. Berlin was seen a *Sündenbabel*. Stefan Zweig, the Austrian poet and novelist, was dumbfounded:

> Even the Rome of Suetonius had not known orgies like the Berlin transvestite balls, where hundreds of men in women's clothes and women in men's clothes danced under the benevolent eyes of the police ... made-up boys with artificial waistlines promenaded along the *Kurfürstendamm* — and not professionals alone: every high school student wanted to make some money, and in the darkened bars one could see high public officials and high financiers courting drunken sailors without shame ... Young ladies

proudly boasted that they were perverted, and to be suspected of virginity at sixteen would have been a disgrace in every school in Berlin.[48]

All this was perhaps exaggerated, but the staging of transvestite and other erotic shows in city nightclubs made people believe that the Republic was decadent and outside the norm of what they regarded as civilised social behaviour.

Belief that proud, traditional German values such as decency and honour were being eroded was also fostered by the changing role of women in society. Their share of the overall workforce did not differ significantly from pre-war levels, but by 1930 the share of female university students had risen to 16 per cent, opening the university and the legal and medical professions to women. They had been given the vote in 1918, and could stand for elections to local councils, state parliaments, or the Reichstag. This allowed them to play a more prominent part in public life. The conservatives felt that this trend should be remedied. The Nazi Party became more successful in elections in the late 1920s because of its demand that Germany's future depended on the return of women to their proper place in the home as wives and mothers. This was an election trump card, particularly in rural and semi-rural areas.

The rise of the cheap 'boulevard press' in the 1920s also proved detrimental to Weimar democracy. Attacks on politicians, often plucked out of the air, alleging sexual or financial misconduct, harmed the Republic. The publicity given to murder trials and police investigations also helped create the impression that society was being submerged in a wave of violence.[49] This impression was reinforced by the increasing street battles between the paramilitary arms of political parties, none more vicious than the clashes between the Nazis' SA (*Sturmabteilung*) and the Communists' Red Front. In short, the average citizen could see few positive achievements in the Weimar Republic.

Gustav Stresemann's foreign policies were successful. He brokered an agreement, signed at Locarno in December 1925, with the foreign minister of France, Aristride Briand, the British foreign minister, Austen Chamberlain, and the U.S. banker Charles Dawes. The agreement recognised Germany's western borders, but not its eastern boundaries. Locarno put Germany on the same footing as France, which, on British insistence, was asked to weaken its alliance system with eastern Europe. It opened the way for Germany to enter the League of Nations in September 1926, where it was immediately given a permanent seat on the league's Council. Germany had gained Great Power status again—no mean achievement on Stresemann's part. Nevertheless, the Locarno Pact was fiercely attacked by the political right for having abandoned German claims in the west. The DNVP left the coalition government, and Stresemann received a great deal of criticism from his own party. But Stresemann was not selling out. Only a few days after the ceremony at Locarno, he offered to repurchase Eupen-Malmedy from Belgium,[50] and not much later he assured the Germans that Locarno did not rule out regaining Alsace-Lorraine.[51]

The Treaty of Locarno, Germany's entry into the league, and the result of the 1928 election, which saw a sharp rise in the vote cast for the Social Democrats, has often been interpreted as evidence that Weimar democracy was stabilising. This was not the case. The DVP had participated in coalition governments, albeit reluctantly, but had begun to shift to the right even before Stresemann fell ill in the late 1920s (he died in October 1929). The DNVP, which had been opposed to Weimar from the beginning, shifted further to the right when Alfred Hugenberg, press baron and, in the Kaiser's day, one of the most outspoken Pan-Germans, became chairman of the party in 1928. Finally, the Catholic Centre, one of the three 'Weimar Coalition' parties, also shifted to the political right under pressure from the Concordat, and had ceased to be a bulwark of Weimar democracy before 1930.[52]

The final act in the life of the trouble-ridden Republic began in October 1929. Aided by the Dawes Plan, the economic performance of Germany's industries had begun to improve by the mid-1920s. Manufacturing, in particular, managed to regain most of its export markets, and by 1928 Germany's industrial output had surpassed pre-World War I levels. The Dawes Plan, however, soon proved a double-edged sword. As stated above, part of the Dawes Plan involved injecting huge sums of American capital into the German economy. This greatly stimulated the nation's economic recovery, but it had inherent dangers. Governments at all levels embarked on a vast spending spree, balancing their budgets with money from U.S. loans. In real terms, a huge deficit was building. Short-term loans were often invested in projects that were designed to return profits in the long term: if the market panicked, and the loans were recalled, grave problems could arise. This is what happened in the last fortnight of October 1929 when the New York sharemarket collapsed. In its wake, American banks and investors stopped lending money and/or started to withdraw their funds from Germany. Within weeks, the German economy was in chaos. Enterprises went bankrupt, banks started to collapse, and unemployment rose. Political consequences soon followed. A 'Grand Coalition', comprising Social Democrats and all the middle-class parties to the left of the DNVP, had formed after the May 1928 election. They united chiefly to secure the passing of the Young Plan in the face of hostile opposition from the far right. Having achieved this, the coalition fell apart. When the middle-class parties demanded an increase in the unemployment-insurance contribution—to meet the rapidly rising costs of unemployment insurance—the SPD-led government resigned in March 1930.

With no majority in the Reichstag, President Hindenburg, who had been elected to the office after Friedrich Ebert's death in February 1925, was repeatedly called upon to rule by emergency decree, in particular by invoking Article 48. The chancellorship went into the hands of the Centre Party leader Heinrich Brüning, who for the next two years governed with a minority.

Brüning was a monarchist at heart, and saw in the monarchy the best system to free government from the interference of political parties. He attempted to solve the economic and political crisis by undertaking drastic cuts in government spending. The budget had to be balanced. Deficits were to be avoided, as was inflation. Because international loans were no longer available in 1930, a balanced budget could be achieved only by raising taxes and cutting expenditure. The government increased taxes on income, turnover, sugar, and beer, and introduced a series of new taxes—for example, a special tax on department-store sales and on mineral water. Even bachelors were taxed. Public servants had their salaries reduced on three occasions during 1931, by a total of 23 per cent. Overall wages were reduced to the level of 1927, a cut of approximately 10 per cent. Unemployment benefits, which had not been particularly generous previously, were cut by about 60 per cent. As a result of these measurers, business declined, and there was a wave of bankruptcies. The collapse of a major banking chain added to the chaos.

In the two years of Bruning's government, unemployment rose from 2 million to 6 million. This was the official figure; it did not include those who, owing to long-term unemployment, had exhausted their claim for benefits. In addition, if the young, female seasonal, and casual workers were included, the total was more like 9 million.

The only sector of the economy receiving government assistance was East Elbian rural estate holders, who managed to win tariffs for their product, thus excluding cheap foreign agricultural imports that might have kept prices down. The combination of extensive unemployment and high food prices brought poverty and suffering to the majority of the German population.

Not surprisingly, Brüning was known as the 'hunger chancellor'. Altogether, about 15 million people received their livelihood through social services or welfare organisations. The unemployed received their small unemployment benefit for about a year, then they had to depend on welfare, which in many cases meant that they could not afford a bed at night. Not unexpectedly, there was great unrest among the population.

The impact of the Depression was worse in Germany than elsewhere, not only in terms of poverty. Historians have referred to the effect of the psychological threat of losing one's job. This is said to have affected about half the wage earners in France and Britain, and just over half in the United States, but virtually everyone in Germany. Moreover, in France and Britain there was relative job security for most white-collar workers, so that the middle stratum of society was less affected than in Germany, and they remained a stabilising, state-supporting element. This stabilising element did not exist in Germany; instead, the middle class became further alienated from the Republic.

An early chronicler of the Third Reich sums it up:

> [A] sense of total discouragement and meaninglessness pervaded everything. Among the most striking concomitants of the Great Depression was an unprecedented wave of suicides. At first the victims were chiefly failed bankers and businessmen, but as the Depression deepened, members of the middle classes and the petty bourgeoisie more and more frequently took their lives. With their keen sense of status, many office workers, owners of small shops, and persons with small private incomes had long regarded poverty as a badge of social degradation. Quite often whole families chose death together. Dropping birth rates and rising death rates led to decreasing population in at least twenty of Germany's major cities … And, as always, such eschatological moods were accompanied by wild hopes that sprang up like weeds, along with irrational

longings for a complete alteration of the world. Charlatans, astrologers, clairvoyants, numerologists, and mediums flourished. These times of distress taught men, if not to pray, pseudo-religious feelings, and turned their eyes willy-nilly to those seemingly elect personalities who saw beyond mere human tasks and promised more than normality, order, and politics as usual—who offered, in fact, to restore to life its lost meaning.[53]

The Nazis gained from the misery of the people. They had done poorly in the May 1928 election, with a mere 2.6 per cent of the vote. By 1930, however, the rank and file had been tightly restructured, and the party was an efficient, well-led organisation. Relying on the oratorical skills of Adolf Hitler and Joseph Goebbels, the NSDAP was ready for the September 1930 election that Brüning had called to overcome the stalemate in the Reichstag. The Nazis did not offer concrete solutions for Germany's economic malaise, but, through 'powerful, simple slogans and images, frenetic, manic activity, marches, rallies, demonstrations, speeches, posters, placards and the like', they were more than just an ordinary party—'they were a *movement* sweeping up the German people and carrying them unstoppably to a better future'.[54] In fact, the Nazis promised everything to everyone. To the people in Germany's rural and semi-rural regions, it was a return to decent, traditional German values; to the people in the cities, it was an end to street violence and a return to law and order.

The September 1930 election result was dramatic. The number of votes cast for the NSDAP increased from

800,000 to 6.4 million, its share of the vote went from 2.6 to 18.3 per cent, and its seats in the Reichstag went from 12 to 107. Although some of the gains may have come from the Social Democrats or the Communists, the majority came from the bourgeois parties. The reason for this big swing to the Nazis does not lie in the Versailles Treaty. All parties rejected the treaty. In contrast to other extreme right-wing parties, as stated above, the Nazis were chiefly concerned with restoring Germany's eastern borders; their demands in the West were confined to the return of Eupen-Malmedy. It was the suffering caused by the Depression, and disillusionment with Weimar politics, that accounted for the Nazis' rise in September 1930 and the subsequent doubling of their vote in November 1932—not the Versailles Peace Treaty. The Versailles peace was not the reason for the political turmoil that led president Hindenburg to swear Hitler into office as reich-chancellor on 30 January 1933. Yet this is the story that has been told by many historians.[55]

Germany has blamed the political and economic malaise of the Republic on outside factors. The failure of democracy was also blamed on outside factors and not on Germany. 'There are two reasons for Hitler', announced the long-time SPD minister-president of Prussia, Otto Braun, shortly after the Nazis seized power: 'Versailles and Moscow'.

CHAPTER SIX

Bonn

By 8 May 1945, the worst of the Nazi nightmare was over. At the headquarters of the Western Allies in Reims, General Walter Bedell Smith, chief of staff to commander of the Western Front General Dwight D. Eisenhower, handed over the documents specifying the unconditional capitulation of the German Wehrmacht. The papers had been signed on behalf of the Germans by General Alfred Jodl, who had used the occasion to give a last speech about the brave achievements and suffering of his people, a heroic effort that he claimed history had never before witnessed. There was not a word of remorse about the violent death of tens of millions and the utter devastation the Third Reich had inflicted upon the countries of Europe and beyond. The capitulation procedure was repeated the next day in Berlin, where Field Marshal Wilhelm Keitel signed in front of Marshal Georgy Zhukov, head of the Soviet forces that had taken the capital.

The Führer had married his longtime partner Eva Braun after midnight on 29 April, and committed suicide with her the next day in the bunker below the Reich Chancellery. His most loyal assistant, propaganda minister Joseph Goebbels, and his wife killed themselves a day later, but not before poisoning their six children. Hermann Göring managed to commit suicide the day before he was to be executed. He was one of 23 prominent Nazis put on trial at Nuremberg for 'major war crimes'. Of these, eleven were given the death penalty. They included Generals Jodl and Keitel, foreign minister Joachim von Ribbentrop, and chief ideologist Alfred Rosenberg. The remainder received lifelong or lengthy prison sentences, but only the Führer's former deputy, Rudolf Hess, died in captivity: he was kept in Berlin's Spandau prison until his suicide in 1987. Also tried at Nuremberg were doctors charged with using and killing humans in medical experiments, and chemists involved in the manufacturing of the poison gas used at Auschwitz and other extermination camps. Viktor Brack and Karl Brandt were sentenced to death for their involvement in the murder of the mentally ill and disabled in the 'euthanasia action'. Few of the others charged at Nuremberg served the full terms of their sentences.

Another 250,000 Nazis were arrested throughout Germany as part of the 'de-nazification program' carried out by the Allies after the war. In the three western zones, 5,000 were eventually sentenced. Of the 806 death sentences, only 486 were carried out. The rest were let off relatively lightly.

Rarely, if ever, had so much damage been done in so little time. Twelve years of Nazi rule had produced enough Orwellian Napoleons, along with their killer dogs, to ensure that only total defeat at the hand of the Allies would bring the nightmare to an end. With the Allies closing in on all sides, and with German cities relentlessly bombed, leaving thousands dead after every raid, Gestapo, SS units, and other self-appointed fighters for 'final victory' unleashed a last wave of terror against alleged political opponents, deserters, defeatists, or anyone who wanted to call a halt to the long-lost war. Tens of thousands perished. In the end, Germany lay in ruins physically, militarily, politically, economically. The nation was ethically and morally bankrupt.[1]

That an Austrian *Hinterwäldler*, a failed novelist from the Rhineland, a Bavarian chicken-farmer, and a morphine addict, supported by a legion of thugs, could usurp the power of the entire German military, political, and economic establishment was a national humiliation. That the regime had committed crimes — as a brave German president admitted forty years later — that have few, if any, parallels in human history was unforgivable.[2] Many people had compromised themselves during the years of Nazi rule, but the professional classes stood out. Lawyers profited as their Jewish competitors were forced to close their offices; likewise doctors, and medical experiments on human beings were not confined to the concentration camps. Academics exulted in fostering the Nazi state — none more than historians. Judges handed out over 16,000 death sentences: voicing opposition to official policies sufficed for the gallows, as did petty theft that allegedly undermined Germany's war effort. Industrialists, too, made a fortune. 'Until the last stages of war, the benefits of the Third Reich to all those sections of industry and finance connected with armament production were colossal'.[3] Shopkeepers benefited as Jewish shops closed, public servants as Jews were sacked, and looting was frequent when Jewish citizens were deported. And there was scarcely an enterprise in Germany that did not benefit from forced labour. The Holocaust and the extermination of the Slavonic 'sub-humans' (*Untermenschen*) was not confined to SS units, but involved the Wehrmacht as well.

For a brief period, it looked as though Germany would not survive as a nation. Plans to dismember it began to emerge in 1942, in particular at the urging of U.S. president Franklin D. Roosevelt. They culminated in a plan drawn up by American secretary of state Henry Morgenthau in September 1944. The Morgenthau Plan provided for the ceding of East Prussia and Upper Silesia to Poland, and of the Saar and adjacent territory to France; for the creation of a federation of German states; for forced labour by German personnel outside Germany by way of reparation; and for the internationalisation of the Ruhr, together with the cities of Bremen, Kiel, and Frankfurt. Finally, all industrial and mining equipment was to be dismantled so that Germany would be transformed into a pastoral economy.

In contrast with the Versailles peace, the Morgenthau Plan would have been a true Carthaginian peace, but it did not come to this. As hostilities ended, the Allies faced a disastrous situation in central Europe, and to avoid a further human disaster they had to rely on the co-operation of the local population. In Germany, utter chaos reigned. The damage was worst in Berlin, but virtually all cities had been bombed. In the Dresden firestorm of 14 February 1945, 35,000 people died in one night. Of Frankfurt's 177,000 houses, only 44,000 remained standing at the end of the war. In Hamburg, 53 per cent of the buildings had been destroyed, and statistics for most other cities were comparable. The fighting on land and Hitler's scorched-earth policy had widened the devastation. Viaducts and bridges, even footbridges over village streams, had been destroyed. Few Germans still lived in their original homes. Millions of people had fled from the bombings into the country, millions had fled from the advance of the Red Army, and others had fled east with the arrival of troops in the west. The population seemed to consist only of women, children, and the elderly. One-and-three-quarter million men had been killed in action, two million were prisoners of war, and a further one-and-a-half million were missing. Food supplies and transport had completely broken down.

In addition, eleven million people from eastern or south-eastern Europe had flooded into Germany, pushed out of their homes for the misdemeanours committed by the Nazis or having escaped from the advancing Red Army. To forestall the possibility of large-scale social and political unrest, the Allies insisted that these refugees had to be integrated as speedily as possible.

Temporarily, Germany was divided into three zones and, when the French were invited to join the post-war administration of the country, into four: three in the west (soon to become West Germany) and the Soviet zone in the east (soon to become East Germany). East Prussia, Silesia, and much of Pomerania were lost to Germany for good.

Economic and political recovery came sooner than expected, in particular for the people in the western-occupation zones. The wartime alliance held as long as there was a common enemy, but given the divergent ideological positions of the victorious powers, the end of hostilities meant the end of co-operation. The failure of Nazi Germany's crusade against Bolshevism had resulted in the establishment of communist governments in the very heart of Europe. Moreover, communist parties in a number of Western countries were experiencing a surge in popularity. Decisive action would be required to stem the further spread of communism. The Western Allies created a single economic entity out of their zones in January 1947. The Marshall Plan, which brought large-scale American investment into Europe, soon followed, and on 23 May 1949 the German Federal Republic constituted itself in the Rhenish city of Bonn. The eastern zone followed suit, establishing itself in East Berlin on 7 October as the German Democratic Republic. The foundation of the two German states marked the beginning of forty years of separation.

Germany's subsequent history stands in striking contrast to the preceding eighty years.

The harmonious development of Western Europe through the second half of the twentieth century was initiated by two conservative statesmen: Konrad Adenauer, the first chancellor of the Federal Republic, and Robert Schuman, the prime minister and foreign minister in several French post-war governments. They were united by their fervent Catholicism, their aim to put an end once and for all to the mutual conflict that had marked the previous 100 years, and their determination to stop any further advance of communism in Europe. Adenauer had been lord mayor of Cologne from 1917 to May 1933, when he was dismissed by the Nazis. He was interned several times during the Third Reich. After the war, he became leader of the Centre Party, which he revamped into the Christian Democratic Union, a conservative party aiming to gain the support of Catholics and non-Catholics alike. Adenauer was able to form a centre-right coalition government following the elections for the constituent assembly of the Federal Republic on 15 August 1949.

His French counterpart, Robert Schuman, was a keen Europeanist. In a declaration made on 9 May 1950, Schuman suggested that the French and Germans pool their coal and steel industries and place them under a common authority (the Schuman Plan). Adenauer, who firmly believed that the Federal Republic's future lay with the West, speedily accepted. As other nations were invited to join less than a year later, France, Germany, Belgium, the Netherlands, Luxembourg, and Italy signed a treaty to form the European Steel and Coal Community (ECSC) in Paris on 18 April 1951. The ECSC having proved a success, the partners agreed to widen their economic co-operation through the formation of a customs union. On 23 March 1957, the six ECSC member nations signed the Treaty of Rome, giving birth to the European Economic Community. Although the treaty laid emphasis on common economic policies, hope was expressed that eventually there might also be political integration. No one at the time could have guessed that the foundation of the EEC would lead within two generations to a transnational political and economic organisation that embraced 28 European states with a population of 500 million.

Improvement in French-German relations during the 1950s was not confined to the economic and political spheres. There were also attempts to bring the two nations closer together culturally. Among other things, this was done through exchange visits that enabled young students to gain a better understanding of their neighbour's culture and lifestyle. It was also agreed that attempts should be made to arrive at a less venomous presentation of the recent past that had seen so much bloodshed. This resulted in a profound change in the way history textbooks treated the causes of World War I and its aftermath. Instead of mutual blame, there was to be a balanced account. The new textbooks still criticised Imperial Germany's rulers for having been too conservative and anti-democratic and too inconsistent in their foreign policies, thus adding to the overall instability of the age, but there was now agreement that national ambitions were characteristic of all major European powers. Imperial rivalry was a common feature of the age, diplomatic mistakes were not confined to Germany, and all nations had been arming in great haste during the last decade of peace. The system of alliances and secret diplomacy contributed to the final disaster. No one, of course, had foreseen how terrible war would be in the twentieth century. All told, the international power structure was balanced precariously, a state often represented as a keg of gunpowder waiting to ignite. The spark was finally provided by the assassination at Sarajevo. Lloyd George's statement that 'we all slid into war' was included in nearly all such accounts.

This 'balanced' explanation for the outbreak of war was not confined to France or the Federal Republic, but has been adopted with minor variations in most Western textbooks, including in the English-speaking world. Once it is agreed that Germany alone did not bear the blame for the outbreak of World War I, criticism of the peacemaking process naturally flows. The Treaty of Brest-Litovsk, which so clearly laid bare the real ambitions of Imperial Germany's rulers, is commonly omitted from the calculation. Nor are references to Wilson's Fourteen Points accompanied by an acknowledgement of the pre-armistice agreement or armistice conditions.

Thus the Versailles Peace Treaty is claimed to have presented the Weimar Republic with unsurmountable economic difficulties, leading to continuous political instability, which in turn undermined and discredited the fledging democratic system, until, finally, and faced with the further threat of Bolshevism, the Germans turned to Adolf Hitler, whose potential for evil no one at the time could have foreseen.

Establishment of harmonious relations with Germany's western neighbours soon brought rewards. The Bonn Republic was a success story virtually from its inception. Economically, the Federal Republic advanced in leaps and bounds during the 1950s and early 1960s. The need to rebuild the damage done by the war was already a powerful stimulus. The proverbial industriousness of the German people and an advanced vocational and scientific education program that fostered innovative approaches in all branches of industry added their share. Soon the term *Wirtschaftswunder* ('economic miracle') was coined to describe the rapid rise in living standards of the whole population, and this assisted with the equally successful establishment of the democratic system. The cataclysmic end of the Third Reich, which had cleansed the nation of its last vestiges of militarism, was another factor. Prussia was finished: its last remnant, the former heartland of Brandenburg, had become part of the German Democratic Republic. Even the names Prussia and Brandenburg were excised, the latter to resurface after re-unification, but the former forever laid to rest. The electoral system worked well. The extreme political right never became a significant force in Germany again, nor did the extreme political left.

But there was another and disturbing side to this success. Economic prosperity and political stability fostered a widespread sense among Germans that the nation had 'come good', and that harping on the past was pointless. In fact, many of the generation that grew up after the Second World War had little knowledge of some of the darker aspects of Germany's recent history. Surveys of young people in the late 1970s and early 1980s revealed that more than half had no or little knowledge of Hitler.

The extent of public ignorance about what had happened in the not-too-distant past could be gauged from the reception accorded to the American television miniseries *Holocaust*. Screened in Germany in early 1979 on the regional Third Program, which normally commanded only a small share of viewers — rarely more than 5 per cent — word of the tragic fate of the Weiss family spread rapidly. Two-thirds of the German television audience watched the final episodes. It was the first time that many had gained a more detailed knowledge of the Holocaust.

Further evidence of widespread complacency about the country's recent past lay in the German judiciary's adherence to its inglorious tradition of dealing out rough justice. The judges' record in punishing culprits of Nazi era crimes is woeful. If the few concentration-camp survivors and the millions of relatives of the murdered held any expectation that penal retribution was to be levied upon those responsible, they were to be disappointed. Given their involvement in the Nazi state, those judges kept in office after the collapse of the regime were disinclined to pull skeletons out of cupboards.[4] But subsequent generations of jurists, with the exception of Frankfurt attorney-general Fritz Bauer, who did manage to put a number of the culprits on trial in the mid-1960s, did little to improve the record. Of the 6,500 SS that had staffed the Auschwitz concentration camps (where over one million people had perished), only 29 received sentences in the Federal Republic.[5] In July 2015, in what was probably the last trial of Nazi criminals, SS Officer Oskar Gröning, then aged 94, was sentenced to four years' jail for his part in the murder of 300,000 Jewish people. The sentence—which raised the number of Auschwitz staff put on trial to 0.48 per cent—was lauded by the international community, as was the judge's condemnation of the German judicial system that had let so many off the hook. The reader keen to gain more knowledge of the trials of Auschwitz mass-murderers is advised to take strong tranquillisers. An SS foreman, for example, in charge of throwing 400 Hungarian children alive into a fire, was acquitted because one of the witnesses was not able to take the stand. 'Those little ones trying to get out of the flames, the SS men kicked back with their boots into the fire … they were like little fireballs', an eyewitness reported, 'trying to escape the stake'.[6]

Little noticed by the broader public, too, was a spectacular confrontation among German historians that took place during the 1960s and 1970s.

Historical controversies

The explanation that the Great War was the product of an international rupture, for which all the major European powers shared responsibility, helped to provide an effective intellectual and cultural basis for the establishment of harmonious relations in Western Europe during the 1950s. This account, however, had one serious shortcoming: it was not compatible with the facts. That Lloyd George's opportunistic 'we all slid into the war' had more to do with the political opportunism of that shifty British statesman[7] than with reality was laid bare in the 1960s, when Fritz Fischer, professor of history at Hamburg University, published a number of lengthy books in which he argued that the course of events leading to the outbreak of war, as presented at the time, was not compatible with the evidence.

In his *War of Illusions*, Fischer contends that Imperial Germany's attempt to join the ranks of the world powers had run into severe difficulties by the end of the first decade of the twentieth century—or, more correctly, that it was felt by the political, military, and economic establishment, and by a large section of the German populace, to have run into severe difficulties. A continuous series of diplomatic setbacks had led to the conviction that the virile German empire was being straightjacketed by its British, French, and Russian rivals. Plans for breaking out of this encirclement through war were being advanced by the powerful German military leadership as early as 1909. The civilian government, though more restrained, was also convinced that French revanchism, Pan-Slavism, and *Handelsneid* (British envy of Germany's economic performance) could not forever stop the empire from becoming a world power.

In Fischer's view, the tendency to take an offensive approach to solving Germany's perceived international isolation was manifested for the first time in early December 1912. The German government had supported the Dual Monarchy in the first Balkan War, and had threatened tsarist Russia with military action should St. Petersburg intervene. This brought an unfriendly response from British foreign minister Edward Grey and war minister Lord Haldane, who pointed out that in case of a German attack upon France, Britain would not remain neutral. As stated above, Wilhelm II was so outraged about the British stance that he called for a meeting of army and navy leaders, where the option of an immediate war against France and Russia was discussed but abandoned.[8]

Nevertheless, to Fischer, the 'War Council' meeting was an indication of how far the will to resort to warfare had taken hold of sections of the German elite. The most contentious part of Fischer's thesis is his account of the crisis of July 1914, in which he blames Germany's military leaders and its civilian government for using the Sarajevo assassination to force a showdown with the continental Entente powers. He argues that Kaiser Wilhelm's 'blank cheque' was followed by a policy of pressuring the Vienna government into taking military action against the Kingdom of Serbia. Fischer furthermore contends that tsarist Russia would not have intervened on Serbia's behalf if the Austro-Hungarians had refrained from a complete annihilation of Serbia. He points out that the tsarist foreign minister, Sergei

Sazonov, attempted to find a diplomatic solution to this new Balkan problem to the very end. Diplomacy failed, and with the Austro-Hungarian declaration of war upon Serbia on 28 July, and Russia's partial mobilisation—and, a day later, its full mobilisation—the German government's vital aim was achieved. A widespread media-fostered campaign of Russophobia, presenting that country as the bastion of evil and reaction, laid the blame on the tsarist government for starting the war—a vital prerequisite to securing the backing of the German labour movement. German troops invaded, without a declaration of war, the Grandy Duchy Luxembourg on 2 August and Belgium on 4 August, having already declared war on Russia on 1 August and on France on 3 August. Chancellor Bethmann-Hollweg's never-tiring attempts to keep Britain neutral, doomed from the beginning, finally failed at midnight on 4 April, after the United Kingdom, citing the violation of Belgium neutrality, declared war on the German empire.

War of Illusions was the follow-up to Fischer's first major monograph on World War I, *Germany's Aims in the First World War*, published in its original version as *Griff nach der Weltmacht* ('Grasp for World Power'). As its title implies, this presents an analysis of German war aims that, to Fischer, were bent on establishing German hegemony in Europe and world-power status. This book had already met with a very hostile response from the community of German historians commonly referred to as the *Zunft*, 'the guild'. One particularly irate colleague claimed that the long list of Germany's war aims presented by Fischer 'was almost the monologue of a deranged person'.[9] *War of Illusions* did little to endear him to the outraged *Zunft*. They claimed that Fischer had completely overlooked the policies of Germany's enemies, as well as the nation's deep longing for peace. They insisted that the empire's policies in July 1914 were of a defensive nature. They also maintained that Fischer's stance had greatly harmed Germany's reputation. The debate soon spread beyond Germany; indeed, with historians from around the world participating, the 'Fischer controversy' took on a global dimension.

Most participants came out in support of Fischer, although sometimes with different arguments. Volker Berghahn, for example, who at the time of the controversy taught at Warwick University in the U.K., maintained that the German chancellor had attempted to seek a localised solution to the Serbian problem — that is, to create a *fait accompli* through a speedy defeat of the Serbs, followed by a peace offensive towards the Entente. According to Berghahn, the chancellor was aware, however, that the plan might misfire, leading to full-scale war. In the end, the bluff did indeed fail, mainly because it took too long for the Central Powers to get their act together. When the ultimatum was finally delivered on 23 July, the Entente partners realised that the Austro-Hungarian government was bent on a military solution, and they began to react accordingly. Now Bethmann-Hollweg was forced into the ranks of the hawks.[10]

Germany's doyen of social history, Ulrich Wehler, accepts the German responsibility for the globalisation of the conflict without qualification, but sees in the motive a *Flucht nach vorn* — a 'forward escape'. By pinning their hopes on a desperate gamble, the empire's power elites attempted to maintain the traditional Prusso-German social and political system—and the privileged position their class held in that system—which they saw threatened by the growing influence of parliamentarism, and even more so by the massive rise of the German labour movement. A victorious war would greatly enhance Germany's status and would take the wind out of the sails of the advocates of constitutional change once and for all.[11] However, as Fritz Fischer also considered the maintenance of the ruling social and political system in his accounts of the outbreak of the Great War, and as Wehler's works also illustrate the growing economic performance of imperial Germany, the difference in their approaches is one of emphasis rather than substance.

The accounts of these 'revisionists' of the outbreak of war in 1914 were supported by a mass of private and official papers from participants and observers in all of the belligerent countries, in neutral countries, and in smaller German states. The selection assembled by Fischer's disciple Imanuel Geiss on the crisis of July 1914 alone amounted to 1,159 documents.[12] So overwhelming was this mass of evidence that attempts to counter it could garner little credibility. A number of traditionalist historians conceded the validity of the evidence that had undermined their original position, but claimed that the German empire had embarked upon a preventive war in August 1914. This, however, presupposed concrete plans on the part of tsarist Russia and France to stage an aggressive war against the Central Powers in 1914, or not much later. Such plans did not exist.[13]

By the mid-1970s, the debate had by and large petered out, at least in academic circles, and few historians kept advancing the 'international crisis' view. Whether the more accurate accounts have penetrated the public mind is difficult to gauge. The Fischer controversy certainly made no measurable impact on textbooks in German schools, which, to the present day, is the domain of the conservative wing of the German historical profession. As accounts there of the outbreak of war differ little from what was written in the 1950s, it follows that there has been no change in the presentation of the 1918–19 peacemaking process.

Notwithstanding a good deal of acrimony and vilification, the debate brought about by Fischer, Wehler, and others remained within the bounds of academic discussion. Common courtesy was not altogether thrown out of the window. This was to change in the early 1980s with the next round of confrontation between West German historians, soon to become known as the *Historikerstreit*, or the 'historians' quarrel'.

Over a generation had passed since the end of the Second World War, and in the main the Nazi past had been treated rather coyly in the Federal Republic. Of course, politicians, public figures, the media, and the churches had expressed their apologies and regrets for the Holocaust, although half of the respondents in a *Der Spiegel* survey had disapproved of chancellor Brandt's kneeling on 7 December 1970 at a memorial to the Warsaw Ghetto uprising. True, some compensation was paid out, but in general the preference seemed to be to let sleeping dogs lie, even as crimes such as the full extent of the extermination war against the Slavonic sub-humans and the inhuman use of slave labour through the whole of the German war industry were coming to light.

In 1982, when, after 13 years, the centre-left governments led by chancellors Willy Brandt and Helmut

Schmidt were superseded by the centre-right government of chancellor Helmut Kohl, a number of West German historians decided to wake the dogs up. The Bonn Republic, approaching its twenty-fifth anniversary, could justifiably claim a successful history. Internationally, the FRG was working towards the widening and enlargement of the European Economic Community. Domestically the country's democratic principles, laws, and institutions had been consolidated.

It was time for a new approach towards Germany's recent past. Kohl's friend and advisor on matters historical, Michael Stürmer, lamented that Germany had lost its positive outlook towards its own past. It had to seek a new identity in order to make a full contribution to the global effort of stopping the communist threat that still emanated from Moscow. While 80 per cent of U.S. citizens were proud of being Americans, and 50 per cent of Britons were proud to be British, Stürmer regretted that opinion polls showed that in Germany only 20 per cent were proud to be Germans.[14] In his accounts of German history, Stürmer once again downplayed German responsibility for the outbreak of World War I, claiming that Versailles had been a fatal error on the part of the Allies that led to the downfall of the Weimar Republic.[15] As he also asserted that the Nuremberg trials were a communist plot (though the chief instigator of the trials was, in fact, the War Department of the United States), his analyses of the past need not be taken too seriously.

Stürmer's writings were mild compared to the outpourings of his fellow Bonn Republic historian Ernst Nolte. He claimed that Auschwitz, the Holocaust, and other crimes committed by Nazi Germany were essentially the fault of the Soviet Union. The Bolsheviks' victory in the Russian Revolution, and the subsequent rise of Stalin and his methods, had forced Hitler's hand and had led to the Final Solution. Auschwitz had its origin in the Gulag Archipelago. Nolte suggested that Hitler perpetrated an 'Asiatic deed'—an act of barbarism akin to the genocide committed by the Turks on the Armenians in 1915, or by Chinese Cheka units who, fighting on the side of the Reds in the Russian Civil War in 1920, are said to have tortured their opponents in rat-cages—because the Nazis thought themselves potential victims of Asiatic terror at the hands of the Bolsheviks.[16] His virtual suggestion 'that the victims of Nazi genocide actually provoked the genocide, that the Jews in certain ways were responsible for their own fate,' is the most appalling of the implications of Nolte's 'revision'.[17]

Almost as unfortunate were the arguments of Andreas Hillgruber, who regarded all efforts by the German leadership, including the continued operation of the death camps, as justified in stopping the advance of the barbarous Red Army into central and east-central Europe. That the Red Army was carrying death and destruction in its baggage was true, but it should have been pointed out that Operation Barbarossa and its aftermath destroyed over 1,700 towns and 70,000 villages, often along with their entire populations; that the Soviet Union lost thirteen million soldiers and seven million civilians; and that of the 5.7 million Soviet prisoners of war captured by the Germans, only 3.3 million survived.[18]

Hillgruber also ranked the expulsion of ethnic Germans from east-central, eastern, and south-eastern Europe, for which he blamed the British government in co-operation with Stalin, as a crime of the magnitude of the Holocaust. It is true that the expulsion was marked by acts of great inhumanity, but Hillgruber's assertion overlooked the important fact that, in contrast to the Holocaust victims, the great majority of those expelled survived. Most, after enduring a period of austerity that was not confined to refugee populations, were able to live a meaningful—and for many even a prosperous—life.

Nolte's and Hillgruber's arguments were received with incredulity, if not downright amazement, outside Germany, and they were also rebuffed by most German historians, but not by all. Renowned German scholars such as Joachim Fest, Karl Dietrich Bracher, and even Imanuel Geiss saw some merit in the work of Nolte, Hillgruber et al., and they were not alone. So bitter did the *Historikerstreit* become that professional academic historians refused to shake hands with each other.[19]

The potential erosion of the tragedy of Auschwitz was also present in a debate that took place in the late 1980s and 1990s, chiefly in the English-speaking world. Here, historians saw themselves confronted with claims that the discipline of history was in effect a meaningless concept. In particular, 'postmodernist' or 'post-structuralist' American scholars had begun to argue that the distinction between fiction and history was breaking down. To them, the notion of scientific history, based on the discovery and use of primary sources, was a false concept. There was no truth in archival documents—only the assumptions that historians brought to them. Historical truth or objectivity was simply whatever a community of historians decided it should be.

'Time itself', some postmodernists argued, 'is a recent highly artificial invention of Western Civilisation'.[20]

The attack on Western civilisation was an important part of postmodernism. This can be traced back to French philosopher-historian Michel Foucault, who had argued that the main purpose of all historical writing and research is to gain power for historians and the political system they represent. As one of his disciples put it, 'History is just naked ideology designed to get historians money in big universities run by the bourgeoisie'.[21] The argument that history is part of Western capitalism has also been advanced by Edward Said, a New York scholar of Palestinian origin, who claimed that works written by Western historians about the other civilisations were flawed and of little value because they failed to understand the mentality of other people. He introduced the concept of the 'Other', meaning the oppressed victims of Western imperialism.

This was not the first time that the discipline of history had faced and survived challenges, and postmodernism, too, failed to finish it off. Nevertheless, there is an inherent danger that postmodernism, with its claims that there is no objective historical truth and its denial of the possibility of establishing concrete relations with our past, could in the last analysis play into the hands of the Holocaust deniers and the Auschwitz relativists.

The collapse of the Soviet system and the re-unification of Germany had raised expectations that peace and harmony, rather than war and conflict, would mark the new century. However, the tragedy of 11 September 2001, and the subsequent wars in Afghanistan, Iraq, and other parts of the Arab world dashed these hopes, while the collapse of Lehmann Brothers signalled the most serious economic crisis since the Great Depression. The attention of historians shifted for two decades or so to history in the making.

Historical controversy erupted in Germany again in 2014 with the centenary of the outbreak of the Great War. Naturally, this included reference to the reasons for the calamity. Many articles by commentators, historians, and self-appointed experts, surprisingly, commenced with the claim that no serious historian would maintain nowadays that Germany was solely responsible for the outbreak of World War I. No one, of course, had ever claimed this literally. Fischer and others had been concerned not with the events of 28 July 1914, when Vienna declared war on Serbia, but with the subsequent expansion of the war into a global conflict. The new commentaries had slipped back into the traditional explanation that 'we all slid into it'. The curious scholar today, seeking to know exactly how the arguments presented in the 1960s and 1970s by historians around the world, in thousands of pages, supported by thousands of documents, had been invalidated, would be disappointed. There was nothing to back up significant corrections to the work of the 'revisionists'. The retirement or passing away of the historians characterised by *Die Zeit* as 'a mixture of liberal, Catholic, democratic, South German, Western-aligned and Communist Prussian critics'[22] seems to have been enough to summon the old wisdoms out of the grave—with the hope, perhaps, that not too many questions would be asked. The case of the Lloyd George revivalists received a boost with the publication by Prussophile Cambridge historian Christopher Clark's book *The Sleepwalkers*.

Into the Great War: half asleep or wide awake?

The German edition of *The Sleepwalkers* was released to paeans of praise from scholars and reviewers early in 2014. By the middle of the year, it had sold 200,000 copies. Books presenting a favourable account of Germany's role in the Great War had always achieved good sales, starting with Keynes's *Economic Consequences of the Peace*, but Clark's lengthy and notably academic monograph broke all records. With most of the German media in the hands of conservative proprietors, *Die Schlafwandler* got plenty of coverage and scores of friendly reviews. Critics of Clark's approach received far less attention, or were swiftly dealt with. When Hans Ulrich Wehler, for example, objected to Clark's pushing the blame for the outbreak of the war upon England, the *Frankfurter Allgemeine Zeitung* dismissed him as an old-fashioned know-all. Clark promoted *Die Schlafwandler* on a tour of leading bookshops across Germany, where teachers are reported to have thanked him for straightening out the facts about the outbreak of war. He was given his own series on Germany's ZDF television network, one of the nation's major free-to-air broadcasters, where at peak viewing time on Sunday evening he ruminated in a cordial and charming manner on the many positive aspects of German history. By the end of 2014 he had become a cult figure in Germany.

The Sleepwalkers opens with a spectacular chapter on the regicide of the Serbian King Alexander and Queen Draga by Serbian Army assassins on 11 June 1903. Embroiled in the conspiracy, intrigue, plotting, purges, liquidations, thuggery, and assassinations that accompanied its quest to re-establish the medieval empire of Stepan Dušan, the kingdom of Serbia was the rogue state par excellence. Easily half of the *The Sleepwalkers'* text deals with the conflict between the Austro-Hungarian empire and Serbia as it was acted out amidst the instability of the Balkans before the First World War. This does not cover new ground, but Clark does add more detail and insight into the many problems this region faced in the pre-war years.

In analysing the Balkan and other conflicts that have troubled Europe since the turn of the twentieth century, Clark is critical of conventional accounts that fault Germany for consistently pursuing ill-conceived diplomacy. Some of his criticisms are legitimate. Nevertheless, the assumptions behind his account of European pre-war diplomacy that the British empire, France, and tsarist Russia could not tolerate a major power in central Europe (evoking the old encirclement theories) are less convincing. Some of his arguments are dubious; others are plain wrong.

Clark maintains that the confrontation between the British and German empires over the latter's naval build-up had run its course with the building of HMS *Dreadnought* in 1906.[23] This is hard to fathom. The construction of a German armada was not the only reason the British government decided to abandon its long-cherished principle of 'splendid isolation' (along with its longstanding German-friendly policies), but it surely played an important part. There was no international rule forbidding aspiring powers from building large and expensive battle fleets, but they had to have a reason. Britain had an empire; Germany did not. In the free-trade world of the century preceding the outbreak of war in 1914, Germany had no need of a huge array of battleships to protect its merchant vessels. The construction of all-big-gun, heavily armoured, steam turbine-powered ships commenced by Britain in 1905 did indeed turn the 'naval race' decisively in its favour. Still, Germany persevered with its costly and eventually futile naval build-up. Nor is political damage once done always easily corrected. All told, Clark does not present evidence to correct the still widely held interpretation of the decline in British-German relations.[24]

Clark's treatment of German and British industrial output and trade performance by the early twentieth century is also questionable.[25] It is true that, in global terms, Britain's share had declined while Germany's had sharply risen. This did not mean, however, that Britain's economy had taken a sharp downward trend. The opposite was the case—it was still growing at the rate of 4.2 per cent per annum during the pre-war years.[26] But the cake of world trade had grown immensely, with the USA now the leading power. No doubt, some branches of British industry were hurt by German competition, but the empire still provided for flourishing trade. To cite a few scaremongers in Britain as evidence for *Handelsneid* establishes little.

The claim that Bethmann-Hollweg nullified the decisions taken at the 'War Council' meeting of December 1912 is wrong. First, other than increasing the size of the army—something Bethmann-Hollweg fully supported—no decisions were made. Second, the chancellor and the civilian government were subordinate to the kaiser, and not vice versa. Clark's overall depiction of Bethmann-Hollweg as a dove is more than questionable.[27]

It also adds little credence to *The Sleepwalkers* that

Clark presents French president Poincaré as a prime mover in the events of July 1914 that led to Russia's mobilisation at the outbreak of war,[28] a claim previously made by German propaganda in the Weimar Republic[29]; or his dismissing as a diversionary manoeuvre the attempts of the Russian foreign minister to find a diplomatic solution to the Serbian problem.[30]

The revisionist arguments of the 1960s and 1970s concerning Germany's responsibility for the outbreak of war are dismissed in a few sentences.[31] Nor does the evidence really support Clark's claim that the Germans were reluctant to make military preparations until the end of July.[32] There is a considerable amount of evidence to the contrary. The German army leadership, and von Moltke in particular, had for months before the Sarajevo assassination been calling for preventive war.[33] The one reference Clark does include, an ultimatum drafted by Moltke demanding that the Belgium government permit a German advance through its territories, was also drawn up well before the end of the month.

The Sleepwalkers did not meet praise exclusively, and its critics were not confined to conservative British military or Eurosceptic historians, as the *Frankfurter Allgemeine Zeitung* would have us believe.[34] British historian and journalist Nigel Jones wondered why the Cambridge historian had not long ago embarked upon his lectures sporting a *Pickelhaube*. Jones accused him of 'Teutonophilism'. *Neue Züricher Zeitung* journalist Ignaz Miller expressed doubt that the reasons for the outbreak of war were to be found in the beds of the wives of French ministers or in the complicated love-life of the Austro-

Hungarian chief of the general staff.[35] Wilhelmine German expert John Röhl accused Clark of playing down Germany's responsibility for the outbreak of war. So, among others, did German historians Gerd Krumeich and Hans Günther Winkler. The latter claimed that Clark was fostering 'apologetic national tendencies' (*nationalpolitische Tendenzen*).[36]

Perhaps surprised by the vehemence of the criticism, Clark is reported to have said at a book promotion in Freiburg that his book was not concerned with the question of war guilt.[37] This is not borne out by *The Sleepwalkers*.

The First World War was not brought about by the alliance system. Christopher Clark is correct when he maintains that '[A]lliances, like constitutions are at best only an approximate guide to political realities'.[38] Clauses in alliances are often ambiguous. There are sub-clauses, side clauses, secret clauses, and whether a 'casus foederis' has been invoked can be differently interpreted. Governments can claim that their country is not yet ready for military involvement; and, finally, there is no international body or institution that can apply penalties if a partner does not meet alliance obligations. The classical case in the First World War was that of the Kingdom of Italy. That nation had entered into a Triple Alliance with Imperial Germany and Austria-Hungary on 20 May 1882, but refused to enter the war on the side of the Central Powers.

The reasons are readily discerned. Italy was seen as a junior partner in the alliance, and treated accordingly. The Italian government was not informed about the policies being pursued by Vienna and Berlin in July and August 1914. Nor was it difficult for the Italian government to present a reason for not supporting the Alliance partners. When the German ambassador in Rome enquired about Italy's stance in regard to the impeding war, he was told by prime minister Giovanni Giolitti that Austria's bellicose policies and their consequences 'had an aggressive character. They were not in line with the defensive purpose of the Triple Alliance. Hence [Italy] would not participate in the war'.[39] The pro-Entente faction in the Italian military and political establishment soon gained the upper hand and, enticed by the prospect of receiving South Tyrol after the war, as well as rich pickings around the Adriatic Sea and Africa,[40] Italy entered the war on the side of the Allies on 24 May 1915. On the topic of alliances, the United Kingdom did not declare war on Germany because of the Triple Entente, but because the German empire violated Belgium neutrality.

The debate about the causes of the Great War is complicated by the fact that there were doves and hawks among both politicians and military in all countries—and that there was not always consistency in the actions of the people involved. Any historian aiming to prove a particular point in regard to the intention to go to war can find belligerent statements by people of power and influence in the military or political establishments to back up his or her claims.

All states take steps to be prepared for war, and plan accordingly. These plans are usually, but not always, of a defensive nature. Governments might enter into alliances if they perceive a threat to their country, or they might increase the size of their armies or the amount and fighting power of their military hardware. The military might put troops on alert, notify their reserves to be prepared for call-up, and place forces at vital positions. All this does not mean that a country is seeking war. The French placement of troops within 10 kilometres of the German border in the last week of July 1914, for example, was a precautionary measure.

Partial mobilisation may also be a precautionary measure. Indeed, even full mobilisation is merely the act of assembling and making troops and supplies ready for war (the Schlieffen Plan provided an exception, as mobilisation was tied to immediate combat action). Mobilisation can also be seen as a last warning that a country is ready for war should means to avoid it fail. Russia's mobilisation on 30 July 1914 did not necessarily mean that the tsar was bent on war. Switzerland and the Netherlands mobilised on the same day. Bethmann-Hollweg himself did not see in the Russian mobilisation an intention to go to war.

Historians, as is the case in courts, must raise the question of motivation. Why should a country take such an extreme and dangerous step, demanding huge sacrifices of its people?

Did Britain want to go to war in 1914? The answer must be in the negative. To put it more bluntly, Britain needed a major war about as much as it needed a hole in the head. The century following the end of the Napoleonic wars had delivered it immense successes. The sun indeed never set upon the British empire. Worldwide trade based on laissez-faire had brought many blessings,[41] and Britain was a pillar of free global economy. In fact, as has been shown above, British policies in the post-war era were guided by attempts to re-establish globalisation, to the benefit of Germany and the detriment of France. A large-scale war, even if only of short duration, would do huge economic and physical damage to Britain's interests. In my opinion, there is still a great deal of validity in Trevor Jones' summary of British motives: that its policy-makers 'had not gone to war on account of the lure of easy pickings ... [but because] ... they had been convinced that at stake was the fulfilment of their national destiny ... [and] ... the defence of their way of life and political values ... against a savage onslaught'.[42]

France did not want war. The French could not reconcile themselves to the loss of Alsace-Lorraine and wanted the provinces back, but they would not go to war over them. The nation had been badly mauled by Prussian Germany in 1870–71, and the relative population sizes, and hence military potential, had further moved in Germany's favour. France had overcome the defeat of the Franco-Prussian war politically and economically, and had reclaimed its position among the world's empires. The entente with Russia, it was hoped, would provide assistance should it once again come to war. France invested heavily in Russia's industrial modernisation, particularly in railways, and the French military worked to improve the fighting quality of the Russian armies. The emphasis, however, was on hope: the Russo-Japanese war of 1904–05 had shown how far tsarist Russia had fallen behind militarily, and French army leaders knew that the Russians were not likely to stand long against the powerful German war machine.

Nor did the tsarist empire seek a full-scale conflagration. The war with Japan was not only a military disaster; it had led to a revolution which almost toppled the tsarist system. Renewed warfare, particularly on a large scale, could be suicidal. According to German military analysts,

Russia would not have been ready for war before 1916, at the earliest.[43] The agrarian reforms to create a prosperous peasantry out of the serfs, introduced by prime minister Pyotr Stolypin in 1906, were working. Why risk everything by embarking upon an aggressive war with both Germany and Austria-Hungary?

Two further recent monographs on the events of 1914 also impute bellicosity to 'the Europeans'.[44] Such interpretations are based, as they have always been, on speculation. More convincing is the conclusion made in a third book on the topic published in 2014:

> The theory of a British-French co-responsibility for the outbreak of war in 1914 fails because of two key facts: the Entente states were in no way militarily prepared to defeat a fully armed opponent of the size of Germany. And the United States with its free press and open society would have never entered the war on the side of the Entente states had they attacked Germany.[45]

The Austro-Hungarian empire did have a motive to resort to war. As Christopher Clark's *The Sleepwalkers* clearly shows, the Kingdom of Serbia, in its quest to establish hegemony over the southern Slavs and other peoples of the west Balkans, consistently strove to undermine the stability of the Danube monarchy. Policies to exploit rising nationalism in order to foster discontent among the Habsburg empire's Slavonic communites were not confined to irredentists and conspiratorial networks such as the 'Black Hand' or the Narodna Odbrana. The

Serbian military establishment, right to the top, was aware of and supported these policies, and as did the kingdom's politicians. In fact, there is sufficient evidence to maintain that prime minister Nikola Pašic was aware of the planned assassination attempt at Sarajevo, but did not, or did not want to, or could not, do anything about it.[46] From Vienna's perspective, a decisive strike would not only quieten its troublesome southern neighbour, but would also take the wind out of the sails of the empire's secessionists. Vienna, however, wanted a local war, confined to the Balkans, and not a global conflict.

A case can be made that Berlin's conviction that rival empires were politically, economically, and militarily bent on preventing Wilhelmine Germany from taking up its rightful place among the leading nations of the world was not the sole motivation behind its decision to force the issue. Germany was economically in dire straits. The huge costs of the military, in particular the construction of the large battle fleet, had led to a spiralling national debt. Imperial indebtedness, which stood at 1.2 billion Reichsmarks in 1890, had doubled to 2.4 billion by 1900, and had more than doubled again by 1914 to 5.2 billion Reichsmarks. As 90 per cent of the Reich's budget was swallowed up by the army and navy, the states and communes were starved of funds. Their liabilities, virtually zero in 1890, had increased to 27.6 billion Reichsmarks by 1914.

Total German debt on the eve of war amounted to 32.8 billion Reichsmarks. Yet the growth of the army from 588,000 soldiers in 1904 to 748,000 in 1913 demanded ever more funds, as did the ceaseless enlargement of the fleet. Levies on consumption, in particular on food and alcoholic beverages, the main form of taxation, had reached their limits, and direct taxes were resented by the propertied classes, as were demands for an inheritance tax. A modest progressive property tax introduced in 1913 made little impact. Only loans could bridge the gap between income and expenditure, but as Germany's credit rating deteriorated, foreign loans were getting harder to come by and were more expensive. A victorious war would lay the burden to pay off the debts upon the shoulders of the defeated enemy.[47]

Only by taking into consideration whether a government 'pulls the trigger'—that is, whether it launches into full-scale combat with or without a declaration of war—can it be established that a nation is bent on going to war. And the states that pulled the trigger in late July and early August 1914 were the Austro-Hungarian and German empires.

'The war that led to the Versailles Peace that led to Hitler'

Even though the Versailles Peace Treaty was not about allocating responsibility for the outbreak of war, such claims linger. Nor did German re-unification in 1990 mean the revival of 'Teutonic supremacy' policies, as some—notably British prime minister Margaret Thatcher—feared. The enlarged Federal Republic was in a league of its own in the European Union in terms of population and, especially, in terms of economic strength. However, all subsequent German governments have handled this new status with consideration and tact. Germany stood behind the positive approach towards EU enlargement in the 1990s and early 21st century, and the German government played a key role in the introduction of the Euro currency. At the time of writing, the government of chancellor Angela Merkel, against considerable opposition from within its own ranks, has resisted attempts to solve the European debt crisis by ousting members, notably Greece. Against even stronger opposition from its Bavarian coalition partner and also most member states of the European Union, the Merkel government insists upon policies that allow a humanitarian approach to the European refugee crisis.

It can no longer be claimed seriously that Germans still shy away from the Nazi past. The Holocaust Memorial in Berlin, which provides a moving record of the tragedy, attracts 500,000 visitors each year, and most German regional and local history museums set aside a section illustrating the fate of their Jewish communities during the Third Reich. Feature films, dramatised television series, and documentaries provide constant reminders of what happened. Germany's leaders attend in full the anniversaries of the key dates of the persecution of the European Jewry, such as Crystal Night and the liberation of the Auschwitz concentration camps.

However, acknowledging the Nazi past is one thing; explaining the reason for Hitler is a different matter. As one German expatriate has remarked, '[T]he German media have a longing for a clean historical account and an ennobling self-presentation'.[48] The tendency to blame the rise of Nazism on outside factors supports this. The last crown prince of the Austro-Hungarian empire, Otto von Habsburg, shortly before his death, described the First

World War as 'the war that led to the Versailles Peace Treaty that led to Adolf Hitler'.

As the centenary of the outbreak of war approached, the presumption that the origin of the war and the peacemaking after it combine to explain the rise of Nazism (and the subsequent Second World War) was not uncommon in German accounts. Commemorating the ninetieth anniversary of the signing of the peace treaty, the news journal *Der Spiegel*, for example, published a lead article under the heading 'The giveaway peace—Why a Second World War had to follow upon the first one'. Its tendentious title notwithstanding, the author's account of the peacemaking at Paris is not unbalanced. In describing the slow train journey of the German delegation to Versailles, it illustrates the apocalyptic impact the German invasion had upon northern France. It acknowledges that von Brockdorff-Rantzau, head of the German delegation, a 'touchy prestige-hungry fellow', still held dreams of German world-domination. It concedes that the hyperinflation of 1923 and the disastrous economic policies of the early 1930s were the fault of the Weimar governments, and that the reparations Germany actually paid were modest.

The author also regards the war-guilt paragraph as harmless, and admits that, in the end, 'the treaty was not so bad'. After all, he points out, Germany remained economically the leading nation in Europe, and was strategically in a stronger position than before the war. The article pokes fun at some of the treaty's clauses, and some do indeed invite ridicule. But whereas the inclusion of '500 stallions, 2,000 oxen, 90,000 milk cows, 20,000 sheep [and] 14,000 sows' may seem petty today, these things were a matter of life and death to French and Belgian farmers after the war. The article puts a great deal of emphasis upon president Wilson's failure to bind the old continent economically and politically to Europe, but this overlooks the deep-seated isolationism of American politicians after 1919—regardless of their affiliation—and of the American public at large. And, in the end, the key question of why Versailles necessitated a Second World War is left unanswered.[49]

The illusion that the Versailles peacemakers are to be blamed for the subsequent disastrous course of history is found not only in contemporary German accounts. In his history of the German occupation of the Channel Islands during World War II, John Nettles, the British actor best known for his role as the redoubtable Inspector Tom Barnaby of *Midsomer Murders*, maintains that 'The victorious Allies imposed a peace on Germany which was not a peace at all ... [but] ... reduced the country to grinding poverty, economic ruin, starvation and great suffering. It was rumoured that mothers in Hamburg were killing their babies because they had no way of feeding them.'[50] Neil MacGregor, the former director of the British Museum in London, in his recent and no doubt excellent book, *Germany: memory of a nation*, maintains that 'in 1919 the victorious powers insisted on declaring Germany guilty, with consequences which ran for the next thirty years'.[51]

These kinds of claims—still a trickle by 2014—will become a torrent in 2019, the centenary year of the Paris peacemaking. The continuous hype surrounding *The Sleepwalkers*—Clark was knighted in June 2015 at the instigation of the British Foreign Office—points in this direction.

This is not just another case of historians quarrelling. Something more is at stake. Margaret MacMillan, in her thoughtful study about the uses and abuses of history, points out that the dividing line between political decisions and historical accounts can be a fine one, and warns us not to allow leaders and opinion makers to use history to bolster false claims and justify bad and foolish policies.[52] Thus she accuses, for example, George W. Bush ('by common consent … one of the most incompetent American presidents of the modern era'[53]) of ignoring the lessons of the American past in his invasion of Iraq and Afghanistan. To her, the United States 'was abandoning its own history of working with others to uphold a world order and … its long history of opposition to imperialism. Worse, as Abu Ghraib and Guantanamo would show, it was going to undermine and compromise its own deep respect for the rule of law'.[54]

Bad history, MacMillan warns, often makes sweeping generalisations for which there is little evidence, and ignores evidence to the contrary because it does not fit the common myth. In her view, accounts of the Treaty of Versailles readily fall into this category. The popular notion that the treaty was so foolish and vindictive that it led inevitably to World War II owed much to the polemical writings of John Maynard Keynes and others. But, she rightly points out, that notion has the severe limitation that it is not compatible with reality. After all, the Germans did lose the war; and they were not nearly as badly treated as they claimed and as many in Britain and America later believed. The reparations were not a major burden, and in any event they were cancelled when Hitler seized power. As economist Étienne Mantoux showed long ago, things were improving economically in Europe in the 1920s. The financial problems Germany faced were of its own making. Likewise the political picture was getting brighter, with the Weimar Republic and the Soviet Union entering the international community. Hence, argues MacMillan:

> Without the Great Depression, which put fearful strains on even the strongest democracies, and without a whole series of bad decisions, including those by respectable German statesmen and generals who thought they could use Hitler once they got him into power, the slide into aggression and then the war might not have occurred. Bad history ignores such nuances in favour of tales that belong to morality plays but do not help to consider the past in all its complexities.[55]

In his recent critical study of counterfactuals ('what ifs?') in history, Richard J. Evans turns his attention to Harvard historian Neill Ferguson's hypothesis about what would have happened had Britain remained neutral in the Great War. In that event, Ferguson reasoned, Germany's war aims would have been less ambitious, she would have won the war, and she would have established hegemony over continental Europe—a desirable state of affairs which, in Ferguson's opinion, occurred anyway a century later with the German domination of the European Union, to the benefit of the Europeans. Consequently, Ferguson posited, the reasons for the rise of Nazism—frustration over the defeat in war and the Versailles Diktat—would have been removed. Hence no Hitler, no Second World War, no

Holocaust, no renewed mass slaughter. There would still be a powerful British empire, rather than the current state of affairs in which, he considered, Britain's position had declined to that of mere adjunct to a German-run Europe.[56]

It was not very difficult for Evans to demolish Ferguson's counterfactual theory. Still, 'what ifs' enjoyed popularity in the 1990s. At a conference held by the German Historical Institute in Washington D.C. to mark the 75th anniversary of the signing of the peace treaty, William R. Keylor, in his paper on 'Versailles and International Diplomacy', raised some 'what ifs' in regard to the peacemaking. What if there had been open diplomacy at Paris? What if the German delegation had been admitted as equal partner? What if all ethnic Germans had been permitted to join the Reich? What if the Allies had settled for Keynes's reparation sums? What if there had been no 'war guilt clause', but all belligerents had accepted to equal blame for the war?[57] Would this have brought peace and harmony to Europe? Keylor, too, had little difficulty in dismissing such counterfactuals as useless mind games that could not be substantiated from the documentary record of the peace conference.

On the contrary, he proposed that anyone interested in evaluating the Versailles Peace should seek to escape from 'the thick underbrush of mythology' that still surrounded the treaty and, instead of indulging in counterfactuals, should approach the topic with a few basic facts in mind. First, the allegedly 'Wilsonian' notion of open diplomacy did not herald a new concept for international relations; rather, it was the last gasp of a 'noble but evanescent aspiration' that gave way to the twentieth century's new diplomacy of utmost secrecy. Second, the much-celebrated principle of national self-determination, believed by many 'Wilsonians', though not by Wilson himself, to be the cure for the world's ills, soon proved to be a bird that could not fly (and, incidentally, in my opinion, was something that contributed significantly to many of the twentieth century's disasters). It is therefore inappropriate to condemn the peacemakers for failing to achieve its universal introduction. Third, there was no war guilt attributed in the treaty. Fourth, the claim that the post-war budgetary policies of France were based on reparation payments constitutes an illusion. Fifth, the British politicians who so recklessly contested the Khaki Election of December 1918 were interested less in the guidelines for the peacemaking process than in exploiting the post-war euphoria—that was soon to abate in any case—to win their seats. And last, but certainly not least, John Maynard Keynes's talk of a 'Carthaginian Peace' was nonsense.[58]

Keylor concluded his paper by raising the question of whether at the centenary conference 25 years away the treaty would have recovered from the 'severe indictment originally issued by disaffected Wilsonians in the interwar period and perpetuated in subsequent generations'. He concluded:

> Will the new scholarly discoveries and interpretations of the 1970s and 1980s finally have been incorporated into the general historiography, and therefore public memory, of the Versailles settlement? Or will the conventional wisdom continue to embrace the condemnatory verdict of those embittered angry young men in the American and English delegation

at Paris who had briefly glimpsed the promised land—or so they thought—only to recede from view as the grim realities of national interest, power, and politics inconveniently intruded into the negotiations to produce a less-than-perfect, that is to say a human, pact of peace.[59]

I hope, with this book, to contribute to the success of the first alternative.

Acknowledgements

I was inspired to write this book by the publications of my compatriots Bruce Kent and Douglas Newton. For the finalisation of the manuscript, I am most indebted to Michael Harrington and Chris Vening. Chris Cunnneen made many valuable comments on the draft, and David Walker's interest in the project was of major benefit. Anna Street and Bernhard Schlegel assisted with overcoming the challenges — faced by many of my generation — presented by computers and the Internet. Arnold Velden's research assistance was invaluable, and Arthur Street provided me with useful material.

A big thanks to my agent, Sheila Drummond, and to Ilka Tampke for recommending me to her.

The publisher, Henry Rosenbloom of Scribe, and his assistant, Anna Thwaites, did a superb job.

In writing this script, I was able to take advantage of the work of fine scholars from North America, the United Kingdom, and Europe I have had not had the privilege of meeting, but whom courtesy demands I acknowledge. These are Margaret MacMillan, Sally Marks, Manfred F. Boemeke, Robert Boyce, William M. Keylor, Antony Lentin, Stephen A. Schuker, and Trevor Wilson. I am grateful for the constructive comments made by Allen Sharp, Roger Moorehouse and Ignaz Miller on the first print of this book.

Finally, thanks to Christine for everything.

Bibliography

Books

Adams, R.J.Q., *The Great War, 1914–1918: essays on the military, political and social history of the First World War* (MacMillan Press, Houndsmill, 1990).

Birdsall, Paul, *Versailles Twenty Years After* (Archon Books, Hamden, Connecticut, 1962).

Boadle, Donald Graeme, *Winston Churchill and the German Question in British Foreign Policies, 1918–1922* (Martinus Nijhoff, The Hague, 1973).

Boemeke, Manfred F., Gerald D. Feldman, and Elisabeth Glaser, *The Treaty of Versailles: a reassessment after 75 years* (Cambridge University Press, Cambridge, 1998).

Bosworth, Richard, *Italy and the Approach of the First World War* (MacMillan, London, 1983).

Boyce, Robert, *The Great Interwar Crisis and the Collapse of Globalization* (Palgrave Macmillan, Basingstoke, 2009).

Clark, Christopher, *Iron Kingdom: the rise and downfall of Prussia,*

1600–1947 (Allan Lane, London, 2006).

Clark, Christopher, *The Sleepwalkers: how Europe went to war in 1914* (Allan Lane, London, 2012).

Dockrill, Michael L. and Douglas J. Goold, *Peace Without Promise: Britain and the peace conferences, 1919–1923* (Batsford, London, 1981).

Dyck, Harvey Leonard, *Weimar Germany and Soviet Russia, 1926–1933: a study in diplomatic instability* (Chatto and Windus, London, 1966).

Eley, Geoff and James Retallack (eds), *Wilhelmism and its Legacies: German modernities, imperialism and the meaning of reform, 1890–1930* (Berghahn Books, New York, 2003).

Evans, Richard J., *In Hitler's Shadow: West German historians and the attempt to escape from the Nazi past* (Pantheon Books, New York, 1989).

Evans, Richard J., *In Defence of History* (Granta Books, London, 1997).

Evans, Richard J., *The Coming of the Third Reich* (Allan Lane, London, 2003).

Evans, Richard J., *The Third Reich at War, 1939–1945* (Allan Lane, London, 2008).

Evans, Richard J., *Altered Pasts: counterfactuals in history* (Brandeis University Press, Waltham, Massachusetts, 2013).

Fischer, Fritz, *Weltmacht oder Niedergang: Deutschland im ersten Weltkrieg* (Europäische Verlagsanstalt, Frankfurt [Main], 1965).

Fischer, Fritz, *War of Illusions* (Chatto & Windus, London, 1975).

Fischer, Fritz, *Der erste Weltkrieg und das deutsche Geschichtsbild: Beiträge zur Bewältigung eines historischen Tabus* (Droste, Düsseldorf, 1977).

Fischer, Fritz, *Juli 1914: Wir sind nicht hineingeschlittert* (Rowohlt, Hamburg, 1983).

Floto, Inga, *Colonel House in Paris* (Universitetsforlaget I, Aarhus, 1973).

Fowler, W.B., *British–American Relations, 1917–1918: the role of Sir William Wiseman* (Princeton University Press, New Jersey, 1969).

Gall, Lothar, *Bismarck. Der weiße Revolutionär* (Propyläen-Verlag, Berlin, 1987).

Gatzke, Hans W., *Germany's Drive to the West* (John Hopkins Press, Baltimore, 1950).

Geiss, Imanuel (ed.), *Julikrise und Kriegsausbruch* (Verlag für Literatur und Zeitgeschehen, Bad Godesberg, 1964).

Geiss, Imanuel (ed.), *Juli 1914. Die Europäische Krise und der Ausbruch des ersten Weltkriegs* (Deutscher Taschenbuch Verlag, München, 1965).

Goldstein, Erik, *Winning the Peace: British diplomatic strategy, peace planning, and the Paris Peace Conference, 1916–1920* (Clarendon Press, Oxford, 1991).

Ham, Paul, *1914: the year the world ended* (William Heinemann, Sydney, 2013).

Horne, John and Alan Kramer, *German Atrocities, 1914: a history of denial* (Yale University Press, New Haven, 2001).

Howard, Michael, *The Franco-Prussian War: the German invasion of France, 1870–1871* (Hart-Davis, London, 1962).

Jaffe, Lorna S., *The Decision to Disarm Germany* (Unwin Hyman, Boston, 1985).

Jeffreys, Diarmuid, *Hell's Cartel: IG Farben and the making of Hitler's war machine* (Bloomsbury, London, 2008).

Kantorowicz, Hermann, *Gutachten zur Kriegsschuldfrage 1914* (Deutsche Verlagsanstalt, Frankfurt, 1967).

Kennedy, Paul, *The Rise of Anglo-German Antagonism, 1860–1914* (Allen & Unwin, London, 1980).

Kennedy, Paul, *The Rise and Fall of the Great Powers* (Unwin Hyman, London, 1988).

Kent, Bruce, *The Spoils of War: the politics, economics, and diplomacy of reparations, 1918–1932* (Clarendon Press, Oxford, 1989).

Kershaw, Ian, *The Nazi Dictatorship* (Edward Arnold, London, 1989).

Kershaw, Ian (ed.), *Weimar Germany: why did democracy fail?* (Weidenfeld and Nicolson, London, 1990).

Kershaw, Ian, *Hitler 1889–1936* (Allen Lane, London, 1998).

Kitchen, Martin, *The Silent Dictatorship: the politics of the German High Command under Hindenburg and Ludendorff, 1916–1918* (Holmes & Meier, New York, 1976).

Kramer, Alan, *Dynamic of Destruction: culture and mass killings in the First World War* (Oxford University Press, Oxford, 2007).

Kučera, Jaroslav, *Minderheit im Nationalstaaat. Die Sprachenfrage in den tschechisch-deutschen Beziehungen 1918–1938* (Oldenbourg, Munich, 1999).

Lentin, Antony, *Lloyd George, Woodrow Wilson and the Guilt of Germany: an essay in the pre-history of appeasement* (Leicester University Press, Leicester, 1984).

Lentin, Antony, *Lloyd George and the Lost Peace: from Versailles to Hitler, 1919–1940* (Palgrave, Basingstoke, 2001).

MacGregor, Neil, *Germany: memories of a nation* (Allan Lane, London, 2014).

MacMillan, Margaret, *Peacemakers: the Paris conference of 1919 and its attempt to end war* (John Murray, London, 2001).

MacMillan, Margaret, *The Uses and Abuses of History* (Profile Books, London, 2008).

Mantoux, Étienne, *The Carthaginian Peace or the Economic Consequences of Mr. Keynes* (Arno Press, New York, 1978).

Marks, Sally, *Innocent Abroad: Belgium at the Paris Peace Conference of 1919* (The University of North Carolina Press, Chapel Hill, 1981).

Marks, Sally, *The Ebbing of European Ascendancy: an international history of the world, 1914–1945* (Arnold, London, 2002).

Martel, Gordon (ed.), *Modern Germany Reconsidered: 1870–1945* (Routledge, London, 1992).

Martel, Gordon (ed.), *The Origins of the Second World War reconsidered: A.J.P. Taylor and the historians* (Second Edition, Routledge, London, 1999).

Miller, Ignaz, *Mit vollem Risiko in den Krieg, 1914–1918* (Verlag Neue Züricher Zeitung, Zurich, 2014).

Moltke, Helmut von, *Erinnerungen, Briefe, Dokumente, 1877–1916* (Stuttgart, 1922).

Mommsen, Wolfgang J., *Max Weber und die Deutsche Politik* (Mohr Verlag, Tübingen, 1959).

Moses, John, *The Politics of Illusions* (University of Queensland Press, St. Lucia, 1975).

Neitzel, Sönke and Daniel Hohrath (eds), *Kriegsgreuel. Die Entgrenzung der Gewalt in kriegerischen Konflikten vom Mittelalter bis ins 20. Jahrhundert* (Ferdinand Schöning, Paderborn, 2008).

Nettles, John, *Jewels and Jackboots: Hitler's British Channel Islands* (Seeker Publishing, Jersey, 2013).

Newton, Doug, *British Policy and the Weimar Republic, 1918–1919* (Clarendon Press, Oxford, 1997).

Pflanze, Otto, *Bismarck and the development of Germany* (Princeton University Press, New Jersey, 1990).

Pflanze, Otto, *Bismarck, Der Reichsgründer* (C.H. Beck, Munich, 1997).

Ritter, Gerhard R., *Das Deutsche Kaiserreich, 1871–1914* (Vandenhoek & Ruprecht, Göttingen, 1975).

Rothwell, V.H., *British War Aims and Peace Diplomacy, 1914–1918* (Clarendon Press, Oxford, 1971).

Scharrer, Manfred, *Die Spaltung der deutschen Arbeiterbewegung* (Edition Cordeliers, Stuttgart, 1983).

Schöllgen, Gregor (ed.), *Escape into War? The foreign policies of Imperial Germany* (Berg, Oxford, 1990).

Sharp, Alan, *The Versailles Settlement: peacemaking in Paris, 1919* (MacMillan, Houndsmill, 1991).

Sharp, Alan, *Consequences of Peace. The Versailles Settlement: aftermath and legacy, 1919–2010* (Haus Publishing, London, 2010).

Shuster, Richard J., *German Disarmament after World War I: the diplomacy of international arms inspection, 1920–1931* (Routledge, London, 2006).

Skidelsky, Robert, *John Maynard Keynes, 1883–1946: economist, philosopher, statesman* (Pan Books, London, 2003).

Stevenson, David, *The First World War and International Politics* (Oxford University Press, Oxford, 1988).

Stevenson, David, *1914–1918: Der Erste Weltkrieg* (Artemis und Winkler, Düsseldorf, 2006).

Tampke, Jürgen, *Czech-German Relations and the Politics of Central Europe: from Bohemia to the EU* (Palgrave MacMillan, Basingstoke, 2003).

Temperley, H.W.V., *A History of the Peace Conference of Paris*, vol. 1. (Oxford University Press, London, 1920).

Terrain, John, *To Win a War: 1918, the year of victory* (MacMillan, London, 1978).

Terrain, John, *The Smoke and the Fire: myths and anti-myths of the War, 1861–1945* (Sidgwick and Jackson, London, 1980).

Tipton, Frank B., *A History of Modern Germany Since 1815* (Continuum, London, 2003).

Tuchman, Barbara W., *August 1914* (London, Constable, 1962).

Wawro, Geoffrey, *The Franco-Prussian War: the German Conquest of France in 1870–1* (Cambridge University Press, Cambridge, 2003).

Wehler, Hans-Ulrich, *Deutsche Gesellschaftsgeschichte 1849–1914* (C.H. Beck, Munich, 2006).

Wehler, Hans-Ulrich, *Deutsche Gesellschaftsgeschichte 1914–1949* (C.H. Beck, Munich, 2008).

Wheeler, Robert F., *USPD und Internationale* (Ullstein, Frankfurt, 1975).

Wheeler-Bennett, John W., *The Nemesis of Power: the German army in politics, 1918–1945* (MacMillan, London, 1964).

Wilson, Keith (ed.), *Forging the Collective Memory: government and international historians through two world wars* (Berghahn Books, Providence, USA, 1996).

Wilson, Trevor, *The Myriad Faces of War: Britain and the Great War, 1914–1918* (Polity Press, Cambridge, 1986).

Wiskemann, Elizabeth, *The Europe I Saw* (Collins, London, 1968).

Articles

Bessell, Richard, 'Why did the Weimar Republic collapse?', in Ian Kershaw (ed.), *Weimar Germany: why did democracy fail?* (Weidenfeld and Nicolson, London, 1990), pp. 120–52.

Boemeke, Manfred F., 'Woodrow-Wilson's Image of Germany, the War-guilt Question, and the Treaty of Versailles', in M.F. Boemeke et al., *The Treaty of Versailles: a reassessment after 75 years* (Cambridge University Press, Cambridge, 1998), pp. 603–14.

Brooks, David, 'Review Lloyd George, for and against', *The Historical Journal*, 24, 1 (March 1981), pp. 223–30.

Bruendel, Steffen, 'Kriegsgreuel 1914–1918. Rezeption und Aufarbeitung deutscher Kriegsverbrechen im Spannungsfeld von Völkerrecht und Kriegspropaganda', in *Kriegsgreuel. Die Entgrenzung der Gewalt in kriegerischen Konflikten vom Mittelalter bis ins 20. Jahrhundert* (Ferdinand Schöning, Paderborn, 2008), pp. 293–316.

Cline, Catherine Ann, 'British Historians and the Treaty of Versailles', *Albion*, 20, 1 (Spring, 1988), pp. 43–58.

Dobschütz, Sigismund von, '"Wir sind dahin gekommen ganze Dörfer niederzubrennen"; Briefe aus dem Deutsch-Französischen Krieg 1870/71 und der Okkupationszeit 1872/73 von Paul Callas an seine Eltern', *Ostdeutsche Familienkunde*, 17, 1 (2006), pp. 321–30; 17, 4 (2006) pp. 454–61.

Dockrill, M. L. and Zara Steiner, 'The Foreign Office at the Paris Peace Conference in 1919', *International History Review*, 2, 1 (1980), pp. 56–86.

Eley, Geoff, 'Bismarckian Germany', in Gordon Martel (ed.) *Modern Germany Reconsidered: 1870–1945* (Routledge, London, 1992), pp. 1–32.

Eley, Geoff, 'Making a Place in the Nation: Meanings of "Citizenship" in Wilhelmine Germany', in Geoff Eley and James Retallack (eds) *Wilhelmism and its Legacies: German modernities, imperialism and the meaning of reform, 1890–1930* (Berghahn Books, New York, 2003), pp. 16–33.

Ferguson, Niall, 'The Balance of Payments Questions: Versailles and after', in M.F. Boemeke et al., *The Treaty of Versailles*, pp. 371–99.

Fest, W.B., 'British War Aims and German Peace Feelers during the First World War (December 1916–November 1918)', *The Historical Journal*, 15, 2 (June 1972), pp. 285–308.

Finke, Carol, 'The Minorities Question at the Paris Peace Conference: The Polish Minority Treaty, June 28, 1919', in M.F. Boemeke et al., *The Treaty of Versailles*, pp. 249–74.

Fischer, Fritz, 'The Foreign Policies of Imperial Germany and the Outbreak of the First World War', in Gregor Schöllgen (ed.) *Escape into War? The foreign policies of Imperial Germany* (Berg, Oxford, 1990), pp. 19–40.

Fischer, Wolfram, 'Die Weimarer Republik unter den weltwirtschaftlichen Bedingungen der Zwischenkriegszeit', in Hans

Mommsen, Dietmar Petzina and Bernd Weisbrod, *Industrielles System und die politische Entwicklung in der Weimarer Republik* (Droste, Düsseldorf, 1974), pp. 26–50.

Fry, Michael Graham, 'British Revisionism', in M.F. Boemeke et al., *The Treaty of Versailles*, pp. 565–601.

Galbraith, John S., 'British War Aims in World War I: a commentary on statesmanship', *Journal of Imperial and Commonwealth History*, vol. 13 (1884–1985), pp. 25–45.

Gelfand, Lawrence C., 'The American Mission to Negotiate Peace: an historian looks back', in M.F. Boemeke et al., *The Treaty of Versailles*, pp. 189–202.

Grimmer-Solem, Erik, 'Imperialist Socialism of the Chair: Gustav Schmoller and German *Weltpolitik*, 1897–1905', in Geoff Eley and James Retallack (eds) *Wilhelmism and its Legacies*, pp. 107–22.

Herwig, Holger H., 'Industry, Empire and the First World War', in Gordon Martel (ed.) *Modern Germany Reconsidered: 1870–1945* (Routledge, London, 1992), pp. 54–73.

Herwig, Holger H., 'Clio Deceived: Patriotic Self-Censorship in Germany After the Great War', in Keith Wilson (ed.) *Forging the Collective Memory: government and international historians through two world wars* (Berghahn Books, Providence USA, 1996), pp. 87–127.

Hewitson, Mark, 'The Wilhelmine Regime and the Problem of Reform: German debates about modern nation states', in Geoff Eley and James Retallack (eds) *Wilhelmism and its Legacies*, pp. 73–90.

Jacobson, Jon, 'Strategies of French Foreign Policy after World War I', *Journal of Modern History*, 55, 1 (1983), pp. 78–95.

Kaiser, David E., 'Germany and the Origin of the First World War', *Journal of Modern History*, 55, 3 (1983), pp. 442–74.

Kennedy, Paul, 'Idealists and Realists: British views of Germany,

1864–1939', *Transactions of the Royal Historical Society*, vol. 25 (1975), pp. 137–56.

Kennedy, Paul and Talbot Imlay, 'Appeasement', in Gordon Martel (ed.) *The Origins of the Second World War reconsidered: A.J.P. Taylor and the historians* (Second Edition, Routledge, London, 1999), pp. 116–34.

Kernek, Sterling, 'The British Government's reactions to President Wilson's "Peace" note of December 1916', *The Historical Journal*, XIII, 4 (1970), pp. 721–66.

Keylor, William R., 'Versailles and International Diplomacy', in M.F. Boemeke et al., *The Treaty of Versailles*, pp. 469–505.

Kitchen, Martin, 'Civil-Military Relations in Germany During the First World War', in R.J.Q. Adams, *The Great War 1914–1918*, pp. 39–68.

Klein, Fritz, 'Between Compiègne and Versailles: the Germans on the way from a misunderstood defeat to an unwanted peace', in M.F. Boemeke et al., *The Treaty of Versailles*, pp. 203–20.

Lentin, Antony, 'A Comment', in M.F. Boemeke et al., *The Treaty of Versailles*, pp. 221–43.

McDermott, John, '"A Needless Sacrifice": British businessmen and business as usual in the First World War', *Albion*, vol. 2 (Spring 1989), pp. 263–82.

McDougall, W.A., 'Political Economy versus National Sovereignty: French structures for German economic integration after Versailles', *Journal of Modern History*, vol. 51 (1979), pp. 4–23.

Marks, Sally, 'Reparations Reconsidered: a reminder', *Central European History*, vol. 2 (1969), pp. 356–65.

Marks, Sally, 'The Myth of Reparations', *Central European History*, 18, No.3 (1978), pp. 231–55.

Marks, Sally, 'The Misery of Victory: France's struggle for the Versailles Treaty', *Historical Papers* [Canada] (1986), pp. 117–33.

Marks, Sally, 'Smoke and Mirrors: In Smoke-Filled Rooms and the Galerie des Glaces', in M.F. Boemeke et al. *The Treaty of Versailles*, pp. 337–70.

Marks, Sally, '1918 and after: the postwar era', in Gordon Martel (ed.) *The Origins of the Second World War reconsidered*, pp. 13–37.

Martel, Gordon, 'The Revisionist as Moralist: A.J.P. Taylor and the lessons of European history', in Gordon Martel (ed.) *The Origins of the Second World War reconsidered*, pp. 1–12.

Mommsen, Hans 'The Disintegration of Germany and the End of World War II in Europe', in John Perkins and Jürgen Tampke, *Europe: prospects and retrospects. Proceedings of the 1995 Biennial Conference of Australian Association of European Historians* (Southern Highlands Publishers, Sydney, 1995), pp. 21–29.

Mommsen, W.J. 'Max Weber and the Peace Treaty', in M.F. Boemeke et al., *The Treaty of Versailles*, pp. 535–46.

Prior, Robin and Trevor Wilson, 'What Manner of Victory? Reflections on the termination of the First World War', *Revue Internationale d'Histoire Militaire*, vol. 72 (1990), pp. 80–96.

Retallack, James 'Wilhelmine Germany', in Gordon Martel (ed.) *Modern Germany Reconsidered: 1870–1945* (Routledge, London, 1992), pp. 33–53.

Schuker, Stephen A., 'The End of Versailles' and 'The Revisionist as Moralist: A.J.P. Taylor and the lessons of European history', in Gordon Martel (ed.) *The Origins of the Second World War reconsidered*, pp. 38–56.

Schuker, Stephen A., 'The Rhineland Question: West European security at the Paris Peace Conference 1919', in M.F. Boemeke et al., *The Treaty of Versailles*, pp. 275–312.

Sharp, Alan, 'The Genie that Would Not Go Back into the Bottle: national self-determination and the legacy of the First World War and Peace-settlement', in Seamus Dunn and T.G. Fraser, *The First*

World War and Contemporary Ethnic Conflict (Routledge, London, 1996), pp. 9–28.

Stevenson, David, 'The Failure of Peace by Negotiations in 1917', *The Historical Journal*, 34, vol. 1 (1991), pp. 65–85.

Stoneman, Mark, 'Die deutschen Greueltaten im Kriege 1870/1 am Beispiel Baiern', in Neitzel Sönke and Daniel Hohrath, *Kriegsgreuel. Die Entgrenzung der Gewalt in kriegerischen Konflikten vom Mittelalter bis ins 20. Jahrhundert* (Ferdinand Schöning, Paderborn, 2008), pp. 223–39.

Trachtenberg, Marc, 'Reparations at the Paris Peace Conference', *Journal of Modern History*, vol. 51 (1979), pp. 24–55.

Trachtenberg, Marc, 'Versailles After Sixty Years', *Journal of Contemporary History*, vol. 17 (1982), pp. 487–506.

Wiegrefe, Klaus 'Der verschenkte Friede. Warum auf den ersten Weltkrieg ein zweiter folgen musste', *Der Spiegel*, 28 (2009), pp. 45–53.

Wiegrefe, Klaus, 'Die Schande nach Auschwitz', *Der Spiegel*, 35 (2014), pp. 28–40.

Wilson, Trevor, 'The Significance of the First World War in Modern History', in R.J.Q. Adams, *The Great War 1914–1918*, pp. 7–30.

Woodward, David R., 'David Lloyd George, a Negotiated Peace with Germany, and the Kühlmann Peace Kit of September 1917', *Canadian Journal of History*, 6, 1 (1971), pp. 75–93.

Woodward, David R., 'The Origin and Intent of David Lloyd George's January 5 War Aim Speech', *The Historian*, vol. 34 (November 1971), pp. 22–39.

Woodward, David R., 'Britain in a Continental War: the civil-military debate over the strategical direction of the Great War of 1914–1918', *Albion*, 12, 1 (1980), pp. 37–65.

Notes

Chapter One: Imperial Germany

1. Cited in Lothar Gall, *Bismarck. Der Weiße Revolutionär*, p. 442.

2. Otto Pflanze, *Bismarck der Reichsgründer*, pp. 486–87.

3. Mark Stoneman, 'Die deutschen Greueltaten im Kriege 1870/1 am Beispiel Baiern', in Neitzel Sönke and Daniel Hohrath, *Kriegsgreuel. Die Entgrenzung der Gewalt in kriegerischen Konflikten vom Mittelalter bis ins 20. Jahrhundert* (Ferdinand Schöning, Paderborn, 2008), p. 227.

4. Sigismund von Dobschütz, '"Wir sind dahin gekommen ganze Dörfer niederzubrennen"; Briefe aus dem Deutsch-Französischen Krieg 1870/71 und der Okkupationszeit 1872/73 von Paul Callas an seine Eltern', *Ostdeutsche Familienkunde*, vol. 17, 4 (2006), pp. 459–60.

5. Pflanze, *Bismarck der Reichsgründer,* p. 487.

6. John Horne and Alan Kramer, *German Atrocities, 1914: a history of denial,* pp. 141–42; Geoffrey Wawro, *The Franco-Prussian*

War: the German conquest of France in 1870–1871, p. 279.

7.   Stoneman, op. cit., pp. 223–39.

8.   Otto Pflanze, *Bismarck and the Development of Germany*, pp. 491–92; Wawro, *The Franco-Prussian War*, pp. 282–83; Gall, *Der weiße Revolutionär*, p. 448. Bismarck took the payment from his secret 'guelph fund', money seized from the Kingdom of Hannover after the second unification war. Ludwig apparently presented this transaction as a partial repayment for the war indemnity paid by Bavaria in 1866. The money did not go into the public treasury, but into his personal accounts, no doubt to assist with the construction of his castles.

9.   Pflanze, *Bismarck and the Development of Germany*, p. 508.

10.   Wawro, *The Franco-Prussian War*, p. 283.

11.   Gall, *Bismarck. Der weiße Revolutionär*, p. 450.

12.   J.H. Morgan, *The German War Book* (John Murray, London, 1915), pp. 54–55.

13.   See pp. 32–33 in this book.

14.   Hans-Ulrich Wehler, *Deutsche Gesellschaftsgeschichte, 1849–1914*, p. 730.

15.   Cited in Wolfgang Mommsen, *Max Weber und die Deutsche Politik*, p. 78.

16.   The most outspoken exponent of this approach was Friedrich Naumann. A number of left-liberal reformers went to Australia and New Zealand, where labour parties by the turn of the century had become politically very influential, and indeed in some states had already gained government. Note the author's *Wunderbar Country: Germans look at Australia, 1850–1914* (Hale and Iremonger, Sydney, 1982), pp. 3–89.

17.   Cited in Mark Hewitson, 'The Wilhelmine Regime and the Problem of Reform: German debates about modern nation states', in Geoff Eley and James Retallack (eds) *Wilhelmism*

and its Legacies: German modernities, imperialism, and the meaning of reform, 1890–1930, p. 77.

18. Treitschke, cited in Eley and Retallack, op. cit., p. 80.

19. Frank B. Tipton, *A History of Modern Germany Since 1815*, p. 245.

20. Cited in Gerhard R. Ritter, *Das Deutsche Kaiserreich, 1871–1914*, pp. 300–1.

21. *Verhandlungen des Reichstages*, XII, vol. 227, *Stenografische Berichte* (Norddeutsche Verlagsanstalt, Berlin 1907), pp. 44–63.

22. Cited in Manfred Scharrer, *Die Spaltung der deutschen Arbeiterbewegung*, p. 21.

23. John A. Moses, *Australia and the Kaiser's War, 1914–18* (Broughton Press, St. Lucia, 1993), p. 10.

24. Richard J. Evans, *The Coming of the Third Reich*, p. 34.

25. Diarmuid Jeffreys, *Hell's Cartel: IG Farben and the making of Hitler's war machine*, p. 49.

26. Horne and Kramer, *German Atrocities, 1914*, pp. 145–51.

27. Op. cit., p. 151.

28. Volker R. Berghahn, *Germany and the Approach of War* (MacMillan, Basingstoke, 1973), p. 207.

Chapter Two: The Great War

1. Barbara Tuchman, *August 1914*, p. 173–74.

2. Op. cit., p. 174.

3. Horne and Kramer, *German Atrocities, 1914*, pp. 10–78; Tuchman, *August 1914*, pp. 247–49, 296–316.

4. See pp. 176–178 in this book.

5. Cited in Jeffreys, *Hell's Cartel*, pp. 55–56.

6. Op. cit., pp. 57–58.

7. Hans-Ulrich Wehler, *Deutsche Gesellschaftsgeschichte: 1914–1949*, p. 143.

8. Cited in Fritz Fischer, *War of Illusions*, p. 518.

9. Cited in Alan Kramer, *Dynamic of Destruction: culture and mass killing in the First World War*, p. 93.

10. Wehler, *Deutsche Gesellschaftsgeschichte: 1914–1949*, pp. 31–38.

11. Fritz Fischer, *Weltmacht oder Niedergang. Deutschland im ersten Weltkrieg*, p. 64.

12. See pp. 82–83 in this book.

13. Robert F. Wheeler, *USPD und Internationale*, p. 25.

14. Fischer, *Weltmacht oder Niedergang*, pp. 98–107; Wehler, *Deutsche Gesellschaftsgeschichte*, pp. 162–74.

15. David R. Woodward, 'Britain in a Continental War: the civil-military debate over the strategical direction of the Great War of 1914–1918', *Albion*, 12, 1 (1980), p. 37.

16. Cited in op. cit., p. 45.

17. Sterling Kernek, 'The British Government's Reactions to President Wilson's "Peace" Note of December 1916', *The Historical Journal*, vol. XII (1976), p. 750.

18. Op. cit., pp. 762–73.

19. Barbara Tuchman, *The Zimmermann Telegram* (Constable, London, 1959), pp. 113–14; Ignaz Miller, *Mit vollem Risiko in den Krieg, 1914–1918*, p. 95.

20. See pp. 76–77 in this book.

21. Cited in Tuchman, *The Zimmermann Telegram*, p. 7.

22. Tuchman, op. cit., pp. 160–64.

23. Paul E. Fontenoy, 'Convoy System', in Spencer C. Tucker (ed.), *The Encyclopedia of World War I: a political, social and military history*, vol. 1 (ABC-CLIO, Santa Barbara, 2005), pp. 312–14.

24. David R. Woodward, 'The Origin and Intent of David Lloyd

George's January 5 War Aim Speech', *The Historian*, vol. 34 (November 1971), p. 25.

25. Op. cit., pp. 25–27; W. B. Fest, 'British War Aims and German Peace Feelers during the First World War (December 1916– November 1918)', *The Historical Journal*, 15, 2 (June 1972), pp. 300–02.

26. Woodward, 'Origin', pp. 34–35.

27. William R. Keylor, 'Versailles and International Diplomacy', in Manfred F. Boemeke, Gerald D. Feldman, and Elisabeth Glaser, *The Treaty of Versailles: a reassessment after 75 years*, pp. 474–76.

28. Wehler, *Deutsche Gesellschaftsgeschichte: 1914–1949*, p. 154.

29. Cited in Doug Newton, *British Policy and the Weimar Republic*, p. 185.

30. The Treaty of Bucharest was signed in the Romanian capital on 7 May 1918 between the Central Powers and Romania. Romania had to cede territories to Bulgaria and Austria–Hungary, and the Central Powers took control of Romania's oil possessions.

Chapter Three: Paris

1. Cited in Antony Lentin, *Lloyd George, Woodrow Wilson and the Guilt of Germany: an essay in the prehistory of appeasement*, p. 4.

2. Op. cit., p. 30.

3. Lawrence C. Gelfand, 'The American Mission to Negotiate Peace: an historian looks back', in Boemeke et al., *The Treaty of Versailles*, p. 189.

4. H.W.F. Temperley, *A History of the Peace Conference of Paris*, vol. 1, p. 433.

5. Op. cit., p. 439.

6.   Ibid.

7.   Alan Sharp, *Consequences of Peace. The Versailles Settlement: aftermath and legacy, 1919–1920*, pp. 101–2.

8.   Alan Sharp, 'The Genie That Would Not Go Back into the Bottle: national self-determination and the legacy of the First World War and Peace-settlement', in Seamus Dunn and T.G. Fraser, *The First World War and Contemporary Ethnic Conflict* (Routledge, London, 1996), p. 9.

9.   Keylor, 'Versailles and International Diplomacy', p. 476.

10. Cited in Lentin, *Lloyd George, Woodrow Wilson and the Guilt of Germany*, p. 32.

11. Cited in Manfred F. Boemeke, 'Woodrow-Wilson's Image of Germany, the War-guilt Question, and the Treaty of Versailles', in Boemeke et al., *The Treaty of Versailles*, pp. 610–11.

12. Boemeke, 'Woodrow-Wilson's Image of Germany', p. 611.

13. Op. cit., p. 612.

14. Keylor, 'Versailles and International Diplomacy', p. 492.

15. MacMillan, *Peacemakers: the Paris conference of 1919 and its attempt to end war*, p. 175.

16. Paul Birdsall, *Versailles: twenty years after* (Archon Books, Hamden Connecticut, 1962), pp. 36–37.

17. *The Times*, 13 December 1918.

18. MacMillan, *Peacemakers*, p. 66.

19. Op. cit., p. 188.

20. Temperley, *A History of the Peace Conference of Paris*, vol. 2, p. 235.

21. MacMillan, *Peacemakers*, p. 56.

22. Cited in W.J. Hudson, *Billy Hughes at Paris: the birth of Australian diplomacy* (Thomas Nelson, Melbourne, 1978), p. 78.

23. Carol Finke, 'The Minorities Question at the Paris Peace

Conference: The Polish Minority Treaty, June 28, 1919', in Boemeke et al., *The Treaty of Versailles*, pp. 252–53.

24. Jürgen Tampke, *Czech-German Relations and the Politics of Central Europe: from Bohemia to the EU*, pp. 32–44.

25. Cited in Jaroslav Kučera, *Minderheit im Nationalstaat. Die Sprachenfrage in den tschechisch-deutschen Beziehungen, 1918–1938*, p. 38.

26. Kučera, op. cit., p. 53.

27. Christopher Clark, *The Sleepwalkers: how Europe went to war in 1914*, pp. 21–22.

28. Margaret MacMillan, *The Uses and Abuses of History*, pp. 86–87.

29. See pp. 79–81 in this book.

30. MacMillan, *Peacemakers*, pp. 249–51.

31. Op. cit., pp. 265–78.

32. Op. cit., p. 300.

33. Trevor Wilson, *The Myriad Faces of War: Britain and the Great War*, pp. 589–91.

34. Lentin, *Lloyd George, Woodrow Wilson and the Guilt of Germany*, p. 14.

35. Hudson, *Billy Hughes at Paris*, pp. 38–39.

36. MacMillan, *Peacemakers*, p. 201.

37. Bruce Kent, *The Spoils of War: the politics, economics and diplomacy of reparations 1918–1932*, p. 67.

38. Keylor, 'Versailles and International Diplomacy', p. 500; Sally Marks, 'The Myth of Reparations', *Central European History*, vol. 11 (1978), p. 232.

39. In the end, it was decided that France would receive 42 per cent of the share, Britain 38 per cent, and the remaining 20 per cent would be divided among the smaller powers.

40. MacMillan, *Peacemakers*, p. 182.

41. Stephen A. Schuker, 'The Rhineland Question: West European security at the Paris Peace Conference 1919', in Boemeke et al., *The Treaty of Versailles*, p. 307.

42. Lentin, *Lloyd George and the Lost Peace*, p. 57.

43. Fritz Klein, 'From a misunderstood defeat to an unwanted peace', in Boemeke et al., *The Treaty of Versailles*, p. 205.

44. Ibid.

45. Sally Marks, 'Smoke and Mirrors: in smoke-filled rooms and the Galerie des Glaces', in Boemeke et al., *The Treaty of Versailles*, p. 350.

46. Op. cit., p. 351.

Chapter Four: Versailles

1. Cited in Lentin, *Lloyd George and the Lost Peace*, p. 84.

2. Marks, 'Smoke and Mirrors', p. 351.

3. Lentin, *Lloyd George and the Lost Peace*, pp. 87–88.

4. Marks, 'Smoke and Mirrors', p. 352.

5. Op. cit., p. 355.

6. MacMillan, *Peacemakers*, pp. 478–80.

7. Fritz Klein, 'Between Compiègne and Versailles: the Germans on the way from a misunderstood defeat to an unwanted peace', in Boemeke et al., *The Treaty of Versailles*, pp. 205–06.

8. Wolfgang J. Mommsen, 'Max Weber and the Peace Treaty', in Boemeke et al., *The Treaty of Versailles*, p. 543.

9. Klaus Wiegrefe, 'Der verschenkte Friede. 90 Jahre nach Versailler Vertrag', *Der Spiegel*, 28, 2009, p. 53.

10. Lentin, 'A Comment', in Boemeke et al., *The Treaty of Versailles*, p. 238.

11. Klaus Wiegrefe, 'Der verschenkte Friede', p. 53.

12. Cited in Temperley, *A History of the Peace Conference of Paris*, vol. 2, p. 276.

13. Op. cit., p. 230.

14. M.S. Anderson, *Europe in the Eighteenth Century, 1713–1783* (Holt, Rinehart and Winston, New York, 1966), p. 31.

15. Robert Boyce, *The Great Interwar Crisis and the Collapse of Globalization*, pp. 53–55.

16. Wolfram Fischer, 'Die Weimarer Republik unter den weltwirtschaftlichen Bedingungen der Zwischenkriegszeit', in Hans Mommsen, Dietmar Petzina and Bernd Weisbrod *Industrielles System und die politische Entwicklung in der Weimarer Republik* (Droste, Düsseldorf, 1974), pp. 28–31.

17. Temperley, *A History of the Peace Conference of Paris*, vol. 2, pp. 300–01.

18. United Nations *Whitaker Report*; 'Germany admits Namibia genocide', BBC News, 14 August 2014. In 2004, the German government recognised and apologised for the event, but refused to pay financial compensation to the victims' descendants.

19. MacMillan, *Peacemakers*, p. 67.

20. These were China, Siam (Thailand), Liberia, Morocco, Egypt, and Turkey.

21. Schuker, 'The Rhineland Question', p. 276.

22. MacMillan, *Peacemakers*, p. 186.

23. Richard J. Shuster, *German Disarmament After World War I: the diplomacy of international arms inspection, 1920–1931*, pp. 111–27.

24. MacMillan, *Peacemakers*, p. 491.

25. Shuster, *German Disarmament After World War I*, p. 116.

26. Harvey Leonard Dyck, *Weimar Germany and Soviet Russia, 1926–1933: a study in diplomatic instability*, pp. 19–22.

27.   Shuster, *German Disarmament After World War I*, p. 79.

28.   John W. Wheeler-Bennett, *The Nemesis of Power: the German army in politics 1918–1945*, p. 98.

29.   Keylor, 'Versailles and International Diplomacy', p. 500.

30.   Wolfgang J. Mommsen, 'Max Weber and the Treaty of Versailles', pp. 537–38.

31.   Temperley, *A History of the Peace Conference of Paris*, vol. 2. pp. 308–11.

32.   Op. cit., p. 313.

33.   Kent, *The Spoils of War*, p. 62.

34.   Fischer, 'Die Weimarer Republik', p. 32.

35.   Niall Ferguson, 'The Balance of Payments Questions: Versailles and after', in M.F. Boemeke et al., *The Treaty of Versailles*, p. 415.

36.   Temperley, *A History of the Peace Conference of Paris*, vol. 2, pp. 321–22.

37.   Sally Marks, 'The Myth of Reparations', p. 235; Marks, 'Smoke and Mirrors', p. 346.

38.   Sally Marks, 'Reparations Reconsidered: a reminder', *Central European History*, vol. 2 (1969), p. 360.

39.   Gaston Furt, De Versailles aux Experts(1925), pp. 133-134, cited in and translated by Sally Marks, op. cit. p. 362.

40.   Op. cit., p. 363.

41.   Marks, 'Myth', pp. 237–38.

42.   Op. cit., pp. 244–45.

43.   See pp. 217–218 in this book.

44.   Boyce, *The Great Interwar Crisis and the Collapse of Globalization*, p. 135.

45.   Marks, 'Myth', p. 247.

46.   Stephen A. Schuker, *American 'Reparations' to Germany 1919–1933* (Princeton Studies in International Finance,

Princeton, 1988), pp. 118–19.

47. Marks, 'Myth', pp. 254–55.

48. Boyce, *The Great Interwar Crisis and the Collapse of Globalization*, p. 37.

49. Marks, 'Myth', p. 235.

50. Fischer, 'Die Weimarer Republik', pp. 29–31.

51. Ibid.

52. Tuchman, *August 1914*, pp. 306–314; Horne and Kramer, *German Atrocities, 1914*, pp. 9–41; Wehler, *Deutsche Gesellschaftsgeschichte*, vol. 4, p. 29.

53. Sally Marks, *Innocent Abroad. Belgium at the Peace Conference of 1919*, pp. 172–73.

54. Op. cit., p. 172.

55. Op. cit., pp. 183–95.

56. Trevor, Wilson, 'The Significance of the First World War in Modern History', in R.J.Q. Adams, *The First World War 1914–1918* (1990, The MacMillan Press, Basingstoke and London, pp. 14–15), reproduced with permission of Palgrave Macmillan.

57. Sally Marks, 'The Misery of Victory: France's struggle for the Versailles Treaty', p. 122.

58. See pp. 213–215 in this book.

59. Cited in Marks, 'Smoke and Mirrors', p. 359.

Chapter Five: Weimar

1. Erhard Lucas, *Märzrevolution im Ruhrgebiet*, 3 vols (Verlag Roter Stern, Frankfurt Main, 1970–78).

2. Richard J. Evans, *The Coming of the Third Reich*, pp. 139–41. Note also Schuker, American 'Reparations'.

3. Op. cit., pp. 83–84.

4. Op. cit., p. 80.

5. Op. cit., p. 135–36.

6. Richard, J. Evans, *In Defence of History*, pp. 132–33.

7. Cited in Volker Berghahn, *Modern Germany: society, economy and politics in the twentieth century* (Cambridge University Press, Cambridge, 1983), pp. 66–67.

8. Holger H. Herwig, 'Clio Deceived: patriotic self-censorship in Germany after the Great War', in Keith Wilson (ed.) *Forging the Collective Memory: government and international historians through two world wars*, p. 97.

9. Imanuel Geiss, foreword to Hermann Kantorowicz, *Gutachten zur Kriegsschuldfrage 1914*, p. 18.

10. Cited in op. cit., p. 32.

11. Walter Schücking and Max Monteglas, 'Deutsche Dokumente zum Kriegsausbruch (DD), Berlin 1927', Appendix iv, p. 2, DD 15, cited in Hermann Kantorowicz, *Gutachten zur Kriegsschuldfrage 1914*, pp. 232–34.

12. Op. cit., pp. 235–36.

13. DD 554 cited in Kantorowicz, op. cit., p. 253.

14. Kantorowicz, op. cit., p. 260.

15. DD 323, DD 395, DD 456, p. 176, cited in Kantorowicz, op. cit., pp. 300–01.

16. Evans, *The Coming of the Third Reich*, pp. 136–37.

17. Richard Bessel, 'Why did the Weimar Republic collapse?', in Ian Kershaw (ed.), *Weimar: why did democracy fail?*, pp. 126–27.

18. Boyce, *The Great Interwar Crisis and the Collapse of Globalization*, pp. 24–29.

19. Robert Skidelsky, *John Maynard Keynes, 1883–1946: economist, philosopher, statesman*, pp. 191–95.

20. Lentin, *Lloyd George and the Lost Peace*, p. 42.

21. Keylor, 'Versailles and International Diplomacy', p. 495.

22. Ibid.

23. Skidelsky, *John Maynard Keynes*, pp. 220–21; Keylor, 'Versailles and International Diplomacy', p. 486.

24. Lentin, *Lloyd George, Woodrow Wilson and the Guilt of Germany*, p. 137.

25. Cited in Étienne Mantoux, *The Carthaginian Peace or the Economic Consequences of Mr Keynes*, p. 5.

26. Mantoux, *The Carthaginian Peace*, pp. ix–xiv.

27. Op. cit., pp. 62–63.

28. Keylor, 'Versailles and International Diplomacy', pp. 501–02; Schuker, *American 'Reparations'*, pp. 18–19.

29. Schuker, op. cit., pp. 10–11.

30. Marks, 'Reparations Reconsidered', p. 361.

31. 'On the morning after the German "election" [the Reichstag election of 29 March 1936] I travelled to Basle; it was an exquisite liberation to reach Switzerland. It must have been only a little later that I met Maynard Keynes at some gathering in London. "I do wish you had not written that book"', I found myself saying (meaning *The Economic Consequences,* which the Germans never ceased to quote) and then longed for the ground to swallow me up. But he said, simply and gently, "So do I."' Elizabeth Wiskemann, *The Europe I Saw*, p. 53.

32. Lentin, *Lloyd George, Woodrow Wilson and the Guilt of Germany*, pp. 145–46.

33. Op. cit., p. 134.

34. Michael Graham Fry, 'British Revisionism', in Boemeke et al., *The Treaty of Versailles*, p. 590.

35. Lentin, *Lloyd George, Woodrow Wilson and the Guilt of Germany*, p. 145–46.

36. Gordon Martel, 'A Comment', in Boemeke et al., *The Treaty of*

Versailles, p. 616; Diane B. Kunz, 'A Comment', in Boemeke et al., op. cit., p. 590.

37. Boyce, *The Great Interwar Crisis and the Collapse of Globalization*, pp. 71–72.

38. Catherine Ann Cline, 'British Historians and the Treaty of Versailles', *Albion*, 20, 1 (Spring 1988), pp. 51–52.

39. Op. cit., p. 50.

40. Ibid.

41. Op. cit., p. 51.

42. Lentin, *Lloyd George, Woodrow Wilson and the Guilt of Germany*, p. 134.

43. Boyce, *The Great Interwar Crisis and the Collapse of Globalization*, pp. 7–8.

44. Op. cit., p. 94.

45. Op. cit., p. 137.

46. Evans, *The Coming of the Third Reich*, p. 106.

47. Op. cit., p. 127.

48. Stefan Zweig, *Die Welt von Gestern. Erinnerungen eines Europäers* (Anaconda Verlag, Colone, 2013), pp. 415–16.

49. Evans, *The Coming of the Third Reich*, p. 120.

50. Marks, 'Misery', p. 120.

51. Manfred J. Enssle, *Stresemann's Territorial Revisionism* (Steiner, Wiesbaden, 1980), pp. 110–17; cited in Marks, 'Misery', p. 130.

52. Evans, *The Coming of the Third Reich*, pp. 90–91.

53. Joachim Fest, *Hitler* (Penguin, Harmondsworth), 1996, p. 74.

54. Evans, *The Coming of the Third Reich*, p. 265.

55. Easily the best: Ian Kershaw, *Hitler: 1989–1936: Hubris*; Richard J. Evans, *The Coming of the Third Reich*.

Chapter Six: Bonn

1. Hans Mommsen, 'The Disintegration of Germany and the end of World War II in Europe', in John Perkins and Jürgen Tampke, *Europe: Prospects and Retrospects. Proceedings of the 1995 Biennial Conference of Australian Association of European Historians* (Southern Highlands Publishers, Sydney, 1995), pp. 28–29.

2. Richard von Weizsäcker, 'Speech to West German Parliament commemorating the fortieth year of the German capitulation', 8 May 1984.

3. Kershaw, *The Nazi Dictatorship*, p. 59.

4. Evans, *The Third Reich at War*, 1939–1945, pp. 741–45.

5. Klaus Wiegrefe, 'Die Schande nach Auschwizt', *Der Spiegel*, vol. 35 (2014), p. 29.

6. Op. cit., p. 34.

7. See pp. 213–214 in this book.

8. Fritz Fischer, *War of Illusions*, pp. 228–30; John Moses, *The Politics of Illusions*, pp. 73–75.

9. Fritz Fischer, *Der erste Weltkrieg und das deutsche Geschichtsbild*, p. 224.

10. Berghahn, *Germany and the Approach of War*; *Sarajewo, 28 Juni 1914. Der Untergang des alten Europa* (Deutscher Taschenbuch Verlag, München, 1997).

11. Wehler, *Deutsche Gesellschaftsgeschichte, 1849–1914*, pp. 1150–68.

12. Imanuel Geiss (ed.), *Juli 1914. Die Europäische Krise und der Ausbruch des ersten Weltkriegs*.

13. Fischer, *War of Illusions*, p. 680.

14. Evans, *In Hitler's Shadow: West German historians and the attempt to escape from the Nazi past*, p. 21.

15. Wolfgang J. Mommsen, 'Max Weber and the Peace Treaty', in

Boemeke et al., *The Treaty of Versailles*, p. 536.

16. Evans, *In Hitler's Shadow*, p. 172.

17. Kershaw, *The Nazi Dictatorship*, p. 176.

18. Evans, *In Hitler's Shadow*, p. 58.

19. Op. cit., p. 22.

20. Cited in Richard J. Evans, *In Defence of History*, p. 141.

21. Keith Windshuttle, *The Killing of History* (Maclean Press, Sydney, 1994), p. 253.

22. *Die Zeit*, 13 August 2015, p. 15.

23. Clark, *The Sleepwalkers*, pp. 148–50.

24. The most detailed and readable account is still Paul M. Kennedy, *The Rise of the Anglo-German Antagonism, 1860–1914*.

25. Clark, *The Sleepwalkers*, p. 165.

26. Wolfram Fischer, 'Die Weimarer Republik', p. 40.

27. Alan Kramer, *Dynamic of Destruction: culture and mass killings in the First World War*, pp. 91–94.

28. Clark, *The Sleepwalkers*, pp. 449–50.

29. Boyce, *The Great Interwar Crisis and the Collapse of Globalization*, p. 119.

30. Clark, *The Sleepwalkers*, p. 483.

31. Op. cit., p. 560.

32. Op. cit., p. 416.

33. Kramer, op. cit., p. 92; Paul Ham, *1914: the year the world ended*, pp. 276, 284; Imanuel Geiss (ed.), *Julikrise und Kriegsausbruch*, documents 23 a and b, pp. 32–33, 84, 124, 138.

34. *Frankfurter Allgemeine Zeitung*, 20 June 2015, p. 12.

35. Ignaz Miller, *Mit vollem Risiko in den Krieg, 1914–1918*, pp. 12–13.

36. *Der Spiegel*, 28 (2014), p. 42.

37. *Badische Zeitung*, 24 November 2014, p. 7.

38. Clark, *The Sleepwalkers*, p. 293.

39. Cited in Miller, *Mit vollem Risiko in den Krieg*, p. 64.

40. Richard Bosworth, *Italy and the Approach of the First World War*, pp. 131–34.

41. Kennedy, *The Rise and Fall of the Great Powers*, pp. 151–58.

42. Wilson, 'Significance', p. 20.

43. Fritz Fischer, *War of Illusions*, p. 543.

44. Margaret MacMillan, *The War that Ended Peace* (Random House, New York, 2013); Paul Ham, *1914*.

45. Miller, *Mit vollem Risiko in den Krieg*, p. 162. Reproduced with permission of NZZ Libro, Neue Züricher Zeitung, Zurich, CH.

46. Clark, *The Sleepwalkers*, pp. 3–64.

47. Miller, *Mit vollem Risiko in den Krieg*, pp. 65–76.

48. Op. cit., p. 13.

49. Klaus Wiegrefe, 'Der verschenkte Friede. Warum auf den ersten Weltkrieg ein zweiter folgen musste', *Der Spiegel*, 28 (2009), pp. 45–53.

50. John Nettles, *Jewels and Jackboots: Hitler's British Channel Islands*, p. 30.

51. Neil MacGregor, *Germany: memories of a nation*, p. 395.

52. MacMillan, *The Uses and Abuses of History*, p. 37.

53. Richard J. Evans, *Altered Pasts: counterfactuals in history*, p. 106.

54. MacMillan, *The Uses and Abuses of History*, p. 167.

55. Op. cit., pp. 36–37.

56. Evans, *Altered Pasts*, pp. 47–48.

57. Keylor, 'Versailles and International Diplomacy', p. 503.

58. Op. cit., pp. 504–05.

59. Op. cit., p. 505.

Index